A School for the People

BEST REGARDS,
LARRY LANDIS

A SCHOOL

Lawrence A. Landis

OREGON STATE UNIVERSITY PRESS   CORVALLIS

for the PEOPLE

A PHOTOGRAPHIC HISTORY OF Oregon State University

For Paul Boller—mentor, teacher, and friend

The paper in this book meets the guidelines for permanence and durability of the Committee on Production Guidelines for Book Longevity of the Council on Library Resources and the minimum requirements of the American National Standard for Permanence of Paper for Printed Library Materials z39.48-1984.

Library of Congress Cataloging-in-Publication Data

Landis, Lawrence A.
    A school for the people : a photographic history of Oregon State University / Lawrence A. Landis.
        pages   cm
    Includes index.
    ISBN 978-0-87071-822-9 (hardcover : alk. paper)
1. Oregon State University—Pictorial works. 2. Oregon State University—History. I. Title.
    LD4346.O433L36 2015
    378.0509795'34—dc23

                           2015021456

Oregon State University Press
121 The Valley Library
Corvallis OR 97331-4501
541-737-3166 • fax 541-737-3170
www.osupress.oregonstate.edu

Contents

Foreword

Oregon State University's status as a land-grant institution is writ everywhere across its seminal documents and photographs. In the spirit of its founding legislation—the Morrill Act of 1862—Oregon State's distinguished faculty and administrators, experiment stations, and extension service have carried out the congressional charge "to promote the liberal and practical education of the industrial classes." A distinctively American institution, land-grant colleges and universities were commissioned to offer instruction in scientific and classical studies, military tactics, and "agriculture and the mechanic arts." The new educational approach suited the needs of an industrializing nation committing itself to higher education on a grand scale. As such, land-grant institutions were truly democracy's colleges.[1]

Born amid the violence of the Civil War, three pieces of complementary federal legislation—the Homestead Act, the Pacific Railroad Act, and the Morrill Act—were designed to promote Western development. The Morrill Act granted each state 30,000 acres of federal land for every senator and congressman (sans the Confederate states) to establish colleges and universities to serve farmers and skilled workers. With an eye to supporting Union forces lacking in military leadership, the legislation included a provision requiring land-grant schools to offer training in "military tactics." When President Abraham Lincoln signed the bill into law on July 2, 1862, he set in motion dramatic changes to American higher education that reflected an industrializing nation's need for a trained workforce.

As an institution hewing closely to the land-grant tradition for a century and a half, Oregon State University has provided students with a post-secondary education and extended its research expertise and useful knowledge to interest groups across the state and beyond. Those conventions of public service and social accountability are rooted in the revolutionary nineteenth-century idea that all classes of people should have access to higher education. From the Midwestern corn belt to the cotton districts in the South and westward to the Pacific coastal states, land-grant institutions have reached into the outback, providing generations of students with the educational prerequisites to take their place as contributing citizens in society. Oregon State President August Strand observed in 1952 that the Corvallis institution was more than gracious lawns and brick-and-stone buildings: "it is a part of the very spirit of the state."[2]

Because land-grant schools originated in a federal initiative, they have always involved federal-state cooperation toward a common purpose—promoting the social good. The cooperative model gained greater traction with the advent of agricultural experiment stations when Congress passed the Hatch Act in 1887 and then followed with federal support for extension services through the Smith-Lever Act of 1914. Both legislative measures represented federal-state coordination, with Smith-Lever designed to make the work of the land grants available to farms, homes, and industrial settings. With the passage of time, extension has become an influential agency in extending education far beyond college and university campuses. When Oregon State University was one of three institutions invited in 1968 to join the National Sea Grant College Program, the consequence was a deepening of the federal-state relationship.

As a land-grant institution, Oregon State has adapted to changing social and economic needs and priorities—developing forestry programs when the lumber industry emerged as a major factor in the state's economy early in the twentieth century and increasing its engineering programs after the Second World War. Those curricular and research endeavors underwent further changes in the late twentieth century with the emergence of ecosystem science (forestry) and the high-tech industry (engineering). President Strand, an exemplar of the land-grant tradition, pointed out that the Corvallis school was addressing the needs of industry, offering its services on matters of agriculture, forestry, nutrition, consumer affairs, budget management, and child development. Oregon State was alive, he reported in 1958, "to the national climate of opinion" when it came to public services. As the portfolio of images in *A School for the People* illustrates, the university's 150 years of teaching, research, and service cast a large net—embracing the story of its built environment, its prominent administrators, faculty, and graduates, its athletic and military cadres, and the evolution of its academic programs.

If a picture is worth a thousand words, Larry Landis's pictorial history speaks volumes about the institution's rich photographic record from its founding to the present. Leafing through the pages of this book reveals a storied past—changing cultural traditions; the effects of distant military conflicts on campus life, the institution's long and proud tradition of training military officers, campus organizations from the first literary societies to the formation of fraternities and sororities to the establishment of several cultural centers since the late 1960s, prominent alumni such as Linus Pauling—and much more. While the photographs tell a story, it is the historical context and the captions to the images that flesh out the larger meaning of events, circumstances, and individuals. "A photograph is a biography of a moment," remarked longtime *Life* magazine photographer Art Shay.[3] But it is providing context and collectively piecing them together to portray a larger narrative that the carefully woven photographs in the eleven chapters of this book accomplish. *A School for the People* creates a striking and moving visual template to celebrate the sesquicentennial of Oregon State University.

WILLIAM G. ROBBINS
Emeritus Distinguished Professor of History,
Oregon State University

Preface and Acknowledgments

Soon after I started at OSU as assistant university archivist in January 1991, it became apparent that the University Archives' photographic collections pertaining to the university's history were superb. I began thinking about a pictorial history for OSU that would complement the venerable but very dated *Orange and Black,* OSU's first pictorial history. It had been published in 1938, seventy years after Corvallis College was provisionally designated as the state's land-grant institution, as a prelude to the college's diamond jubilee anniversary in 1943. It was a groundbreaking work—at the time of its publication, very few colleges or universities had produced a formal pictorial history. *The Orange and Black* was described at the time as "a de luxe pictorial narrative of the romance of the college in all its phases." It has served Oregon State well.

Although there was considerable planning and an impressive slate of activities centering on OSU's centennial celebration in 1968–69, I have not discovered any evidence that a pictorial history was proposed, or even considered, as a part of that celebration. Instead, the centennial committee, chaired by university librarian Rod Waldron, chose to publish a historical essay written by English faculty member James W. Groshong. Seventy historical photographs and documents were interspersed throughout Groshong's excellent narrative, *The Making of a University, 1868–1968.*

More recently, the need for a new, comprehensive pictorial history of OSU had come up in conversations over the years. *Oregon Stater* editor emeritus George Edmonston and I talked about a pictorial history on multiple occasions. We regularly collaborated on pictorial essays that

appeared in the *Stater* throughout the 1990s, including one celebrating OSU's 125th anniversary in 1993.

In 2004, OSU Press director Karen Orchard and I had a casual conversation at University Day about the need for an OSU pictorial history. She recently had come to OSU from the University of Georgia Press, which in 2000 had published a revised and updated edition of that institution's 1984 pictorial history. George Edmonston and I had subsequent conversations with OSU Press acquisitions editor Mary Braun in 2005. Health considerations unfortunately forced George to withdraw from further participation in a potential book project. And at the time, I was involved in two major projects that prevented me from taking on the project by myself.

Fast forward to 2010. By this time, OSU Press had become part of the OSU Libraries. I met with Mary Braun and others in the spring of that year to again discuss the pictorial history idea and brainstorm what would be required. I spent much of the summer laying the groundwork for the project, assisted by former student assistant Doug Schulte. We did a survey of about two dozen recently published pictorial histories and began a preliminary survey of potential images to be included in the work, focusing on many lesser-known collections in our holdings.

The project was delayed yet again when in 2011 University Archives and Special Collections merged into the dynamic Special Collections & Archives Research Center (SCARC). I focused on the merger process for well over a year, though the pictorial history project was always in the back of my mind. With the new department on sound footing by the end of 2012, I developed and submitted to OSU Press a formal proposal for the pictorial history in early 2013. The external reviews of the proposal were positive, and I was off to the races. I spent the summer months of 2013 reviewing tens of thousands of images, selecting a few hundred of them, preliminarily assigning them to chapters, and getting those that were not already in digital form scanned. That fall I began writing the narrative introductions to each chapter, refining the photo selections for each chapter, and writing the detailed captions for each image.

In my first professional position, photographs archivist at what is now the University of Texas at Austin's Briscoe Center for American History, I had developed a strong interest in and deep appreciation of historic photography, and admired the pictorial history of that institution, *The University of Texas: A Pictorial Account of its First Century*, published in 1980. I became acquainted with its author, Margaret Berry, and learned how much work she had put into it.

OSU has a strong photographic tradition dating back to the early 1890s; there is no time period that is not well represented in our collections. I discovered many images that I had not previously seen, despite having worked with many of the collections for more than twenty years. This abundance of visual riches made the selection process both fun and difficult. I would not be exaggerating to say that SCARC's collections could support three OSU pictorial histories of comparable quality. In the end, I strove to include many of the iconic images that Oregon Staters are familiar with, balanced by strong images that very few people have seen before. I have also included pertinent documents, maps, and images of ephemeral items.

Many institutional pictorial histories are chronological in nature, but a thematic format allows each photo to tell its unique story in the context of the other photos around it. Nine of the chapters focus on particular themes. Although the photographs and captions can stand on their own, each chapter begins with a narrative section intended to provide general context for the visual elements. Most chapters also include sidebars—short essays with associated images about unique people, events, and programs.

OSU has no shortage of compelling people—alumni, faculty, staff, donors, friends—who deserve recognition, or at least a mention, in a work of this nature. There are many people who are not included in this book, some of whom perhaps should be. Any oversight of this nature is entirely my responsibility.

Most published volumes are the work of many—not just the author. This is even more the case for a pictorial history. There are literally dozens and dozens of folks who have contributed to *A School for the People*.

My colleagues in the Special Collections & Archives Research Center have been most supportive. Time and time again they took up the slack in departmental affairs when I needed to devote large chunks of time to this project. They also provided advice and insight on particular collections or specific images and reviewed early drafts of text. The well-written and constructed collection guides that my staff have developed over the years greatly simplified the photo selection and background research process. Elizabeth Nielsen, Karl McCreary, Anne Bahde, Chris Petersen, Tiah Edmunson-Morton, Natalia Fernandez, Trevor Sandgathe, Ruth Vondracek, and Ryan Wick—a million thank-yous!

SCARC and earlier University Archives student assistants also played a strong supportive role with the project. I have mentioned Doug Schulte, an award-winning student of history at OSU, whom we were fortunate to have employed in a temporary capacity after he graduated and before he reported for active duty as an officer in the US Air Force. More recently, Mike Dicianna assisted in numerous ways. He was especially adept at tracking down obscure facts related to OSU history, and his knowledge of military history was particularly valuable with developing chapter 10. Amy Woosley, a SCARC student assistant studying photography, gladly accepted a last-minute assignment to photograph the newly opened Austin Hall. She did a great job of capturing the building in late afternoon autumn light. I especially love the sunlight gleaming off the entrance to the building.

The OSU Libraries and Press is fortunate to have a top-notch digital production unit. Brian Davis, Erin Clark, and student assistants Kimberly Laufer and Georgeann Booth digitized hundreds of photographs in many formats for this project. Brian's skill with glass negatives is especially appreciated. Many of those images likely have not been seen for more than a hundred years. They are exquisite!

Several of the more contemporary images are not from SCARC collections. There is typically a lag time of ten to fifteen years between the time a photograph at OSU is taken and the time it ends up in our collections. Theresa Hogue in OSU's News and Research Communications office helped guide me to and through their excellent collection of online photos in Flickr. Theresa is an excellent photographer in her own right, as you will see from the many images in the book that are her work. Steve Fenk at Athletic Communications also provided me with essential assistance. I had access to his department's substantive archive of photographs for athletes not well represented in our collections, and he and his staff tracked down superb images of more recent athletes.

Kip Carlson, OSU baseball expert extraordinaire and a former staffer at Athletic Communications, also lent his expertise to the athletics chapter. He clarified one specific date just days before the final manuscript was due. He also wrote the text for the Knute Rockne sidebar in chapter 5 back in 2000, just before OSU dismantled Notre Dame in the 2001 Fiesta Bowl.

Mary Gallagher, collections manager at the Benton County Historical Society & Museum, provided me with access to that organization's fine collection of photographs, and about a dozen appear in the book. Benton County is fortunate to have an excellent local historical society with professionally managed collections and first-rate public service. Many thanks to Mary and to Irene Zenev, BCHS executive director.

My colleagues at the OSU Press have been a joy to work with. Mary Braun has gently kept me on track throughout the project, Micki Reaman worked her magic with editing the manuscript, and Marty Brown has made the marketing process very easy. Tom Booth always had words of encouragement when he walked by my office during his monthly trips to Corvallis for Press meetings. Book designer Erin New worked wonders with the layout. I knew I was in good hands when, after our initial discussion, she provided me with a mock layout of an early chapter that was knock-my-socks-off good.

Karyle Butcher, university librarian and press director emeritus, was instrumental in supporting the project when it was revived in 2010. Faye Chadwell, the present university librarian and press director, has been a major force in pushing the pictorial history project forward and granting me the necessary time to devote to it. Likewise, associate university librarian Shan Sutton has also been supportive of the project and understanding about the time I've needed to devote to it.

Ben Mutschler, director of the School of History, Philosophy and Religion in the College of Liberal Arts, has provided a very thought-provoking afterword. Ben, who taught a senior seminar in 2013 and 2014 on OSU history, afforded me the opportunity to talk to his classes about the pictorial history project. Two of his 2013 students, Brittany Backen and Todd Moore, contributed content to the book. They both wrote abstracts of their research papers for the class, which appear as sidebars. Brittany's paper was chosen as one of the 2013 winners of the Library Undergraduate Research Award.

Special thanks go to my colleague and friend Bill Robbins, distinguished professor of history emeritus at OSU. Bill, who has been working on a full narrative history of OSU to be published by OSU Press just before the university's sesquicentennial in 2018, was very generous with sharing his research notes, helping clarify key points of OSU history, and offering words of encouragement. His foreword to this book helps set the stage for its focus on OSU's land-grant mission.

My final thanks go to my wife and personal editor, Rebecca. I called upon her superb journalistic skills throughout this project. She edited multiple versions of each chapter, gently making corrections and suggestions. Her understanding of the sometimes complex political issues and policy matters that are interwoven throughout OSU's history was of great help in explaining those issues to a broad audience.

This book has been a labor of love and the fulfillment of a dream that I've had during my twenty-four years at OSU. I hope that through *A School for the People* I have done this amazing place justice.

LARRY LANDIS
Corvallis, Oregon
November 13, 2014

Corvallis College cadet corps, ca. 1873. President Benjamin Arnold established the cadet corps soon after he assumed the presidency of the college in August 1872. Captain Benjamin Boswell assumed command of the cadet corps in 1873—the first United States Army officer on active duty to hold such a position at a western land-grant college. (HC 1344)

An Overview History of Oregon State University

FROM ITS BEGINNING as a struggling preparatory school to its present stature as a Carnegie Foundation top-tier research institution, Oregon State University has exerted a significant influence that today can be seen locally, statewide, nationally, and internationally.

OSU traces its roots to 1856, when the Corvallis Academy was founded as the first community school in the Corvallis area. By 1859, it had developed pretensions that it offered a collegiate-level curriculum, changed its name to Corvallis College, and constructed a building. The college quickly ran into financial difficulties, however, and in 1860 it was sold to Orceneth Fisher, a representative of the Methodist Episcopal Church, South. Under the auspices of that church, Corvallis College began offering a four-year, collegiate-level, liberal arts curriculum in 1865, with the Reverend William A. Finley serving as president of the institution. It also offered a preparatory department, which typically had many more students than the collegiate department.

The US Congress, meanwhile, passed the Morrill Land-Grant Act in 1862, which allowed each state to establish a public higher educational institution that would be supported in part by a grant of federal lands in each state—to be sold to establish an endowment. Introduced by US Representative Justin Smith Morrill of Vermont in 1861, the legislation required that each college established under the act teach agriculture, engineering, and military tactics.[1] President Lincoln signed the legislation on July 2, 1862.

Between 1863 and 1868, the state of Oregon took steps to identify public lands and an appropriate institution, but no firm action was taken until the latter part of 1868.

That year, through the efforts of Corvallis College faculty member William Walter Moreland, who also was a clerk for the Oregon Legislative Assembly, and Benton County members of the assembly, the legislature provisionally designated Corvallis College as Oregon's land-grant institution under the provisions of the Morrill Act.[2] The designation was made permanent in 1870 after a commission identified the land-grant lands. The 90,000 acres of land granted to Oregon in support of the institution were located in south-central Oregon, mostly in what is now Lake County.

Despite the land-grant designation, the small college, under presidents William A. Finley (who left the college in 1872) and Benjamin L. Arnold, constantly struggled with limited enrollment and finances over the next twenty years. The land-grant lands were slow to sell, and financial support from the state was minimal.

The lack of financial support and limited enrollment did not deter the college from doing its best to comply with the provisions of the Morrill Act. Three students graduated in 1870, the first class to complete the collegiate-level course. In 1871 the college purchased a farm of 34.85 acres for $4,500, with funding from more than one hundred local citizens. The original farm is now lower campus and the rise where Benton Hall is located. Courses in agriculture were first offered in 1870 through the chemistry department, and military training began in 1872.

The first agricultural research bulletin was published in 1873 on the topics of white and marl soils. It was included in both the 1872–74 biennial report and the 1873–74 college catalog. The college established an agriculture department

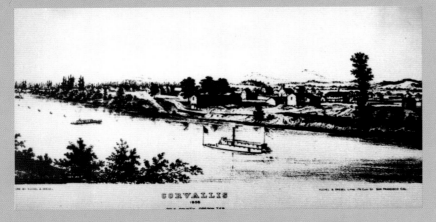

View of Corvallis, 1858. This view was the centerpiece of a series of lithographs made of Corvallis by the renowned San Francisco lithographers, Kuchel & Dresel. The Corvallis College building, with its steeple, is visible just to the right of center. The population of Corvallis at the time was about five hundred. (Courtesy Benton County Historical Society, #20020010080)

Portrait of William A. Finley, ca. 1870. William Asa Finley (1839–1912) served as the first president of Corvallis College. He moved to California from Missouri as a teenager, attended the University of the Pacific in Santa Clara and Pacific Methodist College in Vacaville, and received an AM degree from the latter in 1864. He was appointed president in 1865 by the Methodist Episcopal Church, South, and was president at the time of the college's designation as the state's land-grant institution in 1868. Finley resigned in 1872, purportedly due to his wife's failing health; they returned to California. He later served as the second president of Pacific Methodist College and as president of the Santa Rosa Young Ladies College. (P 1:2)

Morrill Land Grant Act of 1862. Page one of the act that led to the designation of Corvallis College as the state's first public higher education institution. (Courtesy National Archives; Record Group 11, General Records of the United States Government. Downloaded from www.ourdocuments.gov.)

First graduating class, Corvallis College, 1870.
Robert McVeatch, Alice E. Biddle, and James K.
P. Currin posed for this portrait by an unknown
photographer in the spring of 1870.

McVeatch, who delivered the valedictory
address at the graduation ceremony, went on to
serve two terms in each house of the Oregon
legislature and was the 1896 Democratic
nominee for Oregon's congressional seat.
Biddle was the daughter of B. R. Biddle, the
clerk of the college's board of trustees. The
Biddle family had been neighbors of Abraham
Lincoln when they lived in Springfield, Illinois,
prior to coming to Oregon. Alice Biddle
married William W. Moreland in December
1870. (Moreland had been pivotal in Corvallis
College's designation as Oregon's land-grant
institution in 1868.) Currin taught in Missouri
after his graduation from Corvallis College, and
later practiced as a pharmacist. (HC 883)

College or Administration Building, ca. 1889. The first academic
building constructed on the original college farm, now known as
Benton Hall, has been a centerpiece of the OSU campus since it
opened in 1889. The building originally served many purposes—it
included classrooms, labs, faculty offices, the library, a chapel, and the
president's office. In this photo, various agricultural experiment station
test plots are in the foreground, and an orchard is to the right of the
building. (HC 38)

1893-94 football team. Oregon State's first football team was coached by Will Bloss (center, holding the football), son of OAC president John Bloss. He led the team to a 5-1 record that first season, including a 62-0 win over Albany College (now Lewis & Clark College) in the inaugural game. (P25:1390)

in 1883 and named a former graduate, Edgar Grimm (class of 1880), as the first professor of agriculture.

Corvallis College's land-grant designation in 1868 created a bifurcated institution that was a church-controlled entity (its board of trustees were all church appointees) but with an agricultural program that was federally and state supported. The state began working to achieve full control of the college in 1883. Despite legal efforts by church authorities, the end result was state control. Beginning in 1885, the college established a state-appointed board of regents, which included the governor, the state superintendent of public instruction, and the state grange master.[3] The college also began planning to relocate from its inadequate building in downtown Corvallis to its college farm lands west of downtown. A local association was formed in 1885 to raise funds for the construction of a new college building.

The enactments of the federal Hatch Act of 1887 and the Second Morrill Act of 1890 were watershed moments for the college, now known informally as Oregon Agricultural College (OAC), as they provided a regular stream of much-needed additional funding.[4] Construction of the new college building started in August 1887, and the college moved from its downtown Corvallis location to the new building in time for classes in the fall of 1889. The new building, called the Administration Building or College Building (now Benton Hall), served the college in almost every capacity—classrooms, labs, library, president's office, faculty offices, chapel, and more. In 1889 a residence hall, Alpha Hall, was constructed to accommodate many of the college's students.

Benjamin Arnold, who had served as president since 1872 and guided the college through its split with the Methodist Episcopal Church and relocation to the college farm, passed away unexpectedly in early 1892. For the next fifteen years (1892–1907) presidents John M. Bloss, Henry B. Miller, and Thomas M. Gatch directed the college. During President Bloss's tenure (1892–1896), as enrollment grew and the curriculum expanded, several buildings were added to the new campus, including a residence hall for men (Cauthorn Hall) and buildings to support research and teaching. In 1893 Bloss allowed athletic competition at the intercollegiate level. A football team was formed, with the president's son serving as coach and quarterback. In its first season over the fall and winter of 1893–1894, the team won five games and lost one. Farmers' institutes were first held at various locations around the state in 1888 and were supplemented with on-campus short courses for farmers beginning in 1894. What was to become the college's newspaper, the *Barometer*, was founded as a monthly publication in 1896. The domestic science department, established in 1889, grew significantly in the 1890s, as did engineering.

After Bloss's departure in 1896, Regent Henry Miller was appointed college president. Miller served less than a year, from late July 1896 through June of the following year. Following Miller's resignation, the board of regents named Thomas M. Gatch as president. Gatch was a well-known and highly esteemed educator in the Pacific Northwest. He served as OAC's president for ten years.

Gatch's term as president was marked by steady growth in enrollment, academic programs, research, and the physical infrastructure of the college. Enrollment of college-level students in 1897 was 336; by 1907 enrollment had grown to 613 students. International students were allowed to enroll in 1904.[5] New academic programs were established in pharmacy (1898), commerce (1900), mining (1900), and forestry (1906). A self-sustaining music department was formed in 1901; this popular conservatory-style program drew both regularly enrolled students and others. Agricultural research greatly expanded under Gatch's leadership. New investigations were started at the Corvallis campus, and the first branch experiment station was established in eastern Oregon in 1901.

The campus suffered a major, though temporary, setback when Mechanical Hall, built in 1889 and expanded in 1894, was destroyed by fire in September 1898. Board of Regents President John T. Apperson soon began pushing the Oregon legislature for funds for a new Mechanical Hall; the new building was quickly approved and was dedicated on June 30, 1900. Other buildings constructed during

Gatch's presidency included Agriculture Hall (1902), the Gymnasium and Armory (1898), and a new women's dormitory, Waldo Hall (1907).

As enrollment grew, so did extracurricular opportunities for students. The athletic program begun during the Bloss presidency greatly expanded in the Gatch years. Basketball was established for women in 1898 and for men in 1901. Track-and-field competitions began in June 1895 as part of an all-collegiate meet in Salem. Baseball was played sporadically in the 1890s and after the turn of the twentieth century. It gained a foothold as an intercollegiate sport in 1907 with the establishment of a permanent baseball diamond. A student assembly, the forerunner of today's Associated Students of Oregon State University (ASOSU), began in 1900. The *Barometer* moved from its monthly magazine format and became a weekly newspaper starting in fall 1906.

Student organizations have long played a key role in the lives of Oregon State students, and many were established during the Bloss and Gatch administrations. College-sponsored literary societies dated back to the late 1860s and peaked in the 1890s and first decade of the twentieth century. In many respects they were the forerunners of the sororities and fraternities that later developed into a strong Greek system. Today's two-hundred-plus-member marching band has its roots in the early 1890s; for many years it was a component of the ROTC program. A YMCA was established in 1892 and a YWCA in about 1897, and both had a strong presence on campus through the late twentieth century. Clubs centered on living groups and academic areas took root during Gatch's administration. Lecturers were invited to campus, and students and faculty were obliged to attend a chapel period that included songs, prayer, scripture readings, orations, and musical performances.

In late 1906 Gatch announced his retirement. After a national search, the board of regents selected William Jasper Kerr, president of the Utah Agricultural College, as the new president of OAC. Kerr, who ultimately served as president for twenty-five years and transformed the college more than any other president, took office in July 1907.

By the time Kerr left the presidency in 1932, he had led the college from a solid regional school to one of national

Portrait of William Jasper Kerr, ca. 1910. This portrait of President Kerr was taken a few years after he was selected president of the college. Kerr came to OAC in 1907 after having served as president of Brigham Young College (now defunct and not a predecessor of Brigham Young University) and Utah Agricultural College (now Utah State University). He quickly positioned the college for more than two decades of growth in all areas, including academics, research, extension, campus infrastructure, and athletics. By the late 1920s, OAC was one of the leading land-grant institutions in the nation. His accomplishments as president included:

- Raising entrance requirements and securing accreditation of the college by authoritative accrediting agencies
- Initiating summer session
- Organizing the Extension Service in Oregon three years before the federal Smith-Lever Act created the service in all of the states
- Establishing radio station KOAC
- Initiating student government, the student health service, and student loans
- Hiring John Olmsted and A. D. Taylor to OAC to create campus plans—plans that still help shape how OSU develops

Kerr also served as the first chancellor of the State System of Higher Education from 1932 to 1935. He remained closely affiliated with Oregon State until his death in 1947. (P1:17) (P1:29)

importance. When he took office, the enrollment stood at approximately 1,300 students and the faculty consisted of 40 members. By 1930 enrollment was more than 3,300 students and the faculty numbered more than 180. He reorganized the academic structure of the college, establishing the schools of agriculture, commerce, domestic science, and engineering and mechanic arts in 1908; forestry and mining in 1913; pharmacy in 1917; and vocational education and the division of service departments in 1918.

The First World War had a brief, but strong, impact on OAC. In the 1918–20 college biennial report, college editor Edwin T. Reed wrote that the war involved OAC, like other land-grant institutions, "to such an extent as to be a dominant interest even before the declaration of war and long after the signing of the armistice." Nearly two thousand students, faculty, and alumni served in the military, and more than two thousand men enrolled in the Students Army Training Corps and other specialized war training programs in 1918. Housing students in these programs became a priority, and a new YMCA was erected. Most regular student activities were abandoned, and all faculty and staff were required to sign a loyalty oath. A liberty loan bond drive netted $83,000 toward the war effort. OAC agriculture faculty helped increase production of wheat and other grains needed for export, and dean of home economics Ava Milam played a key role in the Federal Food Administration in Oregon. The influenza epidemic that ravaged much of the nation and world in 1918 and 1919 was reported to have been "remarkably well maintained" on campus, though the second floor of Shepard Hall was used as a quarantine infirmary for students and townspeople in early 1919.

The physical plant of the college experienced unprecedented growth in the 1910s and 1920s—growth that was guided by campus plans developed by two of the nation's greatest landscape design and planning companies.[6] Using the design skills of Portland architect John V. Bennes and other architects, the college added twenty-four major buildings totaling more than 1.2 million square feet during Kerr's administration.[7] The most significant of these were a new agriculture hall, built in three phases between 1909 and 1913; a home economics building (1914–1920); men's and women's physical education buildings; a new library;

a massive residence hall for men; and a memorial union, built to honor those Oregon Staters who lost their lives during the Great War and the earlier Spanish-American War. Most of the new buildings were built with red brick and terra cotta (still prevalent on campus to this day), in line with the "uniformity of design" called for in the first campus plan.

New and expanded research programs, particularly in the core land-grant areas of agriculture, forestry, engineering, and home economics, helped OAC become one of the nation's leading land-grant institutions during the Kerr administration. Building on the farmers' institutes and farmers' short courses begun in the late 1880s and 1890s, OAC established an extension service in 1911 *"for the purpose of aiding in extending the advantages of the college to the people of the State. It is known that much of the information in the possession of the experts of the college and the experiment station would be of value to the people of the State who cannot come to the college for it if it could be carried to them."* This was three years before the federal Smith-Lever Act established the Extension Service nationally. In 1922, the college's first radio station, KFDJ, was licensed. Its broadcasts included substantive programming developed by OAC's Extension Service.[8]

Athletics were a vital part of campus life during Kerr's administration, and many teams had considerable success. The football team went undefeated and unscored upon in 1907. The team beat Michigan Agricultural College in 1915 and New York University in 1928, exposing other parts of the country to west coast collegiate football. The OAC men's basketball team won its first Pacific Northwest Conference title in 1909 and another in 1912, and also won titles in the new Pacific Coast Conference in 1916 (co-champion with California) and 1918. The team claimed PCC Northern Division titles in 1924 and 1925.

Several new intercollegiate sports were added in the 1920s, including tennis (1921), swimming (1922), polo (1923), crew (1927), and golf (1928). New or expanded facilities were added for football (1913 and 1924) and basketball (1915). Conversely, OAC women, who had competed in certain sports against other schools for a quarter of a century, were discouraged from doing so starting in 1922.

Curricular conflicts with the University of Oregon and the need for more coordination in Oregon's public higher education led the state legislature to establish the Oregon State Board of Higher Curricula in 1909. Stronger measures were taken twenty years later when the Legislature approved the Oregon Unification Bill in 1929, which

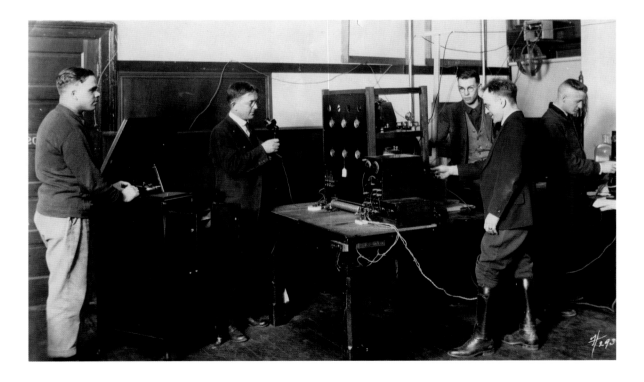

First radio transmitter, 1922. The first transmitter for OAC radio station KFDJ was built by physics professor Jacob Jordan (second from left) in 1922 and was located in Apperson Hall (Kearney Hall). KFDJ became KOAC in 1925. (See chapter 6 for more KOAC history.) Several students assisted Jordan with the transmitter's operation. (HC 598)

consolidated all state-supported colleges and universities into a single administrative structure (the Oregon State System of Higher Education) under a single board (the State Board of Higher Education). Boards of regents for individual schools were abolished. Further refinement and reorganization of the State System of Higher Education in 1932, driven in part by the need to cut costs because of the Great Depression, resulted in William Jasper Kerr's appointment as the first chancellor—not a popular choice with the University of Oregon. This ended Kerr's twenty-five-year tenure as president of Oregon State. He served as chancellor until 1935.

The reorganization effort also resulted in major changes to the curricula of OSC[9] and the University of Oregon. A lower division of liberal arts and sciences and the new School of Science were established at Oregon State; the School of Commerce was transferred to the University of Oregon; the School of Mines was discontinued at Oregon State; and landscape architecture became a joint degree program of the two schools. These changes had consequences that are still felt today—especially the lack of graduate programs in the liberal arts at OSU, particularly at the doctoral level.

Despite financial setbacks and enrollment fluctuations brought on by the Great Depression and the curricular reorganization, Oregon State managed its way through the

1930s under the leadership of George Peavy, the college's longtime dean of forestry, who served as acting president (1932 to 1934) and president (1934 to 1940). In 1931 the college staff had been reduced by sixty-six positions and all salaries were cut. Enrollment dropped from 3,347 in 1930–31 to a low of 1,960 in 1933–34. But enrollment quickly rebounded, and by the 1936–37 school year, OSC had set a new enrollment record of 3,785 students.

The Depression put the brakes on the rapid growth of the campus infrastructure experienced in the 1910s and 1920s. A number of planned buildings were delayed or cancelled. Two buildings were constructed in the 1930s, both funded with federal Public Works Administration dollars. In 1936 the Student Health Services Building was completed, and in 1939 a new chemistry building opened its doors.

Agricultural research, supported by federal funding, continued to be strong, especially in insect pest and plant disease control; farm crops breeding, selection, and production; and fruit, vegetable, and nut production. The School of Forestry strengthened its position as one of the premier programs in the country in 1932 with the acquisition of several hundred acres northwest of Corvallis through benefactor Mary McDonald, forming the nucleus of its research forest named for her.

Academically, OSC fared well during Peavy's years as president. The college reached a milestone with its first

McDonald Forest entrance sign, ca. 1940. Mary J. McDonald's 1932 donation of 520 acres a few miles north of Corvallis formed the nucleus of the McDonald Research Forest. Funds from McDonald's estate enabled the subsequent purchase of additional lands for the research forest. (P61:7)

Oregon State's first PhD recipients, June 1935. Herbert L. Jones (left) and Alfred Taylor were two of four recipients of the first PhD degrees awarded by Oregon State. Jones studied physics and Taylor studied zoology. The other recipients were Karl Klemm (chemistry) and Clarence Burnham (soils). (HC 1878)

four doctoral degrees, awarded at the 1935 commencement exercises. Sigma Xi, the national honor society for science, formed an OSC chapter in 1937. At the close of the decade, the School of Home Economics and the School of Engineering celebrated their fiftieth anniversaries.

Athletics continued the success it had experienced in the 1910s and 1920s. Its "Iron Men" football team of 1933 tied the powerful University of Southern California 0-0 while using only eleven players the entire game. The basketball team, led by All-American center Ed Lewis, won the 1932–33 Pacific Coast Conference title.

As the 1930s drew to a close, so did Peavy's presidency. Frank L. Ballard (class of 1916), from OSC's Extension Service, was selected as the college's new president by the State Board of Higher Education and assumed office on July 1, 1940. Health problems forced Ballard to resign about a year later. Dean of Science Francois Gilfillan (class of 1918) was appointed acting president, and he served from September 1941 to October 1942. August L. Strand, president of Montana State College, became the next president in October 1942 and served nearly nineteen years.

The United States' entry into World War II in December 1941 quickly changed the face of Oregon State. Many male students took leave from school to enlist in the armed forces. Though not large in number, OSC's Japanese-American student population was forced to leave school in the spring of 1942 because of federal Executive Order 9066.

The OSC football team, which won the right to play in the Rose Bowl (its first) against Duke, was almost denied the chance. The game in Pasadena was cancelled due to the prohibition of large public gatherings on the west coast. Fortunately Duke offered the use of its stadium and the game was played—a 20–16 upset victory for OSC.

OSC played a key role in many aspects of the war effort during World War II. The college commissioned more ROTC cadets as officers than any other non-military institution in the United States and trained 3,023 servicemen as part of the Army Specialized Training Program. Several faculty members taught ASTP courses, served in the armed forces, or conducted research directly related to the war effort. Students raised money for war bonds, participated in scrap drives, and sponsored blood drives. The Extension Service promoted victory gardens, developed labor-saving techniques for the farm and home, and coordinated a massive farm labor program to counter the agricultural labor shortage in Oregon caused by military enlistments and work in the war industries. President Emeritus Peavy served as the local civil defense coordinator.

Returning servicemen in the years immediately after the war created another enrollment boom (enrollment reached nearly seventy-five hundred students in 1947–48), resulting in the hiring of many additional faculty members. All

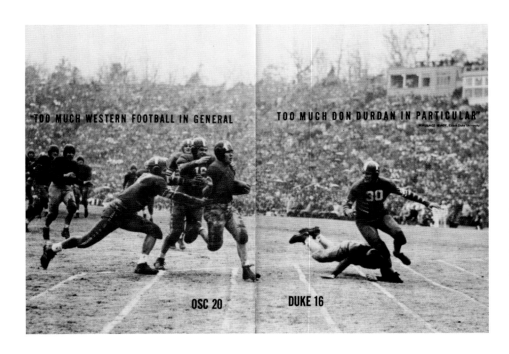

1942 Rose Bowl spread in the *Beaver* yearbook. Oregon State's first Rose Bowl appearance—and only victory to date in that iconic bowl game—received considerable attention in the 1942 yearbook. The quote on the pages was attributed to Duke University football coach Wallace Wade. (1942 *Beaver* yearbook, 186–187)

Coeds in a hops field, 1944. These OSC women participated in the massive wartime farm labor program coordinated by the OSC Extension Service. Utilizing housewives, retirees, children, guest workers from Mexico and Jamaica, soldiers on leave, and even prisoners of war, Oregon's Emergency Farm Labor Service (EFLS) made more than 900,000 farm labor placements from 1943 to 1947. The EFLS was one of Oregon State's major contributions to the war effort on the homefront. (HC 972)

available space was used to accommodate students. Parts of the Memorial Union were used as temporary student housing, and facilities at the former Camp Adair military cantonment just north of Corvallis were used to house returning vets and their families. Quonset huts seemed to appear almost overnight in many locations across the campus.

New construction, based in part on the updated campus plan developed by architect A. D. Taylor in 1945, commenced in the late 1940s and continued throughout Strand's administration. A new women's residence hall, Sackett Hall, opened in 1948—the first new permanent residence hall since completion of the Weatherford complex twenty years earlier. New academic buildings completed in the late

1940s and early 1950s included an electrical engineering building (Dearborn Hall), food science building (Wiegand Hall), and animal science building (Withycombe Hall). Athletics received a boost with new facilities for basketball (Gill Coliseum), which opened in late 1949, and football (Parker Stadium), which opened in 1953. Several college-owned cooperative houses were built, giving students who wished to live on campus alternatives to the standard dormitory experience.

Research in a variety of disciplines was established or expanded in the 1940s and 1950s. A seafood lab in Astoria and a forest products lab on campus provided new research facilities. The schools of agriculture and forestry benefitted from the acquisition of 6,200 acres that had been part of Camp Adair during World War II. Oregon State entered the computer age when the Oregon State College Electronic Analog Computer went online in the mid-1950s. The Science Research Institute was created in 1952 to promote individual and team-based scientific research and the pursuit of research grants. Oceanographic research was greatly expanded with grant funding from the Office of Naval Research starting in 1954. By 1959 oceanography was established as a department. Nuclear research took a major step forward in 1958 when OSC received $250,000 from the Atomic Energy Commission to purchase an AGN-201 nuclear reactor.

OSC was not immune to the effects of the Cold War. In February 1949 President Strand declined to renew two faculty members, chemistry professor and Linus Pauling protégée Ralph Spitzer and economics professor Laurent R. LaVallee. Strand claimed that both had Communist sympathies. The OSC firings, similar to faculty dismissals at other universities, put OSC in the spotlight of national debates over academic freedom. It also caused a decades-long rift between Pauling and OSC, as Pauling supported Spitzer and was greatly displeased by Strand's action. Ultimately Pauling renewed his relationship with Oregon State, and in 2012 OSU President Ed Ray issued a formal apology to Dr. Spitzer.

Curricular changes resulted from the establishment of new or expanded degree programs. Business training returned to OSC in 1943 after having been moved to the University of Oregon in 1932. The pharmacy curriculum

Coliseum interior construction, 1949. This photo shows Gill Coliseum under construction just a few months before the first events were held in the facility in November 1949. (P16:873)

AGN-201 nuclear reactor in Dearborn Hall, 1961. OSU's first nuclear reactor, purchased for $250,000 in 1958, was relocated to the newly built Radiation Center a few years later. (P82:92 #2620)

was shifted from a four-year to a five-year program in 1951—one of the first in the country. A joint degree program in education was established with the Oregon College of Education (now Western Oregon University) in 1953. ROTC added Naval and Air Force detachments in 1946 and 1949. The most significant curricular change in the postwar era was the 1959 establishment of the School of Humanities and Social Sciences, which was authorized to grant BA and BS degrees.

During the postwar years OSC began developing a strong international presence, especially in the Pacific Rim. In 1950, President Strand was appointed by President Harry Truman to a five-person commission to study economic conditions in the Philippines. In 1954, OSC signed a contract with Kasetsart University in Bangkok, Thailand, to provide it with technical assistance. Several OSC faculty participated in the contract work under the leadership of Godfrey Hoerner and Robert Henderson, each of whom served as chief adviser of OSC staff at Kasetsart between 1955 and 1960. OSC faculty conducted a sports clinic in Japan in 1956. The college's international student population grew quickly in the 1950s, from 107 students from twenty-four countries in 1949 to 207 students from thirty-six countries in 1958.

Athletics continued to achieve success in a number of sports. After a down period in the early 1950s, the football team bounced back under coach Tommy Prothro and played in the 1957 Rose Bowl. The baseball team under coach Ralph Coleman made its first appearance in the College World Series in 1952. Basketball coach A.T. "Slats" Gill continued to put competitive men's basketball teams on the court. His teams won seven conference titles between 1940 and 1960, and made three NCAA playoff appearances, including its first Final Four appearance in 1949. Student Ken Austin donned a beaver head and made his debut as Benny Beaver in the fall of 1952.

As was true at other universities, the 1960s can be characterized as a decade of significant change for Oregon State. In March 1961, Oregon Governor Mark Hatfield signed legislation that renamed Oregon State College to Oregon State University. President Strand stepped down in August 1961, and Iowa State's provost, James H. Jensen, was selected as his successor. OSU's student enrollment nearly doubled

Benny Beaver and the Rally Squad, 1952. According to the *Barometer*, Benny Beaver made his live debut on September 18, 1952. Pictured here is Ken Austin, purportedly the first student to don the Benny the Beaver costume. Benny is one of many long-standing traditions at OSU. (P17:32)

during the decade, from 7,900 in 1960 to 15,200 in 1969. The makeup of the student body also began to change, as more students of color and international students came to OSU, though racial strife would surface in 1969. Academically, the 1960s brought expanded degree programs in the social sciences and humanities and a new library building that opened in 1963.

The 1960s proved to be a landmark decade for research at OSU, with the establishment of several centers and institutes. These included the Water Resources Research Institute (1961), the Transportation Research Institute (1962), the Nutrition Research Institute (1965), the Nuclear Science and Engineering Institute (1966), the Environmental Health Sciences Center (1967), and the International Plant Protection Center (1969).

Perhaps no OSU research program grew more quickly and developed a stronger national reputation than oceanography. An oceanography building was completed in 1964. New research vessels were commissioned, including the *Acona* in 1961, the *Yaquina* in 1964, and the *Cayuse* in 1968. A new marine science center was established in

Governor Mark O. Hatfield signs legislation changing the name of Oregon State College to Oregon State University, March 6, 1961. With Governor Hatfield (seated) were, from left: C. R. Hoyt, state representative from Benton County; Francis Ziegler, state senator from Benton County; Richard A. Seideman, president of the Associated Students of Oregon State University; Robert White (class of 1940), state senator; President A. L. Strand; Harry Bolvin, president of the Oregon Senate; John Fenner (class of 1940), Alumni Association president; and Anthony Yturri, state senator. (HC 2227)

Newport and dedicated in 1965. And in 1968—the university's centennial year—OSU was one of just three universities nationally selected to take part in the new federal Sea Grant program.

Steady growth of the student population and an expanding research program in the 1960s required additional physical facilities. Several residence halls were built to accommodate on-campus living; these included West Hall (1960), Orchard Court apartments (1961), the McNary/Callahan/Wilson complex (1963–64), Avery and Dixon Lodges (1966), and Finley Hall (1967). In the centennial year of 1968 a new mechanical engineering building (Rogers Hall) and dairy barn were opened. The Milne Computer Center went online in 1969.

Campus life changed dramatically in the 1960s, as it did at many colleges and universities across the nation. In 1962, ROTC at all land-grant institutions shifted from two years of mandatory participation to voluntary participation. ROTC at OSU remained strong. Greek organizations continued as a significant part of student life. Toward the end of the decade, there was a growing recognition of students of

OSU research vessel *Yaquina*. The *Yaquina*, OSU's second oceanographic research vessel, was commissioned on September 28, 1964, in Portland. (P25:2082)

March in memory of Dr. Martin Luther King Jr.
OSU students and faculty paid tribute to King after his assassination
on April 4, 1968. (P120:5013d)

A civil handshake between rival coaches, 1962. OSU
football coach Tommy Prothro received congratulations from
University of Oregon coach Len Casanova after OSU's 20–17
victory in the 1962 Civil War. All-Americans Terry Baker (OSU
no. 11) and Steve Barnett (Oregon no. 77) are behind their
respective coaches. (P25:3116)

color and students from various ethnic and cultural backgrounds. The Black Student Union (BSU) was organized in 1968 to give a voice to the campus's African American community. The BSU organized a march after the assassination of Rev. Martin Luther King Jr. in April 1968, and led a walkout in early spring 1969 to protest the mistreatment of an African American football player. Although divisive at the time, the walkout led to the formation of committees and organizations that were the forerunners of OSU's strong diversity programs today. The war in Vietnam was on students' radar screens in the late 1960s, but it did not yet evoke the emotions seen in protests at other colleges and universities. That would change in the early 1970s.

Paralleling the university's expanded research agenda in the 1960s was the visibility of athletics. Teams played in two football bowl games and in several NCAA basketball tournaments. The basketball team was integrated under new coach Paul Valenti.

Perhaps the most visible sports in the 1960s were OSU's track and field and cross-country teams. The 1961 cross-country team gave OSU its first NCAA national championship. Under coach Berny Wagner, the track and field team became a national powerhouse between 1966 and 1975. OSU's athletic pinnacle of the 1960s was high jumper Dick Fosbury's gold medal win at the 1968 Summer Olympics in Mexico City. His distinctive "flop" style revolutionized the high jump as a track and field event.

The 1960s also saw other Oregon Staters honored nationally and internationally. 1922 graduate Linus Pauling won the 1962 Nobel Peace Prize—his second unshared Nobel prize, coming less than ten years after he was awarded the 1954 chemistry prize. Former English faculty member Bernard Malamud, who taught at Oregon State from

Linus Pauling's Nobel Peace Prize medal. Pauling was the recipient of the 1962 Nobel Peace Prize, which was awarded to him in Oslo, Norway, on December 10, 1963. (MSS-Pauling Papers, 1963h2.1)

1949 to 1961, won the 1967 Pulitzer Prize for fiction for his novel, *The Fixer*. And alumnus and former faculty member Willi Unsoeld was part of a team of the first Americans to scale Mount Everest in May 1963.

President Jensen resigned in June 1969 to become vice rector of Kasetsart University in Thailand. Dean of Research Roy A. Young was appointed acting president and served for a year. After Robert W. MacVicar was selected as president in 1970, Young was appointed OSU's vice president for research and graduate studies—the university's first-ever vice president position.

MacVicar, who came to OSU from Southern Illinois University, led the university in the 1970s and the first half of the 1980s. His administration was marked by the construction of several new academic and administrative

buildings and student housing; the establishment of new cultural centers for students of color; the elevation of schools to colleges; and a new administrative structure—yet tempered with fluctuations in enrollment and the university's budget. It was also a time of contradictions and change for the university's athletic teams, with the start of what would be a nearly three-decade downward spiral for the football team, a rise in unmatched prominence for the men's basketball team, and the formalization of women's athletics under federal Title IX.

Student enrollment stood at 15,500 when MacVicar assumed OSU's presidency. It peaked at about 17,700 in 1980 and had fallen to 16,100 when he left office. MacVicar instituted administrative changes, upgrading several administrative dean positions to vice presidents and creating a faculty senate office. The new Administrative Services Building opened in early 1972, replacing the Camp Adair buildings that had been dubbed as temporary when they were moved onto campus twenty-five years earlier. It housed virtually all of OSU's administrative and student support functions, as well as some state system of higher education offices. In 1980 the Office of International Education was created to coordinate OSU's growing international student and scholar population.

A major downturn in Oregon's economy in the late 1970s and early 1980s had consequences for OSU. Reflecting significantly reduced state income tax revenues, OSU's state support was reduced by $6.4 million during the 1981–82 and 1982–83 academic years. In a precursor to similar circumstances that would play out ten years later, tuition quickly rose and enrollment dropped.[10] Academic losses included the closure of the Department of Architecture and Landscape Architecture, elimination of the graduate degree program in general science, and the end of general fund support for Summer Session.

Other academic changes during the downturn were more positive. The departments of oceanography and veterinary medicine and the division of health and physical education were promoted to school status in the 1970s, and by 1983 all schools (except education) had been given college status. In 1982, OSU and Western Oregon State College established a jointly administered school of education—the only one of its kind in the nation.

New OSU President Robert MacVicar talks to Lloyd Smith on Larry Wade's ranch near Condon, summer 1970. Just two weeks after assuming office, MacVicar undertook a five-day swing through eastern Oregon visiting ranches and agricultural projects. This photo appeared on the cover of the September 1970 *Oregon Stater*. (P57:5283)

Research programs under MacVicar continued the momentum achieved under President Jensen. Additional research centers, institutes, and labs were established, including the Survey Research Center, the Environmental Remote Sensing Application Laboratory, the Climate Research Institute, and the Human Performance Lab. A Center for the Humanities was created in 1984 to support humanities-related teaching, research, and scholarship. Oceanographic programs continued to expand, with additional facilities at the Marine Science Center (renamed the Mark O. Hatfield Marine Science Center in 1983), a new research vessel (the *Wecoma*, commissioned in 1975), and the establishment of the Hinsdale Wave Research Lab on the main campus in 1983.

Individual faculty achievements included Harold J. Evans, professor of plant physiology, becoming the first faculty member from OSU elected to the National Academy of Sciences in 1972, and crop scientist Warren Kronstad releasing Stephens wheat in 1981, a new variety that quickly became the most widely planted variety in the Pacific Northwest. Alumnus Milton Harris (class of 1926) established OSU's first fully endowed faculty chair in 1984, in polymer chemistry.

Several new buildings were constructed to support teaching and the expanding research agenda. Nash Hall was completed in 1970 as the new home of the fisheries and wildlife department, and Wilkinson Hall opened in 1973 to house geology and geography. Forestry moved into Peavy Hall in 1971, a new facility built to replace the 1917 Forestry Building. The Crop Science Building opened in 1981. Veterinary medicine received a new facility, Magruder Hall, in 1979 as part of its upgrade from a department.

Students benefitted from a new residence and dining hall complex, Bloss and Arnold Halls, completed in 1972. A recreation center was built in 1976, and several cultural centers opened new facilities. Student programs were enhanced with a move to larger quarters in a former residence hall, Snell Hall, and its 1973 addition. The entire campus community benefitted from the opening of the cultural and conference facility, the LaSells Stewart Center, in 1981. At the time, this building was the largest gift-funded construction project at an Oregon public college or university, and it set the stage for the use of gift monies to underwrite most subsequent major building construction projects at OSU.

Athletics during the MacVicar years were a mixed bag. The strong football teams of the 1960s under coaches Tommy Prothro and Dee Andros gave way to weaker teams and support in the 1970s—consequently resulting in twenty-eight consecutive losing seasons (1971 through 1998) and several coaching changes. Men's basketball moved in the opposite direction. Paul Valenti stepped down as basketball coach after the 1970 season. Ralph Miller, who had success at Wichita State and the University of Iowa, was brought in as OSU's new coach; he served through the 1989 season and took eight teams to the NCAA tournament. By the late 1970s, Miller's teams were nationally ranked, and his 1980–81 team was ranked first in the nation for twenty-five weeks.

Although women had competed in intercollegiate athletics since before the turn of the twentieth century, federal legislation known as Title IX literally changed the face of athletics at most colleges and universities, including OSU, in the early 1970s.[11] Before the passage of Title IX, OSU women competed in volleyball, field hockey, gymnastics, pistol and rifle, skiing, and bowling, mostly at the club sport level. By 1976, four years after Title IX's passage, OSU women also competed at the intercollegiate level in basketball, track and field, gymnastics, softball, swimming, golf, and tennis. The women's basketball, gymnastics, and track and field teams had notable success during the MacVicar years. Basketball player and future Olympian Carol Mencken played for OSU for three seasons (1979 to 1981), leading the team to an NIT championship. Mary Ayotte and Laurie Carter won individual gymnastics national titles in the early 1980s. And Joni Huntley, another Olympian, was the best high jumper in the nation in 1975 while at OSU.

President MacVicar retired in November 1984. His successor, John V. Byrne, had been an oceanography faculty member at OSU and had just completed a term as the administrator of the federal National Oceanic and Atmospheric Administration (NOAA). Byrne also had served OSU as the first dean of oceanography and vice president for research and graduate studies before heading to NOAA. He quickly put his own stamp on the university's

Students rallying in opposition to Ballot Measure 5, fall 1990. The ballot measure, which was passed by Oregon voters on November 6, 1990, capped local property taxes. The net result was significantly reduced funding for most state functions, including higher education. (P3)

administration, including the establishment of the provost and a vice president for university relations. Byrne created OSU's first formal long-range plan in 1987, a document titled "Preparing for the Future," and in 1990 implemented Total Quality Management (TQM). OSU received a first place Innovative Management Achievement Award in 1994 from the National Association of College and University Business Officers for its TQM efforts.

The most significant challenge during Byrne's eleven years as president was passage of the statewide Ballot Measure 5 in November 1990. This measure limited local property taxes, leading to a substantial shift of state financial resources to public K-12 schools from all other programs. As a consequence, OSU and other public higher education institutions raised tuition and cut programs, which caused severe reductions in enrollment. OSU's tuition fees nearly doubled between 1990 and 1995; conversely, its enrollment fell from just over 16,000 in fall 1990 (prior to the passage of Measure 5) to 13,800 in fall 1996, a decrease of nearly 14 percent. Because of Measure 5, President Byrne

ordered an outside review of OSU's administrative costs and structure.[12]

The Byrne years included both gains and losses for academic programs. Prior to Measure 5, the first graduate degrees in the College of Liberal Arts were approved, as were new undergraduate curriculum and graduation requirements known as the Baccalaureate Core. Class of 1986 graduate Knute Buehler became OSU's first Rhodes Scholar in 1987. But in 1991, in response to Measure 5, OSU merged the colleges of home economics and education and eliminated several departments and programs, including journalism, religious studies, hotel and restaurant management, general science, and the honors program. The university's Horner Museum was closed in 1995.

There were bright spots in academics during Byrne's final years as president. A new degree program in international studies received approval and was initiated in fall 1993. The ethnic studies department and a new Honors College began in 1995. Debra Walt was selected as OSU's second Rhodes Scholar in 1995. Academics received a major boost in 1995 when the Wayne and Gladys Valley Foundation[13] pledged $10 million toward the university's library expansion campaign.

OSU's research agenda made significant progress during the Byrne years despite the limitations of Measure 5. Research grant funding increased. In 1987 OSU received more contract dollars from the US Agency for International Development (USAID) than any other university, and in 1988 OSU opened the nation's first marine experiment station, the Coastal Oregon Marine Experiment Station, at the marine science center in Newport. A new fish disease lab and a new sheep research facility opened in 1990. The following year OSU was designated as a space grant university, and in 1992 a new family study center was completed, underwritten in part with funds from alumnus Mercedes Bates. Zoologist Jane Lubchenco received OSU's first-ever MacArthur Fellowship in 1993 and the following year was named Oregon Scientist of the Year.

The physical infrastructure of the campus continued to expand during Byrne's administration, although at a slower pace and with more reliance on private funding. In 1988 OSU added a new electrical and computer engineering building, financed with state lottery funds. The

Agricultural and Life Sciences Building was dedicated in 1992, providing the College of Agricultural Sciences and the Department of Biochemistry and Biophysics with new teaching and research facilities. Parker Stadium received a new press box, skyboxes, and a grandstand roof in 1991. In addition to its pledge of $10 million for an expanded library, the Valley Foundation also funded the renovation of OSU's former theater into a world-class gymnastics training facility (Valley Gymnastics Center) and the construction of a new training and administrative facility for the football program (Valley Football Center). The CH2M HILL engineering firm, founded in 1946 by three alumni and their major professor, pledged $2 million toward a new alumni center in 1993.

As in MacVicar's administration, athletics were a study in contrasts during the Byrne years. In a pre-Measure 5 budget-cutting move, men's and women's track and field and cross country were eliminated, ending ninety years of participation as one of the stronger programs in the region and a worthy rival to the University of Oregon. Football continued to struggle, as it had since the early 1970s.

Basketball continued its powerhouse ways in the late 1980s, led by All-American Gary Payton, but it also fell from its pedestal in the early 1990s. In women's athletics, gymnastics continued to be a top-tier program nationally, finishing in the Top Ten nine times and producing four individual national champions during the Byrne years. Under coach Aki Hill, the women's basketball team reached the NCAA tournament in 1994 and 1995, led by two-time Pac-10 player of the year Tanja Kostic.

John Byrne retired at the end of 1995. Paul G. Risser, president of Miami University of Ohio, was selected to succeed him as president. During Risser's six years as president, OSU's declining enrollment trend was reversed, major buildings were constructed or expanded, and in 1999 the football team experienced its first winning season since 1970. A new higher education funding model implemented in 1999 led to modest increases in OSU's state appropriation, though just two years later OSU's budget was again faced with a shortfall.

Additions to the campus during the Risser years included an expanded Valley Football Center (1997), the completion

Gymnast Joy Selig about to perform a vault routine, winter 1989. Many consider Selig to have been the greatest gymnast in OSU history. She won three individual national titles—the balance beam in 1989 and 1990 and the floor exercise in 1990—and was a seven-time All-American. (P3, 1989 *Beaver*)

Students at commencement, June 2001. The 2001 commencement ceremony was the first to be held outdoors, in Reser Stadium. (P3, Accession 2005:064)

Students in the Valley Library rotunda, summer 1999. The $40 million renovation and expansion of the Valley Library was completed in the spring of 1999. The library quickly became a popular space for study and relaxation. The Valley Library was the first academic library to receive *Library Journal*'s Library of the Year Award (in 1999). (P83, Accession 2004:052)

of the CH2M Hill Alumni Center (1997), a renovated and expanded Valley Library (1999), the College of Forestry's Richardson Hall (1999), and Cascades Hall at OSU's new Central Oregon campus (2002). Two major floods in 1996 played havoc with Corvallis and OSU; record rain in November 1996 flooded ten OSU buildings and caused power outages and heat losses in others.

Enrollment began to grow again in 1997, when 14,118 students were tallied, reversing six years of decline. In fall 2002, when President Risser left OSU, enrollment had grown to 18,034 students.

During the Risser years, academics regained some of the ground lost in the early 1990s when several programs were eliminated. The new Honors College graduated its first class in 1997. New degree programs included Environmental Sciences (graduate) and New Media Communication. The

home economics and health and human sciences colleges merged in March 2002, and the School of Education was re-established as a separate academic entity. OSU engineering students had a higher pass rate on the Fundamentals of Engineering professional licensure exam than 99 percent of students in engineering programs in the United States. In 1999 OSU was named one of America's one hundred most wired universities. And OSU's first outdoor commencement was held in the newly renamed football stadium, Reser Stadium, in June 2001.

The 1996 relocation of the Linus Pauling Institute of Science and Medicine to OSU from Palo Alto, California, was a boost to OSU's research program. Food science took center stage with the opening of the Seafood Research Center in Astoria in 1998 and the Food Innovation Center in Portland in 1999. In 2000, OSU's office of Extension and

Experiment Station Communications won thirteen awards at the Agricultural Communicators in Education meeting, more than any other member organization.

Athletics received a big boost when the 1999 football team, directed by new coach Dennis Erickson, went 7-4 and played in the Oahu Bowl. The next year the team compiled a record of 10-1 and went on to defeat Notre Dame in the Fiesta Bowl. In 1996 football achieved a national championship of sorts—its athlete graduation rate of 95 percent was the highest in the nation. During the late 1990s and early 2000s men's and women's basketball struggled at times, though the gymnastics and baseball teams were consistent winners. The baseball field received a major facelift through $2 million in gifts. In 1999 alumni Al and Pat Reser (class of 1960), pledged $5 million toward an expansion and upgrade of the football stadium, which was renamed in their honor.

In February 2002, the State Board of Higher Education selected OSU to develop a new branch campus in Bend. The campus included the University of Oregon and Eastern Oregon University as Oregon University System partner institutions, and Linfield College, Oregon Health and Sciences University, and Central Oregon Community College as non-OUS partners. Classes started in September of that year—initial enrollment was 487 students[14]—and construction started on the $3.4 million Cascades Hall.

Risser departed OSU in late 2002 to become the chancellor of the Oklahoma University system. Provost Tim White was named interim president, a position he held until the end of July 2003. Edward Ray, who had been an Ohio State University faculty member and administrator for thirty-three years, was selected as Oregon State's new president and began on July 31, 2003.

The hallmarks of Ed Ray's presidency have been significant growth in enrollment, campus infrastructure, and research funding. He initiated a robust strategic planning process and embarked the university on a $1 billion capital campaign, which was completed in 2014.

Enrollment growth was fueled in part by the national recession of 2008, as well as growth in Ecampus, OSU's distance education program, new international students, and the Cascades Campus. OSU's total enrollment in fall 2003 stood at 18,979 and by fall 2008, it had risen to 20,320.

But after 2008, enrollment exploded, reaching just under 28,000 in fall 2013.[15]

OSU entered a building boom to accommodate the new students and expanded research programs. Major construction projects completed during Ray's first eleven years included an expansion of veterinary medicine research and training facilities in Magruder Hall, a complete renovation of Weatherford Hall for use by the College of Business's Austin Entrepreneurship Program, the Kelley Engineering Center, a $93 million expansion of Reser Stadium, complete restoration and renaming of Apperson and Education Halls (two of OSU's early twentieth-century buildings), a new residence hall focusing on the needs of international students, and a new home for the College of Business, Austin Hall. OSU's central campus area was designated in 2008 as an historic district on the National Register of Historic Places, making OSU one of just a few campuses nationally with such a designation. In the fall of 2013, OSU selected a site in southwest Bend as the permanent home of the Cascades Campus.

OSU's recent growth has not been without controversy. The rapid growth has at times created tension between the university, the City of Corvallis, and neighborhoods adjacent to campus. These issues were nothing new, as "town and gown" conflicts can be traced to the early twentieth century. Most recently, privately built housing developments for students have impinged on existing neighborhoods. New on-campus housing has helped to mitigate the impact but has not kept pace with the growth of new students. Parking has been another pressure point, as OSU's shift of parking to the southwest part of campus resulted in more OSU-related parking on neighborhood streets. Despite these issues, OSU has maintained a cordial relationship with the City of Corvallis, with several faculty and staff having served as mayor, city councilors, and on citizen commissions.

In January 2004, OSU was one of five universities selected to participate in the Sun Grant initiative, a program to develop sustainable and renewable agricultural products based on the sun's energy. Other key research initiatives included the establishment of the Oregon Nanoscience and Microtechnologies Institute (ONAMI) at the Corvallis Hewlett-Packard campus.

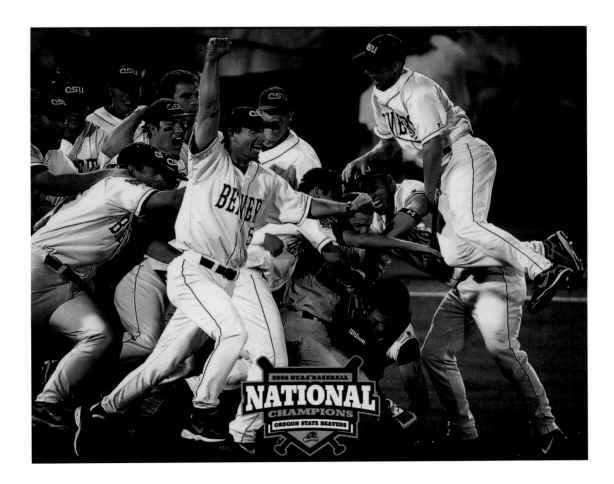

OSU baseball team celebrates after winning the 2006 College World Series, Omaha, Nebraska, June 26, 2006. OSU's team, led by coach Pat Casey (arm raised), creates the traditional "dogpile" in celebration of the win. OSU defeated North Carolina 3–2 in a thrilling game to capture the first of two consecutive College World Series titles. OSU defeated North Carolina again for the 2007 title. This image is the cover of the 2007 OSU Baseball Media Guide. (Courtesy of OSU Athletic Communications)

Athletics took the national spotlight with back-to-back baseball national championships in 2006 and 2007. Football teams participated in eight bowl games between 2003 and 2013. Track and field and cross country returned to OSU in 2004 with the re-establishment of women's programs in those sports. In 2008, OSU hired Craig Robinson, the brother-in-law of US Senator Barack Obama who was elected president of the United States in November of that year, as the new men's basketball coach. A new basketball practice facility was completed in 2013, providing a major boost to both the men's and women's programs. Gymnastics and wrestling were consistently ranked nationally, and the 2006 softball team played in the College World Series. On the club sports level, OSU fielded strong men's rugby teams and the coed racquetball club won national championships in 2006, 2008, 2009, 2010, 2011, and 2013.

Today OSU is considered one of the greenest universities in the nation. It draws students from all fifty states and one hundred countries. Students can choose from more than two hundred undergraduate and eighty graduate degree programs. More than 170,000 alumni are a part of Beaver Nation. It is the only university in Oregon to hold both the Carnegie Foundation's top research institution designation and its community engagement classification. OSU has a presence in all Oregon's thirty-six counties with a statewide economic footprint of more than $2 billion annually. It is truly Oregon's statewide university.

Corvallis College building, ca. 1868. This carte-de-visite photograph of the original Corvallis College building, built in 1858–59, was taken by photographers Stryker & Dohse. It is the earliest known photograph of what was to become Oregon State University. In 1868 the campus was located on Fifth Street between Madison and Monroe in downtown Corvallis, the same block on which Corvallis City Hall is located today. President Finley is one of the men by the fence on the right side of the photo. Stryker and Dohse opened their Corvallis photography gallery in 1868. It was located above B. R. Biddle's drug store on Main Street (now Second Street). Biddle was a member of the college's board of trustees. (HC 1344)

"Let Us Flee from Debt as from the Grave"
OSU's Early Years, 1858–1889

ALTHOUGH BENTON COUNTY was identified as the potential home of a state institution of higher learning even before Oregon became a state[1], the history of Corvallis College's evolution into a state agricultural college reveals a somewhat turbulent start—especially financially—for the institution known today as Oregon State University.

The local Baptist church established a Corvallis Academy in 1856, though it is not known how long this school was in existence. A school named Corvallis College was incorporated on January 20, 1858, by the territorial legislature.[2] It had no religious affiliation and offered classes that were at a "preparatory," or high school, level, rather than the collegiate level. This was true for many other "colleges" and academies founded during Oregon's territorial period.[3] John Wesley Johnson was one of Corvallis College's first teachers—an ironic twist of fate, as he later became the first president of the University of Oregon.

After the college's 1858 incorporation, local citizens raised funds to construct a building for the school. The site selected was the block bounded by Fifth and Sixth Streets on the east and west, and Madison and Monroe Streets on the south and north. The building was finally completed in 1859, and classes were held in the Baptist Church while the building was constructed. Beginning in 1858 the school began encountering severe financial difficulties, despite various attempts at fundraising. Because payments to carpenters and others who had constructed the building were delinquent, a judgment was made against the Corvallis College trustees on April 10, 1860. This judgment led to in the school being sold at a sheriff's sale on May 16, 1860, to Orceneth Fisher, a representative of the Methodist Episcopal Church, South, who bid $4,500.

The school, still called Corvallis College, reopened in November 1860 with Reverend W. M. Culp as principal. Tuition ranged from $8 to $16 per quarter, with course work mostly at the high school level. Fisher sold the college to the new board of trustees on January 1, 1861, and he continued to serve the college as its agent during that year.

In 1865 the school officially became the property of the Methodist Episcopal Church, South, and that year the church named Reverend William A. Finley of Santa Rosa, California, as its president. Finley is considered to be the institution's first president. Despite continued financial difficulties, it began offering collegiate-level classes in 1866. Most of the students continued to be enrolled at a sub-collegiate level.[4]

The passage of the federal Morrill Act in 1862 was a watershed for higher education in the United States, incorporating agriculture, engineering, and military instruction into the curriculum and making higher education more accessible to the "industrial classes." Throughout the 1860s, Oregon governors reiterated the need for the Legislative Assembly to move on accepting the provisions of the Morrill Act. As time was running out in 1868, the Legislative Assembly finally took action.

The 1868 session was the last in which Oregon could accept the conditions of the Morrill Act. Corvallis College had well-placed friends in the Legislative Assembly who ultimately outmaneuvered Willamette University during the session for temporary designation as the state's land-grant college. B. F. Burch, the college's agent and member of the board of trustees, was president of the senate. William W. Moreland, who directed the college's primary department, was the assistant clerk for the House of

Representatives and is credited with engineering legislative action on the Morrill Act.

The legislation as it was introduced designated Willamette University as the land-grant school. Willamette, founded in Salem in 1842, should have had a considerable edge given that it was a much more established institution. According to local historian John E. Smith's 1953 treatise on Corvallis College, the bill was delayed in the state senate due to wrangling over land grants to the state's two major railroads. During this delay, Charles B. Bellinger[5] Benton County representative and member of the majority Democratic Party[6] "experienced little difficulty in striking out the words Willamette University [from the bill] and inserting Corvallis College." The bill passed in the Legislative Assembly on October 24, 1868, was signed into law on October 27, and was accepted by the board of trustees of Corvallis College on October 31. Corvallis College was provisionally Oregon's land-grant institution.

The legislation stipulated that a Board of Commissioners be appointed to locate the lands "to which this State is entitled by Act of Congress, for the purpose of establishing an Agricultural College," and that they report the locations to the Oregon secretary of state. Joseph C. Avery, who had served on the original board of trustees in the late 1850s, was named commissioner along with J. F. Miller and J. H. Douthit. Oregon received a grant of 90,000 acres, 30,000 each for its representative and two senators. The lands were to be sold, at not less than $2.50 an acre, to create an endowment to support the college's agriculture and mechanic arts courses of study. The commissioners located 89,907 acres, mostly in Lake County.[7]

After the commissioners filed their lands report with the secretary of state in 1870, the Legislative Assembly passed legislation on October 27, 1870, to permanently locate the state's agricultural college at Corvallis. The board of trustees accepted the legislation on October 29.

But even after the permanent designation in 1870, the board learned that funds—whether from community "subscriptions," interest on the land trust, state appropriations, or tuition from farm families—would be hard to come by for many years. The land-grant lands sold very slowly, and monies appropriated to the college by the legislature for "state students" were slow in coming—$5,000 appropriated

in 1871 took more than a year to make its way to the college. The continual financial woes greatly disappointed President Finley and were likely at the heart of his decision to resign in June 1872.[8]

Despite the college's precarious financial position, it did manage to graduate its first class in June 1870 and acquire a college farm in 1871. One of the requirements of the Morrill Act was that each institution provide a college farm of at least 35 acres to support agricultural instruction. During 1870, the board of trustees solicited subscriptions for underwriting the cost of the farm. Enough of the $4,500 needed to make a substantive down payment on a farm had been raised by early 1871, and in March, 34.85 acres just west of downtown Corvallis were acquired from George and Elizabeth Jane Roberts. The purchase encompassed what is now lower campus and the knoll where Benton Hall is located, and included a dwelling, barn, and orchard. Many prominent local citizens and most of the board of trustees were subscribers. The largest subscription, $500, was provided by Greenberry Smith, the largest landholder in Benton County at the time.[9] Farming began on the land on April 12 under the direction of William Moreland, though was abandoned temporarily due to lack of funds and the need for Moreland to return to coordinating the preparatory department—a major source of tuition income for the college.

The college's second biennial report, written by faculty member, trustee, and interim president Joseph Emery in August 1872, outlined the college's successes, such as the purchase of the college farm. But Emery made it clear that additional financial support was necessary for the college to meet its needs, especially for agricultural instruction and for establishment of a military department: "To meet all these wants and demands, and to stock the farm with team, wagon and the necessary implements of agriculture, will require an appropriation by the legislature of not less than five thousand dollars a year, for the next two years."

Benjamin L. Arnold was appointed as president to replace Finley, and he assumed office in late summer 1872. He guided the college for nearly twenty years, including the turbulent period when the state assumed full control of the college from the Methodist Episcopal Church, South. Arnold took over an institution that was in debt, had few resources, and lacked the infrastructure for basic scientific instruction.

"Let us flee from debt as from the grave," wrote President Arnold in his 1873 annual report to trustees, given at a meeting in which they sought to consolidate the college's debts. Indebtedness continued as trustees placed a series of mortgages on the original thirty-five-acre college farm, and much of it was often leased out, leaving little room for agricultural experiments.[10] Despite periodic reports to the legislature that the college was free of debt, trustee minutes suggest that the college was in debt to Arnold and others throughout much of its period of church control.

In addition to a lack of ongoing financial support, another difficulty facing Corvallis College was its dual role as an instrument of both the church and the state. The college operated under the auspices of the Methodist Episcopal Church, South, though the church did not require college trustees to be members and insisted that it never sought to teach that church's "distinctive doctrines." But allegations that the agricultural college was operated in a parochial or sectarian manner surfaced periodically, especially in several of the state's newspapers, and the debate was sometimes tinged with Civil War politics and even internal church politics. Such continuing complaints led to fears that Benton County could lose the state agricultural college altogether.

Although the agricultural college was supposed to be a separate program within Corvallis College, the college's catalog was general in nature and made little distinction between students taking the regular curriculum and those taking the agricultural curriculum. Longtime faculty member Frederick Berchtold, who joined the college in 1884, recounted late in his career that the agricultural college relied heavily on the rest of the institution between 1870 and 1885. Conversely, the college's biennial reports to the legislature mostly addressed the agricultural program, creating an illusion of two separate institutions.

The condition of the college began to slowly improve during the early years of Arnold's administration. The legislature made an appropriation of $5,000 in October of 1872; military equipment also arrived that fall, enabling the college to begin military instruction and drill under Arnold's direction. An alumni association was established in June 1873, and another full-time faculty member was added that year, as was a farm manager. Additional space was necessary to accommodate enrollment growth, particularly in the preparatory department. Plans were made for an addition to the college building, which was completed in 1876, roughly doubling its size. And in 1874, the college issued its first agricultural research report—fourteen years before the formal establishment of experiment stations that would undertake agriculture research.

As a means to stabilize the college's financial situation, the board of trustees filed supplemental articles of incorporation with the Oregon secretary of state on January 4, 1876. The articles enabled the college to "execute and deliver notes, checks, deeds, mortgages, etc., and to buy and hold property for the institution up to the value of $500,000." They also articulated the college's sources of revenue—legislative appropriations, proceeds from the sale of endowment lands, interest from the sale of these lands, and rental of college property (the farm).

By 1884, college trustees were prepared to turn over the farm's title to the state in return for a larger appropriation to fund mechanical arts and a guarantee that the agricultural college would remain in Benton County. The regional church conference[11] initially supported the trustees' action and further agreed to end the relationship with the state if its agent could not raise $25,000 for a building in a short period of time. A church historian, struggling to explain the 1884 action, said the conference "must have been mesmerized, or bereft of its senses." A year later the conference disavowed the transfer and for many years fought state takeover in the courts, even after others had effectively taken over the college.

In 1885, state senator Thomas Cauthorn sponsored legislation that would separate the agricultural college from Corvallis College, as the church conference had not raised the $25,000 necessary for the new college building. The Legislative Assembly approved the legislation on February 11, 1885, which stipulated the relocation of the college to a new building at the college farm, the establishment of a new board of regents, and the creation of a course of instruction meeting the tenets of the Morrill Act. A board of regents was established,[12] and a State Agricultural College Association was formed to raise the $25,000 for the new college building to be constructed on the farm.[13] In his 1885 annual report to trustees, President Arnold tried to remain upbeat: "This year has been a stormy one in our external relations, but as smooth as usual within the school itself; how we have held the school together, I know not; both the students and Faculty deserve credit."

Even though a board of regents had been established to direct the state agricultural college, it served as a place-holder for its first two years, and the board of trustees continued to direct the business of the college. The church conference and college trustees made attempts to reassert control of the college. The tipping point came in early 1888, when Governor Pennoyer, himself an ex officio regent, designated the "board of regents of the agricultural college as the proper authority to receive and expend the $15,000 per annum" appropriated by the federal Hatch Act, which authorized the establishment of experiment stations at the land-grant colleges and universities. The act required the treasurer or other duly appointed official of the institution to receive the funds. At its June 1888 meeting, the board adopted bylaws and began acting in an official capacity.

Meanwhile the cornerstone of the new agricultural college building was laid on August 17, 1887, and construction was completed on July 1, 1888, repre-senting the "combined efforts of the faculty and President of Corvallis College (financial contributions as well as moral support), many members of the board of trustees, and many public-spirited

citizens." On July 2, 1888, Governor Pennoyer notified the board of regents of his acceptance of the college farm and college buildings on behalf of the state of Oregon and handed the keys of the college building to the president of the board.[14]

Chosen by the regents of the state-controlled board as their president, Arnold began the 1889–90 school year lead-ing a larger faculty in the new building on the hill, known today as Benton Hall. Despite ongoing litigation, the state agricultural college was now effectively separate from Corvallis College. The agricultural college regents used a fresh infusion of federal and state support to buy more land, build additional structures, and expand the curriculum; in addition to the $15,000 annually from the federal Hatch Act, this soon included another $15,000 annually from the Second Morrill Act of 1890.[15] The college also requested $30,000 from the legislature in 1888 to establish a "broader foundation for agriculture and the mechanic arts."

Meanwhile, the trustees of Corvallis College struggled without state support to sustain a preparatory boarding school in the downtown building, seeking church collections to raise the balance of a teacher's $500 annual salary in 1890 and 1891. After reporting a circuit court victory in 1891, the minutes of the board of trustees end abruptly.

Although the involvement of Corvallis College and the Methodist Episcopal Church, South, ended in the early 1890s, the history of Oregon's state agricultural college had just begun.

Letterhead seal, 1889. This seal was adopted by the board of regents in 1888. (MC—University Seals)

Portrait of Rev. Orceneth Fisher, 1858. Fisher (1803–1880) was born in Vermont, became a Methodist minister, and served as the chaplain of the Republic of Texas in 1844 and 1845. He was transferred to the Pacific Conference in 1855. On May 16, 1860, on behalf of the Methodist Episcopal Church, South, he purchased Corvallis College at a sheriff's auction for $4,500 after outbidding a representative of the local Baptist Church by $500. On January 1, 1861, Fisher sold the college to its trustees; Fisher remained affiliated with the college as its agent. This image is the frontispiece of Fisher's work, *The Christian Sacraments*, published in 1858. (HC 2970)

Marriage photograph of William A. and Sarah Finley, 1866. Finley was appointed president of Corvallis College in 1865. In the summer of 1866 he made a visit to Santa Rosa, California, where he had lived prior to coming to Corvallis. While there, he married Sarah Latimer on August 7. They returned to Corvallis together via steamer from San Francisco to Portland. In 1930, Sara Finley recounted that trip:

The sea was rough and our course was perilous near shore, always fraught with possible disaster . . . When about to cross the Columbia Bar a heavy fog delayed our purpose; and here, without a sign of the "cup that cheers" we lingered for hours . . . A boat at Portland and then around the Willamette Falls in a diminutive box car drawn by an amiable donkey along iron rails . . . For lovers to sit on the deck of one of those river boats and glide over the beautiful Willamette was the essence of poetry . . . (HC 224)

Portrait of Joseph C. Avery, ca. 1868. Avery (1817–1876) was one of the founders of Corvallis and played multiple roles in the early history of the college. He was one of the original investors in the first incarnation of Corvallis College in the late 1850s and one of the trustees who chartered the school on January 20, 1858. In 1868 he was one of three commissioners named in the act that provisionally selected Corvallis College as the state agricultural college to locate the land-grant lands in accordance with the Morrill Act. Avery also contributed $200 toward the purchase of the college farm in 1871 and served on the college's board of trustees in the 1870s, until his death in 1876. Several of Avery's children attended Corvallis College, either as preparatory or college-level students. Avery was not without controversy; he was the editor of the pro-slavery newspaper *Occidental Messenger*, published in Corvallis from 1857 to 1859. (*Portrait and Biographical Record of the Willamette Valley, Oregon*, p. 868)

View of Main Street, Corvallis, ca. 1870. This view of what is now Second Street in Corvallis, one of the first photographs of its business district, was taken around the time that Corvallis College received permanent designation as the state's land-grant institution. Corvallis's 1870 population was estimated to be 1,200. (HC 596)

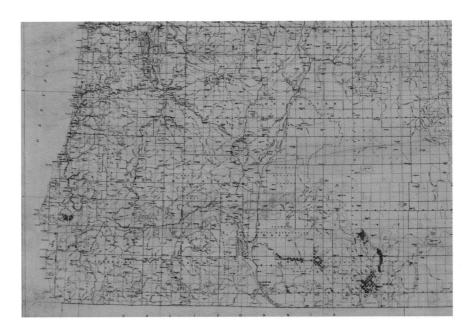

Map showing OSU's original land-grant lands. Most of the lands (indicated in red) were located in Lake and Klamath Counties, remote locations in Oregon in 1870. This map may have been prepared in the 1960s for either the centennial of the Morrill Act in 1962 or OSU's centennial in 1968. (MAPS—OSU Campus)

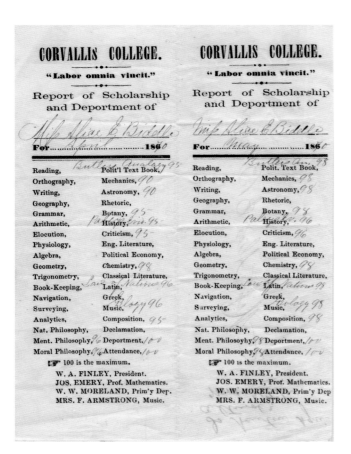

Alice Biddle's grade reports, April and May 1870. Alice Biddle, a member of the first graduating class in 1870, completed the college curriculum in three years and graduated at age sixteen. Biddle took classes in the college's preparatory department prior to taking collegiate level classes. (MC—Biddle, Alice)

Corvallis College students in front of the college building, ca. 1872. This image shows some of the preparatory and college-level students enrolled at the time. The 1872–73 college catalog lists ninety-eight students at all levels, including twenty-six "agricultural students." (HC 1344)

View of Corvallis from the residence of D. G. Clark, April 1871. This photo, taken around the time of the purchase of the college farm in spring 1871, includes some of the lands that became the farm. The view is looking east to Corvallis from the ridge on the west end of the farm. The college building can be seen slightly left of the center of the image. The steeple was painted a dark color. (Courtesy of Benton County Historical Society, #19800850049p)

Portrait of Ida Burnett, ca. 1881. Burnett (1863–1932) had a nearly lifelong association with Oregon State. She literally grew up at Corvallis College, starting at the school around 1870 as a primary department student. She graduated with a bachelor of science degree in 1881. Her father, John Burnett, was a local attorney who served on the college's board of trustees. In 1883 Ida Burnett began working as an assistant in the preparatory department and had responsibility for the primary students for two years. In 1889 Ida Burnett married Thomas Callahan. She later served as principal of OAC's preparatory department (1894–95), as dean of women (1906–07), and as an instructor of English from 1896 until her death in 1932. Callahan Hall is named for her. (HC 817)

Corvallis College faculty, 1883. The faculty consisted of (from left) Edgar E. Grimm, professor of agriculture and chemistry and an 1880 graduate of the college; Ida Burnett, assistant in the preparatory department and an 1881 graduate; President Benjamin L. Arnold, professor of moral philosophy and physics; B. J. Hawthorne, professor of languages; Joseph Emery, professor of math and natural sciences, and W. W. Bristow, preparatory department. (HC 170)

Portrait of Joseph Emery, ca. 1885. Emery (1833–1924), who was William A. Finley's brother-in-law, served on the Corvallis College faculty from 1867 to 1885. He was acting president of Corvallis College between the Finley and Arnold administrations and submitted Corvallis College's first biennial report to the governor. During his eighteen years at the college, Emery taught mathematics, physics, geology, and physiology. Like Finley, he was an ordained minister. Emery helped raise funds for the purchase of the original college farm and also served on the college's board of trustees. He left Corvallis College in 1885 to become an agent for the US Indian Agency near the Klamath reservation. (HC 1516)

State Agricultural College advertisement, *Willamette Farmer,*
October 19, 1883. Ads were frequently used by the college in
the 1870s and 1880s to attract new students. The *Willamette
Farmer* was published in Salem from 1869 to 1887. (Courtesy of
the Oregon Digital Newspaper Program)

Corvallis College building, ca. 1888. The building had been remodeled and expanded
in 1876 to accommodate a year-round preparatory department and an additional faculty
member. Much of the lumber for the addition was donated by a member of the board of
trustees, R. W. Brock of Corvallis. (HC 1344)

Commencement invitation, 1887. This invitation was sent by Robert E. Cooper, one of the graduating seniors, to Bertha Davis, who graduated in 1889. Commencement was held in the Corvallis City Hall. (MC—Commencement)

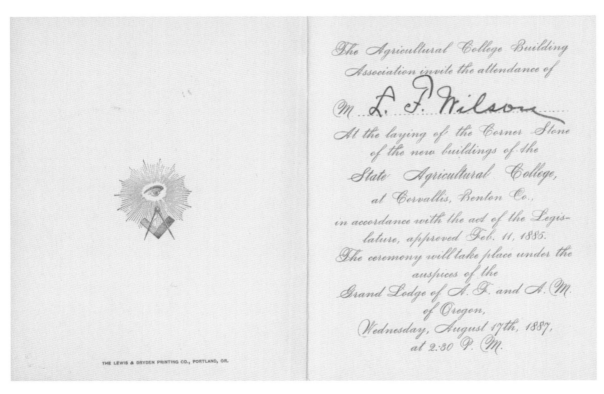

Invitation to the laying of the cornerstone of the new college building, August 17, 1887. This invitation was sent to Lewis F. Wilson, a local brick maker and the father of student and future board of regents member Eddy E. Wilson. Lewis Wilson supplied the brick used in the construction of the building, completed in 1888. It is now Benton Hall. (MC—Buildings-Benton Hall)

Senior portrait of James Collins, 1888. James Collins (class of 1888) was one of the first Native American graduates of Oregon State. He was affiliated with the Confederated Tribes of Siletz and was an educator for much of his career, including serving as the superintendent of schools in St. Helens, Oregon. His brother, Benjamin, was a member of the class of 1886. (P135:004)

Campus view, 1899. This photo, which appeared in the 1898–99 college catalog, shows OSU as it appeared on the eve of the twentieth century. The buildings, from left, are the Gymnasium and Armory, Wilson House, Cauthorn Hall (in background with tower), Withycombe House, Station Building, Administration Building, Alpha Hall, and Mechanical Hall. Note the windmill just to the left of Mechanical Hall. (P25:1259)

Architectural Harmony and Function
Development of OSU's Campus

3

The original Corvallis College building in downtown Corvallis, completed in 1859, served the institution in its various roles for nearly thirty years. With the construction of what is now Benton Hall on the western edge of the college farm in 1888, OAC was poised to develop a physical infrastructure that would carry it into the twentieth century and beyond. The college completed the move from its downtown Corvallis building to the new college building in 1889, in time for the start of classes on September 12. Earlier that year, the college had purchased 119 acres to the west of the college farm for agricultural experimentation. Three buildings approved by the board of regents at its April 1889 meeting also were constructed that year—Alpha Hall, the first residence hall; Mechanical Hall, which included "tools and other means for giving instruction in the mechanic arts, such as joining, turning, forging, machine work, etc."; and an octagonal barn.[1]

Additional lands were purchased when opportunities arose and funds were available. Several new buildings were constructed in the 1890s, and a few more were built in the first few years of the twentieth century.[2] By 1910, the land area of campus had grown to nearly 224 acres and included eighteen major buildings. Several hundred acres also had been acquired for three branch experiment stations around the state.

Considerable growth occurred during President Kerr's administration (1907–1932). Kerr had the foresight to develop a campus plan that would guide the growth of the campus in a rational and efficient manner. In 1909 Kerr engaged the services of the Olmsted Brothers firm of Brookline, Massachusetts. John and Frederick Law Olmsted Jr. were sons of Frederick Law Olmsted, who designed New York's Central Park. John Olmsted was in the Pacific Northwest in 1909 overseeing the development of the Alaska-Yukon-Pacific Exposition in Seattle. He visited OAC in June and spent a number of days on campus. In October, he issued his report—a sixty-page document that made dozens of recommendations.[3]

Many of Olmsted's recommendations were adopted.

- A president's residence "suitable for entertaining on a much larger scale than is expected of professors and other officials of the college"
- Locating dormitories along the college's periphery (though the periphery extended outward as the campus grew)
- Maintaining the former college farm (Lower Campus) as a "broad, imposing park meadow" to secure "a dignified frontage and to open up the College to view from the city and from trains"[4]
- Constructing separate men's and women's gymnasiums once the number of students had greatly increased
- East and west quadrangles
- Continued employment of an "architect or firm as long as he or they are satisfactory"
- Simple, classically designed buildings of red brick with terra cotta trim that can be easily enlarged or added to

He also recommended that the college consider developing a new campus once enrollment reached twenty-five hundred. Just nine years later, enrollment surged past that number. It is doubtful that Kerr considered that recommendation.

Most of the buildings constructed during Kerr's administration were designed by one architect—John V. Bennes of Portland—in line with one of Olmsted's recommendations. Bennes's designs were almost all red brick with terra cotta ornamentation and flourishes, also called for in the Olmsted plan. Bennes designed more than thirty-five buildings for Oregon State between 1907 and 1941.

The physical development of the college was not limited to the campus area. A branch experiment station was established in 1901 at Union in northeast Oregon with a $10,000 appropriation from the legislature. Several additional branch stations were added from the 1910s through the 1930s.[5] In 1925–26 the college acquired 341 acres just north of Corvallis for use as an arboretum and research forest. Additional land acquisitions in the 1930s and 1940s increased the research forests to more than 6,500 acres by 1950.

The 1920s were a golden age of development on OSU's central campus. Many of the landmark buildings were constructed during this period, including the Women's Building (1926), the Memorial Union (1928), and Weatherford Hall (1928). Several new fraternity and sorority houses were constructed adjacent to campus in the 1920s, enlarging the overall campus community. In 1925 President Kerr acquired the services of renowned landscape architect Albert D. Taylor of Cleveland, Ohio, to complete an update of the 1909 Olmsted campus plan.[6]

Taylor's January 1926 plan retained many of the core elements of the Olmsted plan, such as maintaining the lower campus area as open space. Taylor had several other significant recommendations.

- Grouping of buildings by function or academic discipline, with a quad being a center point for each building group[7]
- Moving all farm buildings west of Thirtieth Street
- Developing Thirtieth Street as a boulevard to define the western edge of the core campus
- Creating separate men's and women's recreational areas
- Confining football and baseball facilities to a definite area
- Maintaining the Chemistry Building (Furman Hall) and Apperson Hall (Kearney Hall) as part of the

campus, acknowledging their contributions as some of the earliest structures on campus

Taylor also called for limiting vehicle traffic on campus:

So far as possible the development of streets carrying traffic other than traffic catering to the immediate needs of college activities should be strongly discouraged. . . . Student use of automobiles on the campus proper, should be discouraged between certain hours of the day, preferably 7:30 in the morning to 5:30 or 6:00 in the afternoon.

He advised the college on landscaping, suggesting that

Trees should be planted in rows, parallel with the walks and roads. . . . Vistas should be created and enhanced, and groups and specimen trees should be scattered about the quadrangles to develop that interesting play of light and shadow which gives life to any landscape picture.

Taylor completed an update of his 1926 plan in 1945.

The Great Depression, with its resulting reduced student enrollment and financial constraints on the college budget, slowed campus development to a crawl. Plans for new buildings were shelved. Only two major buildings were constructed between 1930 and 1940—the Student Health Services Building (Plageman Hall) and the Chemistry Building (Gilbert Hall). Both were funded in part by the federal Public Works Administration (PWA). However, the Depression also deflated local property values, which gave the college an opportunity to make strategic land purchases of properties adjacent to campus at cut-rate prices.

With the end of World War II and the resulting surge in enrollment, plans were quickly drawn up for new buildings to accommodate teaching, research, and student housing. Immediately after the war, the college made use of surplus wartime buildings from nearby Camp Adair and Quonset huts, a new type of temporary building developed during the war. A few of the Quonset huts are still in use today, such as the Naval ROTC Armory. The Adair Tract, 6,200 acres that had been part of Camp Adair, was acquired in 1948 for research use by the schools of forestry and agriculture. By 1950, a new dormitory (Sackett Hall), basketball arena (Gill Coliseum), and electrical engineering building (Dearborn Hall) had been constructed, as well as a building that housed the Forest Products Lab. Planning for or construction of two buildings for agricultural sciences was also underway.

During the 1950s the campus infrastructure echoed the steady growth of enrollment. The college acquired additional properties adjacent to campus for future growth. Oregon State began offering co-op housing opportunities, constructing three during the decade and acquiring a former sorority house for use as another co-op. Traditional dormitory housing continued to be the mainstay of on-campus living—a new quad of four residence halls, another residence hall for women, and a cafeteria for Weatherford Hall were added in the late 1950s. Several academic and research buildings were added, reflecting the college's quickly expanding research activities. A new football facility, Parker Stadium, opened in 1953 to replace the venerable, but unsafe and outdated, Bell Field.

The steady growth of the 1950s continued into the 1960s. Five new dormitories were erected between 1960 and 1970, including the Wilson/Callahan/McNary complex on the east side of campus during the early 1960s. It was built on land that had been a residential area acquired by OSU as an urban renewal project, essentially replacing one type of student housing with another. Additions to the east and west ends of the Memorial Union, for use as a bookstore and eating commons, were completed in 1960. New married student housing was built in 1961. Many other properties were purchased in the 1960s and 1970s and banked for future growth.

Two significant building projects of the 1960s were the construction of a new Kerr Library, completed in 1963, and the development of a marine research facility in Newport, now known as the Hatfield Marine Science Center. The new library replaced the 1918–1941 library, nearly doubling its square footage. The marine science center was needed to support the college's quickly growing oceanographic program and later included cooperative partners from federal and state agencies. Also supporting marine science research was a new oceanography building completed on the Corvallis campus in 1964. OSU's nuclear science program took a major step forward in 1964 with the opening of the Radiation Center, designed to house the university's Triga research nuclear reactor. As they had done with the

marine science center, OSU also partnered with state and federal agencies to co-locate complementary programs on the Corvallis campus. During the 1960s, facilities were built on campus for the United States Forest Service (1962) and the Environmental Protection Agency (1966).

Through the years, OSU has had to cope with its share of fires, floods, and other natural disasters. OSU experienced several events of this nature in the 1960s. In 1962, western Oregon bore the brunt of the remnants of a hurricane. Known as the Columbus Day storm, it did significant damage to campus trees and to some buildings. A major flood in December 1964 paralyzed much of the state, including Corvallis, though the direct impact on OSU was lessened by final exams having concluded earlier in the month. In 1968 OSU's dairy program suffered a major setback when its massive dairy barn complex burned. It was rebuilt the next year. And in late January 1969, western Oregon experienced near record-setting snowfall; some locations received more than thirty inches between January 25 and 30. OSU cancelled classes for the first time in more than fifty years. Snow and ice storms also closed campus in January 2004 and February 2014. Local floods in the 1990s and 2010s limited access to campus and directly affected the farm, crew facilities, and Trysting Tree Golf Course on the east side of the Willamette River across from downtown Corvallis.

In 1972, a new administrative services building was completed, replacing the temporary Camp Adair structures north of Milam Hall that had been in use since 1947. Another dormitory and a dining center were built in the early 1970s—the last to be built until 2002, though OSU did purchase an apartment-style residence hall in 1975. Facilities for cultural centers opened during the decade, as well as a new student recreation center. Facilities at the Marine Science Center expanded in the 1970s, and a building for the newly designated School of Veterinary Medicine opened in 1979. Wayne Valley Field opened in 1974 as a state-of-the-art facility for track and field.

Planning for an OSU cultural and conference center began in the 1960s, though ground was not broken for the facility until August 1979. Dedicated in April 1981, the LaSells Stewart Center—built exclusively with private funds—was the largest privately funded construction project at a public university in Oregon up to that time. Statewide budget issues significantly slowed construction projects on campus in the early 1980s. A new crop science building was completed in 1981, but no major new buildings came online until 1988, when a new electrical and computer engineering building (now Owen Hall) opened. That same year OSU unveiled the Trysting Tree Golf Course, developed on land adjacent to the experimental farm land that had been acquired in the late 1940s and early 1950s, just across the Willamette River from Corvallis. An updated campus plan was unveiled in 1984—the first new campus plan in twenty years.

New research/classroom buildings for agriculture/life sciences and family studies were planned in the late 1980s, and both were completed in 1992. Despite budget issues caused by the 1990 passage of the property reduction initiative known as Ballot Measure 5, several additional campus buildings were constructed in the 1990s—though most relied heavily on major gifts from alumni and other donors. The Wayne and Gladys Valley Foundation, established by two Oregon Staters who attended OSC in the 1930s, funded two significant athletics facilities and provided $10 million toward a major expansion and renovation of the 1963 library building. The expanded library, dedicated in May 1999, was named the Valley Library in their honor. The CH2M HILL engineering firm, founded by OSU alumni, pledged $2 million toward a new alumni center in 1993. That facility was completed in 1997.

OSU's research capacity was greatly enhanced by two projects completed in the late 1990s. A new state-of-the-art seafood research center opened in Astoria in 1998, and the next year a 97,000-square-foot forestry research and teaching facility, Richardson Hall, was dedicated. The latter part of the 1990s also saw a significant improvement to OSU's baseball facilities and a major donation from alumni Al and Pat Reser to begin the upgrade of the football stadium, which was renamed after them.

In 2001 the State Board of Higher Education authorized OSU to establish a branch campus in Bend, which had been pushing for a more robust higher education presence for many years. The new campus was named OSU-Cascades. OSU partnered with Central Oregon Community College and constructed a multi-purpose building on its campus; Cascades Hall opened in September 2002. In 2013, OSU selected a site in southwest Bend for construction of a permanent campus.

Increased enrollment at the Corvallis campus required additional student housing. Three new residence halls were built between 2000 and 2014. Carrie Halsell Hall, named for OSU's first female African American graduate, opened in 2002. Halsell graduated in 1926 with a BS degree in commerce. The International Living-Learning Center, focused on meeting the housing and other needs of OSU's expanding international student population, opened in 2011. William Tebeau Hall, named for OSU's first male African American graduate, who received an engineering degree in 1948, opened in the fall of 2014. Co-operative housing was de-emphasized, and after the end of spring term of 2014, all of OSU's co-operative houses were closed.

OSU's growing student population and research agenda required additional and upgraded classroom and research facilities. The Kelley Engineering Center, funded in part by a $20 million gift from alumni Martin and Judy Kelley, provided state-of-the art teaching and research facilities for the School of Electrical Engineering and Computer Science. It received the gold designation from LEED.[8] Austin Hall, which opened in September 2014, was named for alumni Ken and Joan Austin, major contributors to the new building and longtime supporters of the College of Business's Austin Family Business Center and Austin Entrepreneurship program.

Close to Austin Hall, the Learning Innovation Center (LinC) opened in fall 2015, providing additional classroom, collaboration, and study spaces for several academic programs. The Beth Ray Center for Academic Support opened in 2013 to provide services and facilities to help ensure the academic success of OSU's students. The Student Experience Center, completed in early 2015 just east of the Memorial Union, provides new and improved spaces for many student-related programs that had been housed in Snell Hall. The Linus Pauling Science Center opened in the fall of 2011 as the new home of the Linus Pauling Institute. In Portland, OSU collaborated with Oregon Health and Sciences University (OHSU) in 2006 to co-locate part of the pharmacy program in OHSU's Center for Health and Healing. In July 2014 the Collaborative Life Sciences Building opened on the OHSU campus. A partnership between OSU, OHSU, and Portland State, the building includes a large theater-style lecture hall, classrooms and practice labs, research labs, and faculty offices for the College of Pharmacy.

The campus master plan received a major update in 2005, and in 2015 a new OSU District Plan was developed in collaboration with the City of Corvallis and community stakeholders. One of the hallmarks of the 2005 plan was a greater emphasis on preservation and recognition of historic buildings as a unique asset. To that end, OSU applied for and received National Register status for its core campus in 2008.

As a part of OSU's recent emphasis on preservation, several historic buildings have undergone restoration and transformation. Weatherford Hall, closed for nearly a decade, was renovated and restored as the home of the Austin Entrepreneurship Program. It reopened in 2004 as OSU's first LEED-certified building. Apperson Hall was restored and expanded, complete with twenty-first century technology. In 2005 it was renamed Kearney Hall

after alumni Lee and Connie Kearney, whose $4 million gift helped fund the restoration. Likewise, Education Hall, which had such severe seismic issues with its exterior sandstone façade that it had to be wrapped in fencing in the mid-1990s, received a new limestone exterior that matched the old sandstone piece by piece. The interior was completely updated to better serve the College of Education, and the building was renamed Furman Hall in memory of alumnus Joyce Collin Furman. It reopened in early 2012, and in 2013 won one of the first DeMuro Awards from Restore Oregon.[9] A transformation of the interior of Strand Agriculture Hall began in early 2014.

University campuses rarely remain static. That is certainly true for OSU. A new campus for OSU-Cascades is underway in Bend. Research and teaching facilities at the Hatfield Marine Science Center in Newport are in the planning stage. Oregon State University's main campus will continue to evolve, blending new buildings with updated, state-of-the-art historic and older buildings to support a twenty-first century university.

View of the west side of the Administration Building, 1891. This rare early view of the west (back) side of the Administration Building also shows the lower campus area and downtown Corvallis. (P16:685)

Alpha Hall and residents, ca. 1890. Alpha Hall, the first dormitory built on the new campus, was constructed in 1889 and originally housed both men and women. Note the male students in their gray cadet uniforms. The board of regents announced in December 1889 that the "Students Hall and Dormitory was full to overflowing," necessitating the rental of the Episcopal Church parsonage to accommodate extra students. A separate men's dormitory, Cauthorn (Fairbanks) Hall, was constructed in 1892. Alpha Hall was used as a women's dorm until 1907, when Waldo Hall opened. It was used for the next several years for the pharmacy department. Originally located where Gilkey Hall is today, it was partially deconstructed and moved to another location about 1912. This photo was taken by the Pernot Bros. Studio. (HC 44)

Lower campus, 1892. The baseball diamond on the right was one of the college's first athletic facilities. The Experiment Station gardens are to the left. In the distance is downtown Corvallis; prominent buildings include the Benton County Courthouse (upper left) and Central School. Just to the right of the school is the old Corvallis College building.

Station Building, ca. 1892. This photo was taken soon after construction was completed. The building accommodated the offices of the agricultural experiment station, established in 1888; the station's chemistry lab was in the basement. This building has housed many programs over the years, including the co-op bookstore, the student health service, the campus police headquarters, a paleontology lab, and (since 1973) the Women's Center. The building was expanded in 1920. (P25:1)

Mechanical Hall, soon after expansion, 1894. The three-story wood frame section of the building was added in 1894. The original structure, built in 1889, is the two-story brick building behind the new addition. The 1896–97 college catalog described the building as containing "the college and station printing office, the physical laboratory, class rooms for military tactics, mechanical drawing and theory of mechanics, as well as the blacksmithing, woodworking, and machine shops," as well as the electrical works and pumping station for the entire college. A wing of the building was also used as a gymnasium for a period of time. This photo, taken by photography instructor Emile Pernot, first appeared in the 1893–94 college catalog. (HC 63)

Students at Cauthorn Hall, ca. 1900. Cauthorn Hall, constructed in 1892 as a dormitory for male students, was designed by Salem architect W. D. Pugh. The building was named for Thomas Cauthorn, a former state senator and member of the OAC board of regents. It could accommodate more than one hundred students and included water, steam heat, electric lights, and a dining room and kitchen. It was later known as Kidder Hall, and in 1964 its name was changed to Fairbanks Hall. Today it houses art and sociology, and walking on the third-floor ledge is frowned upon. The Douglas fir tree on the left side of the photograph is today a prominent feature of Fairbanks Hall's front lawn. (P25:1407)

Agricultural Hall, soon after construction, 1902. The 1901–02 college catalog proclaimed this building to be the largest and finest structure on campus. Designed by Albany architect Charles Burggraf, it was built to provide classrooms and labs for the agricultural departments and also included the experiment station director's office, a stock judging room, and a museum. In 1909 it was repurposed for science classrooms and labs; this is the building in which Linus Pauling spent considerable time and met his future wife, Ava Helen Miller. The College of Education has occupied the building since 1940. In 2011 it was completely renovated and renamed Joyce Collin Furman Hall. (P25:1191)

Octagonal barn and dryer house, ca. 1900. This barn, built in 1889, was the first agricultural building constructed by the college. An addition was constructed about 1893. Prior to this the college used existing buildings from an earlier farmstead on the site. This served as the primary barn until about 1908, when a new barn was constructed to house beef cattle and dairy cows. The house-like structure on the right was the drying house, used for prune drying. (P25:1620)

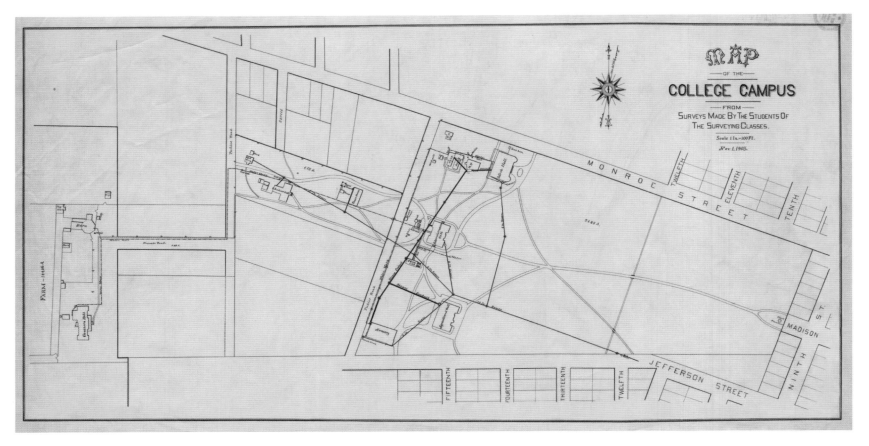

Map of the OAC Campus, November 1903. This map of campus, an original pen-and-ink drawing, is one of the earliest. It was compiled using survey data gathered by students. In addition to buildings, roads, and pathways, it shows the campus utility system as it existed at the time—water, steam, and sewer lines; wells; and windmills and water storage tanks. (MAPS—OSU Campus)

Armory and gymnasium, ca. 1905. Completed in 1898, this building provided facilities for physical education, special events, and the college's growing military science program. The basement included a bowling alley. In the 1930s the building was used as rehearsal space for musical groups, and the basement housed the Horner Museum. In the early 1950s it was transformed into the college playhouse, a role it served for nearly forty years. Almost doomed to demolition, the building was repurposed in 1992 into a world-class gymnastics training facility, funded in part by the Wayne and Gladys Valley Foundation. (P25:1179)

Waldo Hall, ca. 1910. This view of Waldo Hall was taken just a few years after the building was completed in 1907 to serve as a women's dormitory. It also housed the domestic science department on its first floor, and single women faculty members were allowed to live there. Waldo Hall was designed by Albany architect Charles H. Burggraf and named for Clara Humason Waldo (1858–1933), the first woman to serve on OAC's board of regents (1905–1919). Waldo, the wife of Oregon Supreme Court Justice John Waldo, was a champion of agricultural education, the traveling library, and other causes. Waldo Hall served as a residence hall until 1965, when the first three floors were remodeled for use as classrooms, labs, and faculty offices. The fourth floor was vacant until remodeling in 2010. Today Waldo Hall is the home of the anthropology and public health programs, the Educational Opportunities Program, the Center for Teaching and Learning, and the Academic Success Center. (HC 36)

New Armory under construction, 1909. A new armory was built to accommodate OAC's growing cadet corps and replace the armory constructed in 1898. An April 1910 newspaper article stated that it was "one of the largest in the entire country" and included "some of the heaviest and longest steel spans in the West." The spans are clearly visible in this photograph. The building was designed by John Bennes—one of the few OAC structures designed by him that was not red brick and terra cotta. (P17:1328)

Portrait of architect
John V. Bennes, ca. 1916.
(From *Photographic Business and
Professional Directory*, Portland,
Oregon, 1916)

Between 1907 and 1941, Portland architect John V. Bennes designed more than fifty new buildings, building additions, and building renovations for Oregon State College. He also designed at least three houses for the college's fraternities and sororities.

Born in 1867 in rural Illinois and raised in Chicago, Bennes studied architecture at Prague University. He worked as an architect in Chicago from about 1890 to 1900 and was a contemporary of Frank Lloyd Wright. Bennes migrated to Oregon in 1900 and spent six years working in Baker City. His major design projects there included a makeover of the Geiser Grand Hotel, the 1903 City Hall, the St. Francis Academy, and the hotel at Hot Lake Resort. Bennes moved to Portland in 1906 and joined two other architects in the firm Bennes, Hendricks & Tobey. He is credited with introducing the Prairie Style of architecture to the firm—evidence of the influence of his fellow Chicago architect Wright.

Bennes's OSU designs form the core of the OSU Historic District and include many well-known buildings on campus. They include the Armory (1910; now McAlexander Fieldhouse), Agriculture Hall (1909, 1911, 1913; now Strand Agriculture Hall), Men's Gymnasium (1915, 1920; now Langton Hall), the Library (1918; now Kidder Hall), the Women's Building (1926), and Weatherford Hall (1928). His designs were highly regarded; landscape architect Alfred D. Taylor noted in his 1926 OAC campus plan that "with the exception of the original College buildings, all of the permanent buildings in the campus development possess a unity of design which is exceptional. . . . I have come in contact with no college campus where buildings over a considerable area and during a considerable period of time, have been designed and located with so much uniformity as here." There is no doubt that Taylor was referring in large part to the buildings designed by Bennes.

Bennes's firm did design work for other public colleges and universities, including the administration buildings at Southern Oregon, Eastern Oregon, and Western Oregon universities. He and his partners were prolific architects—they completed scores of designs for buildings in Portland and other communities throughout Oregon. Many have been listed on the National Register or are part of historic districts. These design projects include Portland's Broadway Hotel (1913), Hollywood Theatre (1926), and Aaron Maegly House (1914); Astoria's Liberty Theater (1924); the Heppner Hotel (1919); and the Bexell House in Corvallis (1927).

During his career, Bennes was active in the Oregon Chapter of the American Institute of Architects and the Oregon State Board of Architectural Examiners. He retired to Los Angeles in early 1943, and died there on November 29, 1943.

New dairy barn, 1909. This barn, the first of six designed by Portland architect John Bennes for OAC, was built in 1908–09. It was a frame building with brick pilasters. Although built as a general barn, its primary use was to support the dairy program. The west wing housed the farm mechanics shop until about 1913. After a new dairy barn was built in 1937–38, the structure became the Agricultural Utilities Building. Over the next fifty years, it was utilized by several departments (agricultural engineering, horticulture, computer science) and the USDA. It was razed in 1989 to make way for the Agricultural and Life Sciences Building (HC 41)

John Bennes and Ruth Glassow on the steps of the new Women's Building, 1926. The Women's Building is considered one of Bennes's most significant designs on the OSU campus. His firm's partner, Harry Herzog, also contributed to the design. Ruth Glassow was the director of women's physical education at OAC. This photo appeared in the December 1926 issue of the *OAC Alumnus*. (HC 1514)

Agriculture Hall and the Dairy Building, ca. 1912. Agriculture Hall was built in three stages—the agronomy wing (center of the photo), 1909; the main section (left), 1911; and the horticulture wing (partially visible, far left), 1913. The Dairy Building, just to the north of Agriculture Hall and under construction in this photo, was completed in 1912. Both buildings were designed by John Bennes. Agriculture Hall was renamed Strand Agriculture Hall in 1984 for former president A. L. Strand. The Dairy Building became Social Science Hall in the early 1950s, and was named for Gordon Gilkey in 2001. (P25:1232)

Mines Building and Shepard Hall, ca. 1914. These two buildings were some of the first built on what became Campus Way. Shepard Hall (Tudor-style building, center left) was privately constructed in 1908 as the home of the YMCA and YWCA organizations serving the OAC community. Much of the fundraising for the building was done under the leadership of Claiborne Shepard, secretary of the YMCA during his OAC student days. He died of tuberculosis in 1906, before the building was constructed. Shepard Hall is the current home of speech communication, a program in the School of Arts and Communication. The Mines Building, designed by John Bennes, was completed in 1913 for OAC's School of Mines. In 1965 it was named for James H. Batcheller, head of the school from 1919 to 1942. Today it houses some of the College of Engineering's administrative programs, classrooms, and faculty offices. (P16:398)

Landscape crew planting trees, ca. 1915. One of the hallmarks of the OSU campus is its beautiful landscaping, which has been a key element of the campus master plans over the years. This tree was planted on the northeast corner of what is now Campus Way and Memorial Place. (HC 603)

President's home, ca. 1921. This grand residence, located just north of Shepard Hall, was acquired by OAC in 1921 for use as the president's home. It had been the Lambda Chi Alpha fraternity house prior to its acquisition by the college. Presidents Kerr and Peavy lived here. From 1950 to 1957 it was used as the zoology department's physiology lab. In the fall of 1957 the structure was demolished to make way for new campus buildings. (P96:58)

Mechanical Arts building, ca. 1915. This building complex, designed by John Bennes, was constructed in 1908. The building on the middle right was a heating plant built in 1900. Today the outer L-shaped building remains and is named Merryfield Hall for Fred Merryfield, OSC faculty member and one of the founders of the CH2M HILL engineering firm. (P16:40)

Looking east on Jefferson Street, ca. 1918. Pictured, from right, are the Forestry Building (completed in 1917), Men's Gymnasium (first phase completed in 1915), and the 1907 Waldo Hall. The Forestry Building was renamed Moreland Hall in 1973 after early faculty member William W. Moreland; today it is the home of the School of Writing, Literature, and Film. The Men's Gymnasium, which housed the exercise and sport science program and the physical activities class program, was named for Clair Langton in July 1973. Langton was a longtime director of health and physical education (1928–1964). (P25:1238)

New college library, January 1919. The new library had been open for about two months when this iconic wintertime view of the building was taken by Ball Studio. Built in 1918 to replace the library's cramped and inadequate quarters in the Administration Building (Benton Hall), the building was expanded in 1941, named the Kerr Library in 1954, and served as OSU's library until 1963. Today it is Kidder Hall, named for OSU's first professional librarian, Ida Kidder. The water fountain in the foreground was a gift of the class of 1916 and is similar to the famous Benson Bubbler water fountains in Portland, designed by architect Albert E. Doyle. Today this fountain is located on the west side of the Valley Library, close to its original location in front of Strand Agriculture Hall. (P16:262)

Farm Mechanics Building and Horticultural Products Building, ca. 1919. The Farm Mechanics Building was constructed in 1912 and included an open main floor area suitable for demonstrating heavy farm machines. The building suffered a devastating fire in 1938 and was subsequently expanded and remodeled. Today it is known as Gilmore Hall and is the home of the biological and ecological engineering department. The Horticultural Products Building was the first home of what is now food science and technology. It was expanded in 1923 to include a small production-level canning operation. It subsequently housed the farm crops and computer science departments. Today the building, named Hovland Hall in honor of C. Warren Hovland, professor emeritus of religious studies, houses faculty in the philosophy and religious studies programs. Both buildings were designed by John Bennes. (P96:23)

Commerce Hall, ca. 1923. Designed by John Bennes, Commerce Hall was one of the largest buildings on campus when it opened in 1922. In addition to being the home of the School of Commerce, it also housed the president's office, the college press and editor's office, student publications, and the industrial journalism department. It was renamed Bexell Hall in 1966 in memory of John A. Bexell, OAC's first dean of commerce. The College of Business, successor to the School of Commerce, occupied the building until 2014, when Austin Hall opened as the college's new home. (P16:592)

Engineering Laboratory, ca. 1925. Depicted is the Monroe Street (now Avenue) entrance to the building, which was built in 1920. It originally included a materials lab, a hydraulics lab, and a steam and gas engine lab, all served by a five-ton electric crane. The building, designed by John Bennes, was named for alumnus and long time engineering faculty member Samuel Graf, who was chair of the mechanical engineering department from 1934 to 1954. (P16:705)

Steam plant, ca. 1925. A new steam plant was built just south of the Armory in 1923 to provide steam to the rapidly growing campus. This facility, which could burn either fuel oil or hogged fuel (wood chips), replaced two older and smaller steam plants—one on the south end of the Armory and the other on the campus's north side near the engineering buildings. The smokestack was a campus landmark for many years, until it was removed in 1994 due to seismic concerns. (P16:553)

Women's Building nearing completion, 1926. The Women's Building is considered one of the masterpiece buildings designed by John Bennes and his partner at the time, Harry Herzog. The Italian Renaissance building was constructed of brick manufactured in Monroe, Oregon; it is likely that the red brick for other buildings built during this era came from the same source. The building originally included a thirty-by-seventy-foot pool, dance studio, assembly room with a fireplace, and a posture room with equipment for corrective body building. Today the building, which has retained most of its original charm, is the home of the College of Public Health and Human Sciences. Marys Peak, the highest point in the coastal mountains, is in the background (upper right). (P16:884)

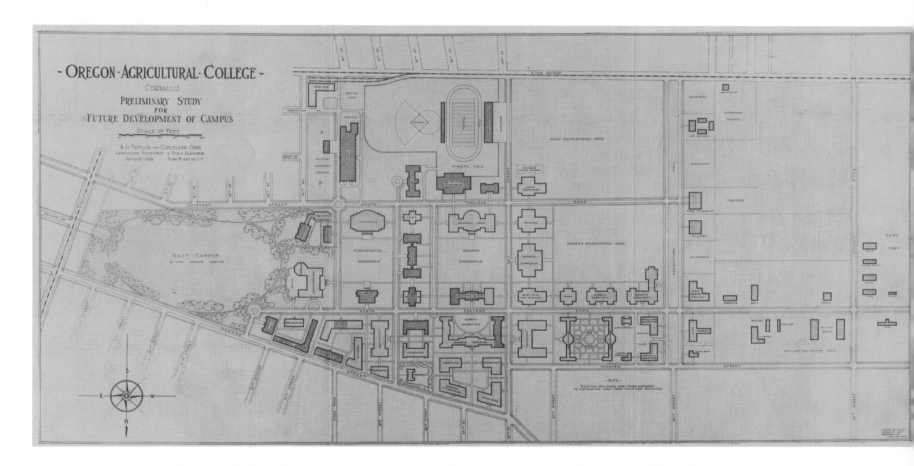

Map of A. D. Taylor's campus plan, January 1926. Taylor's campus plan built on the 1909 Olmsted plan, retaining what are now the Library and Memorial Union quads, as well as East Campus (lower campus today) as a park-like front lawn. He also called for making Thirtieth Street a boulevard to mark the western edge of the main campus, and moving all agricultural buildings west of Thirtieth Street. Many aspects of both the Olmsted and Taylor campus plans are still evident on campus and are components of OSU's current campus master plan. (MC– Campus Planning)

Memorial Union, 1929. This image was likely taken in the fall of 1929, about a year after the building opened and just a few months after it was dedicated on June 1. The building served as a memorial to Oregon State students, faculty, and alumni who lost their lives in the Spanish-American War and World War I. It was funded through donations and fees that students assessed themselves. The building was designed by Lee Thomas, a 1907 graduate of OAC. Today the Memorial Union is considered one of the finest examples of Neoclassical architecture in Oregon. (HC 34)

Veterinary Dairy Barn, 1935. This barn was the last of six designed by John Bennes, and was completed in 1930. It was a classic barn design with a gambrel roof, similar in style to the earlier beef and horse barns. It is the only pre–World War II barn that remains on OSU's main campus. (HC 41)

Men's Dormitory, 1934. Designed by Bennes and Herzog, the new men's dormitory replaced temporary barracks constructed during World War I. The building was actually five interconnected buildings, each with a separate name— Cauthorn, Poling, Buxton, Hawley, and Weatherford (center tower). The entire complex was renamed Weatherford Hall in 1957, and the other four names given to a new dormitory quad just to the west. Because of deferred maintenance issues, the building was vacated in the early 1990s. In 2004 it received a $20 million restoration to serve as the home of the Austin Entrepreneurship Program, financed in part by alumnus Ken Austin and his wife, Joan. (HC 57)

Entrance to the new Chemistry Building, ca. 1940. Completed in 1939, the building provided new quarters for the chemistry department. It was the second of two PWA buildings constructed on campus and was John Bennes's last new building design project for Oregon State. An addition was completed in 1980, and today the building is known as Gilbert Hall, named for longtime chemistry department chair Earl C. Gilbert. (P16:407)

Campus gates dedication, May 9, 1941. Chancellor and president emeritus William Jasper Kerr is presenting the gates to the college community during Mothers' Weekend. The gates were designed by renowned metal artist O. B. Dawson in the late 1930s. After a fundraising campaign, the gates were constructed as a Works Progress Administration project at the eastern edge of lower campus near Ninth Street. Seated on the podium to Kerr's left are E. C. Sammons, representing the State Board of Higher Education; Frederick M. Hunter, chancellor of the Oregon State System of Higher Education; and Albert D. Taylor, renowned landscape architect from Cleveland, Ohio, who developed the 1926 and 1945 campus plans for Oregon State. (HC 1477)

Arrival of temporary buildings from Camp Adair, March 1947. The decommissioning of the Camp Adair military cantonment north of Corvallis after World War II provided a huge stock of temporary buildings and building materials to public and private organizations and individuals throughout Oregon. Oregon State acquired several buildings that had been part of the naval hospital at Camp Adair to use as temporary administrative and faculty offices. The building complex was located on the northwest corner of Campus Way and Memorial Place, directly across from the Home Economics Building (Milam Hall). "Temporary" became a misnomer, as the structures were used for about twenty-five years. In all, seventy-nine buildings from wartime centers were brought to campus for temporary use. (P82:10 #507)

Sackett Hall and women's athletics field, ca. 1950. Sackett Hall, completed in 1948, was the first permanent dormitory constructed at Oregon State after World War II. A women's residence hall, it was named for State Board of Higher Education member Beatrice M. Sackett, who died in May 1947. The hall is located on the west side of the former women's athletic field, beyond the Women's Building. The athletic field was used for women's physical education instruction and later for intramural sports. Today Austin Hall and the Learning Innovation Center are on the site of the field. The straw bales on the field were used to secure archery targets. (Courtesy Benton County Historical Society, #20020910015)

Withycombe Hall, 1953. Withycombe Hall was constructed in 1952 as the home of the animal husbandry and dairy husbandry departments. The large section of the building at the far right was the dairy lab and was renovated in the early 1990s to serve as the new university theatre. The animal and rangeland sciences department currently uses the rest of the building. It is named for James Withycombe, OAC agriculture faculty member and experiment station director from 1901 to 1914. (He later served as governor of Oregon.) (P82:61 #1274)

Intramural fields and tennis courts, February 1948. The open area southwest of the Weatherford Hall dormitory complex, long used for military drills and intramurals, was formally developed for intramural purposes in the 1930s. Included were track and field facilities, football fields that included goalposts, and tennis courts, which were constructed about 1937. The building at the far end of the field is Dryden Hall, which housed the poultry science department. The lower buildings were the Mall Apartments, constructed as temporary housing in 1946 and demolished in 1961. Today this area is still used for intramural sports; it was redeveloped in 2011 and named Student Legacy Park. (P82:64 #402)

Cauthorn and Poling Halls, spring 1959. Steady enrollment growth at OSC in the 1950s necessitated more residence halls. A dormitory quad was built in 1957–58 and took the names Cauthorn, Poling, Buxton, and Hawley Halls. Cauthorn and Poling Halls were the third dormitories at Oregon State to bear those names. (P82:47 #2449)

Cordley Hall, ca. 1960. Like several OSU buildings through the years, Cordley Hall was built in stages. It housed many of the college's science and agriculture departments, including zoology, botany and plant pathology, microbiology, and entomology. The first section was completed in 1957 and the second in 1966. The car on the drive is a Studebaker Lark station wagon. (HC 1946)

Columbus Day Storm aftermath, October 1962. A major extratropical storm that was in part the remnants of a typhoon hit the west coast of the United States on October 12, 1962. Much of western Oregon was affected by the storm, including the OSU campus. Wind gusts reached at least 127 miles per hour in Corvallis, and total damage in the state topped $200 million (in 1962 dollars). There was some building damage at OSU, but the most noticeable damage was to campus trees. Fifty-five campus trees were destroyed, and another forty-three, including the Trysting Tree, were damaged. This tree on the Memorial Union quad, just south of Milam Hall, was sheared in half by the winds. (P82:78 #2728)

Wilson Hall, ca. 1965. Wilson Hall was part of a three-dormitory-and-dining-center complex built in 1963 and 1964 (Wilson, Callahan, and McNary Halls and McNary Dining Center). It was named for Eddy E. Wilson, alumnus and longtime member of the college board of regents (see chapter 4). The land for the dorm complex, acquired by OSU as part of an urban renewal project, had previously been a residential neighborhood that included student housing. (P57:2240)

Aerial view of the OSU campus, looking southwest, ca. 1965.
In the center is the new Kerr Library, completed in 1963. (Courtesy
of Benton County Historical Society, #19820950028)

Marine Science Center complex and dock, ca. 1970. The first buildings at the center—the hexagonal visitors center, the main buildings (east and west wings), and the dock—were dedicated in 1965. The building on the far left was constructed in 1970 for the Oregon Department of Fisheries and Wildlife. Prior to 1965, research vessels were docked at Newport's municipal dock; research vessels first had a presence in 1961 when the *Acona* was launched. Two research vessels can be seen at the dock. (P114:273)

Peavy Hall, ca. 1972. Peavy Hall was completed in 1971 as the new home for OSU's School of Forestry. It was named for George Peavy, longtime dean of forestry and president of Oregon State from 1932 to 1940. Today it houses most of the classrooms, computing labs, specialized labs, and central administrative services (including the dean's office) for the College of Forestry. (P170)

Construction of the Cultural and Conference Center, February 26, 1980. Planning for an events center at OSU began as early as the late 1960s. Construction of this building began in 1979, and it was dedicated in 1981. At the time of its construction, this was the largest building on any public college or university campus in Oregon that was built with private funds. One of the major donors was alumnus Loren L. "Stub" Stewart; the building is named for his father, LaSells Stewart. (P187)

Administrative Services Building, November 1984. It opened in 1972 and replaced the "temporary" Camp Adair buildings that had been used for the previous twenty-five years. The building housed almost all of OSU's administrative and student services, including the president's office, as well as the State System of Higher Education's Controllers' Division. It was renamed the Kerr Administration Building in 1996. (P57, Accession 2006:046)

President John Byrne teeing off during the Trysting Tree Golf Club dedication ceremony, June 2, 1988. The golf course, located on the east side of the Willamette River just across from Corvallis, was built on 175 acres of land that OSU had acquired in 1951 for that purpose. The course became a reality after alumnus N. B. "Nat" Giustina (class of 1941) championed the cause in the 1970s and made the lead gift. It was designed by Ted Robinson, a noted golf-course architect. The club, home to OSU's men's and women's golf teams, is a popular public golf course. It was named in honor of OSU's iconic campus tree, the Trysting Tree. (P92:1336g)

Magruder Hall, 1989. Magruder Hall was constructed in 1980 to accommodate the School of Veterinary Medicine, established in 1975, which prior to that time had been a department in the School of Agriculture. The building, named for state representative Richard Magruder, instrumental in securing funding for its construction, included classrooms, labs and a large-animal clinic. Magruder Hall was enlarged in 2004, adding a small-animal clinic that was a key component of the newly established Lois Bates Acheson Veterinary Hospital. Photo by Kevin Morris. (P94, Accession 2006:004)

Bates Hall, 1992. Bates Hall serves several family studies programs in the College of Public Health and Human Sciences. The building was funded in large part by home economics alumnus Mercedes Bates (class of 1936), a General Mills executive who turned the "Betty Crocker" brand into a household name. (P57, Accession 2006:046)

Agricultural and Life Sciences Building nearing completion, 1992. The building provided new quarters for several agricultural and science programs and centers that had outgrown Cordley Hall (right). Today it houses horticulture, biochemistry and biophysics, and the Center for Genome Research and Biocomputing. (P57, Accession 2006:046)

Valley Library, 2000. An expansion and complete renovation of the 1963 Kerr Library, the Valley Library was named in 1995 for Wayne and Gladys Valley, whose foundation made a gift of $10 million to the project. Groundbreaking took place in May 1996 and the project was completed in May 1999. The Valley Library, which remained open during construction, has won numerous awards and is consistently named the best place on campus to study. (P247)

Richardson Hall, ca. 2001. Richardson Hall, opened in 1999, houses the wood science and engineering and forest science departments. The building includes many research labs and a GIS computing classroom/laboratory. It is named for Kaye Richardson, an Oregon forester who provided a major gift for construction of the building. (P61, Accession 2011:024)

Dedication of Cascades Hall, OSU Cascades Campus, September 22, 2002. State Representative Ben Westlund of Bend, at the podium, was a strong advocate for creation of the Cascades Campus. He was one of several speakers at the dedication of Cascades Hall, which houses the campus's administrative and faculty offices, classrooms, and labs. Photo taken by the author. (P16:1351)

Interior of the Kelley Engineering Center, October 2009. The center, completed in 2005, was funded in part by a $20 million gift from 1950 engineering alumnus Martin Kelley and his wife, Judy. The center, home of the School of Electrical Engineering and Computer Science, features many collaborative research and learning spaces. The building received LEED gold certification in 2006; its environmental features include a rainwater catchment system that reduces water use by about 372,000 gallons a year, photovoltaic panels, solar hot water panels, and a design that encourages alternate forms of transportation. (Photo by Amy Charron, courtesy of OSU IMC Network)

Front entrance of the CH2M HILL Alumni Center, ca. 2010. The alumni center, completed in 1997, was funded in part by a major gift from the CH2M HILL engineering company, founded by an OSU faculty member and three of his students. Prior to the center's construction, the Alumni Association was located in the Memorial Union. In addition to housing the offices of the Alumni Association staff, the center's meeting rooms and conference space host a variety of events. (Photo courtesy of the OSU Alumni Association)

International Living-Learning Center, September 7, 2011. The center, completed in late summer of 2011, houses approximately 320 international and domestic students. Its learning spaces include twenty-six classrooms and an auditorium. It also is the home of the INTO OSU Center and parts of the university's International Programs department. Collaboration between OSU and INTO University Partnerships significantly increased the number of international students coming to OSU and fueled demand for the center. (Photo courtesy of OSU News and Research Communications)

View of Carrie Halsell Hall from the International Living-Learning Center, May 2012. The first new residence hall at OSU in almost thirty years, Halsell Hall opened in the fall of 2002. Built to house students in suites and apartment-style rooms—a relatively new concept at the time—the hall was named for Carrie Halsell, a 1926 commerce student who was Oregon State's first African American graduate. Like many students of color throughout the first six decades of the twentieth century, Halsell lived off campus. (Photo by Nancy Raskauskas for University Housing and Dining Services, courtesy of the OSU IMC Network)

Austin Hall, late afternoon, November 10, 2014. The new home of the College of Business, Austin Hall opened in early fall 2014 and was dedicated on October 31 of that year. The building features ten classrooms, including a 250-seat auditorium; an MBA suite for collaborative and team work and study; a business research suite; more than seventy faculty offices; suites for programs such as the Austin Family Business Program; a student study/collaboration/meeting space called the "marketplace"; and state-of-the-art technology. It was named for Ken and Joan Austin, longtime supporters of OSU and the College of Business, who provided a gift of $10 million that funded its construction. (Photograph by Amy Woosley.)

Linus Pauling Science Center, fall 2011. The new home of the Linus Pauling Institute as well as many chemistry faculty members opened in the fall of 2011. It includes a 180-seat auditorium and multiple labs. More than $31 million in private gifts—$20 million from the Wayne and Gladys Valley Foundation—helped fund the $62.5 million building. (Photo by Karl Maasdam, courtesy of the OSU Foundation)

Two land-grant college presidents, June 1926. William Jasper Kerr and Ernest O. Holland were presidents of the two Pacific Northwest land-grant colleges, Oregon Agricultural College and Washington State College. Kerr served as president of OAC from 1907 to 1932. Holland, like Kerr, was his institution's longest-serving president; he guided WSC from 1916 to 1944. Holland gave OAC's 1926 commencement address. (HC 388)

Builders of a Great University

4

Since its designation as the state's land-grant institution in 1868, hundreds of people have served Oregon State University in leadership capacities. These leaders provided the framework and vision for OSU's evolution from a church-affiliated institution that was not much more than a preparatory school to the top-tier Carnegie Foundation–designated research institution that it is today.

OSU has had nineteen presidents since 1868, including five acting presidents. Although most presidents were selected from outside the university, more than a few have been OSU faculty, and two were alumni.[1] Some of the earliest presidents and other leaders were ordained ministers—not surprising given the institution's affiliation with the Methodist Episcopal Church, South. OSU's presidents have had a broad range of academic backgrounds, from agriculture to forestry to oceanography to economics. All have been male, though women have played key roles in other high-level administrative positions—as deans of schools and colleges and as vice presidents.

Through the years, most of OSU's deans and vice presidents have been drawn from its faculty. Frederick Berchtold, a longtime faculty member, served as the first dean of the college from 1895 to 1901. The holders of other early administrative positions were also designated as deans, such as the dean of women and dean of men, established circa 1900 and 1924, respectively. The first dean of administration, E. B. Lemon, was appointed in 1943, replacing the executive secretary position established by William Jasper Kerr in 1907.[2] Schools and colleges have had academic deans since President William Jasper Kerr's 1908 reorganization of OAC's academic structure into schools.

Vice president positions are relatively new at OSU; the first was the vice president for research and graduate studies, established in 1970 by President Robert MacVicar and held by Roy Young. This position, as well as other vice presidential posts, grew out of similar positions that had been deans. The position of provost was established in 1985, the result of a reorganization of OSU's central administration by President John Byrne. Graham Spanier was appointed as OSU's first provost in 1986 and served until 1991.

In 1945 the Administrative Council, established in 1908 to advise the college president on administrative and policy issues, created the Faculty Council to serve as the governing body of the institution, responsible for academic policies, educational standards, curricula, academic regulations, and faculty welfare. It became the Faculty Senate in 1957. It was the first faculty body at Oregon State to have elected representatives. From 1945 until 1978, the college/university president served as chair of the faculty council and the senate; the vice-chair was elected by the faculty. The senate changed its bylaws in 1977 to allow for the election of a president and vice-president/president elect, though the university president retained certain veto powers. Warren Hovland served as the first president of the Faculty Senate in 1978.

From 1868 until 1888, the college was governed by a board of trustees, appointed by the Columbia Conference of the Methodist Episcopal Church, South. The board, which often included as many as twenty members, typically consisted of officials of the Columbia Conference, other ministers, local businesspeople, and occasionally politicians. The college president was also a trustee, as were some of the faculty.

When the state began assuming control of the college in February 1885, it established a new board of regents that consisted of nine members; this board first met in 1886, though it served only as a placeholder until 1888. The governor, state superintendent of public instruction, secretary of state, and state grange master were ex officio members. The other five regents, appointed by the governor, included businesspeople from around the state and state representatives or senators from the mid-Willamette Valley. In 1889 the Oregon legislature increased the number of regents to thirteen, with nine appointed by the governor.

Several regents served for multiple decades; James K. Weatherford, a member of the college's class of 1872, served as a regent from 1886 to 1929. The first female regent, Clara Humason Waldo, was appointed in 1905 and served through 1919. Oregon State had its own board of regents until 1929, when Oregon established the State Board of Higher Education. The new board became effective on July 1, 1929, and consisted of nine members. Only one member, B. F. Irvine, had served on OAC's board of regents.

The 2013 legislature once again provided for individual boards of trustees—at OSU, the University of Oregon, and Portland State University. The board of trustees of Oregon State University can include eleven to fifteen members appointed by the governor and confirmed by the Oregon senate. Members include civic, business, and educational leaders; one student; one faculty member; and one non-faculty university employee. OSU's president serves as an ex officio, non-voting member. The board's responsibilities include:

- Establishing policies for all aspects of the university's business;
- Establishing tuition and fees;
- Controlling academic programs;
- Approving the university's budget for submission to the state; and
- Appointing and employing OSU's president in consultation with the governor.

The new board met for the first time on January 9 and 10, 2014, and assumed full governance duties on July 1, 2014. Alumnus and donor Pat Reser (class of 1960) was chosen as the board's first chair.

Carte de visite portrait of Benjamin L. Arnold, ca. 1880. Arnold (1839–1892) was selected as president of Corvallis College in the summer of 1872. He graduated from Randolph-Macon College in 1861, served briefly in the Confederate Army during the Civil War, and subsequently taught at several small colleges in the southern United States, including West Tennessee College, where he served as president for four years. While president of Corvallis College, Arnold taught a variety of courses, including physics and English. In 1872 he established the cadet corps, as required by the Morrill Act. Arnold's first wife died in 1871, and he later married Minnie White, an 1876 graduate of the college. Despite his ties to the Methodist Episcopal Church, South, Arnold weathered the separation of the college from the church, and he served as president of the college until his death on January 30, 1892. This photo was taken by Corvallis photographer L. Goldson. (P1:3)

Captain John T. Apperson, ca. 1890. Apperson (1834–1917) was a member of the OAC board of regents from 1888 to 1917 and served as its president from 1894 to 1901. In early adulthood, he spent time in the gold fields of California and piloting a steamboat on the Willamette River. After the start of the Civil War, Apperson enlisted in the 1st Oregon Cavalry in the fall of 1861, ultimately earning the rank of captain. In the 1870s and early 1880s he served as a state representative and state senator from Clackamas County, and from 1874 to 1876 was sheriff of that county. During his tenure as an OAC regent, he helped secure state funding to rebuild the college's Mechanical Hall, which burned in September 1898. The new building was named for him in 1920, three years after his death. (P25:1210c)

Portrait of regent Wallis Nash, 1892. Nash (1837–1926) was a Benton County lawyer and entrepreneur. One of the original members of the board of regents, he was appointed in 1886 and served as secretary. Nash, a native of England who counted Charles Darwin as a friend as well as a client of his law firm, came to Oregon in 1879. He later purchased 1,800 acres in the coastal mountains west of Corvallis and established the community of Nashville. As a regent, Nash assisted in the hiring of several key faculty members, including horticulturalist and fellow Englishman George Coote and Margaret Snell, who established OAC's household economy and hygiene program (home economics). Nash was involved with the development of the college's farmers' institutes, which provided information and basic training to farmers throughout the state—essentially the start of today's Extension Service. He also played a key role in the selection of a new president, John Bloss, in 1892. Nash authored several books; his most popular was his travelogue volume, *Oregon: There and Back in 1877*. One of his daughters, Dorothea, an 1895 graduate of OAC, was the first head of music when it became a separate department in 1897. Two of Nash's sons, Percival and Desborough, played on OAC's first football team in 1893–94. Nash Hall is named for Wallis Nash. (HC 1726)

President John McKnight Bloss with students, ca. 1894. Bloss (1839–1905; front row, second from right) served as OAC's president from 1892 to 1896. He graduated with an AB degree from Hanover College in Indiana in 1860. During the Civil War he fought in the Army of the Potomac's 27th Indiana Volunteer Infantry and is credited with finding "Lee's Lost Dispatch" during the Battle of Antietam. From 1865 to 1892, Bloss was an administrator of several schools and school systems in the Midwest, serving, for example, as Indiana's state superintendent of public instruction from 1880 to 1882. As president of OAC, Bloss was director of the Agricultural Experiment Station and professor of mental and moral science, teaching courses in political economy, psychology, and ethics. With his health failing, Bloss resigned the presidency of OAC in 1896 and returned to his farm north of Muncie, Indiana. Both of Bloss's children spent time with him in Corvallis. Son Will, though not a student at OAC, was the coach and quarterback of its first football team. This photo was taken on the steps of the Administration Building (Benton Hall). (P25:1423)

Henry B. Miller, ca. 1890. Miller (1854–1921), a successful Oregon politician and businessman, was appointed to the OAC board of regents in 1895. The next year the board selected him as president of the college after John Bloss's resignation, a move that was seen by some as being fraught with politics, given Miller's political connections. From 1879 to 1895 he managed lumber businesses in Josephine County and was one of the first fruit growers in the Rogue River Valley. He served in the Oregon legislature in the early 1890s. Miller's presidency of OAC lasted less than a year. He resigned in 1897 to assume leadership of the State Board of Horticulture, and later served as the consul-general in China (1900–1905); Yokohama, Japan (1905–1909); and Belfast, Ireland (1909–1910). From 1914 to 1917 he served as the director of extension and publishing programs for the University of Oregon's School of Commerce. (P1:7)

John Richard Newton Bell on the OAC campus, ca. 1905. Bell (1846–1928) was a member of the Corvallis College board of trustees and the OAC board of regents for many years, starting in 1874. He was also an ordained Presbyterian and Methodist minister, known as the "marrying parson" for the more than one thousand weddings that he performed. Bell served in the Confederate Army during the Civil War and spent time in a Union prisoner-of-war camp. He also published three newspapers in Oregon. After his service as a regent, Bell remained an ardent supporter of OAC. He became the official "mascot" of the college, best known for throwing his hat into the Marys River after each Civil War football victory over the University of Oregon. He purportedly established this ritual with OAC's first victory over Oregon in 1894, though some sources indicate 1907. OAC renamed its athletic field Bell Field in 1921 in his honor. (Courtesy Benton County Historical Society, #20100700006)

Portrait of Thomas Milton Gatch, ca. 1900. Gatch (1833–1913) was a highly respected educator in the Pacific Northwest when he assumed the presidency of OAC in 1897. He received AB and AM degrees from Ohio Wesleyan University and a PhD from Indiana Asbury University (now DePauw University) in 1874. He twice served as president of Willamette University (1860–1865 and 1870–1880) and as president of the University of Washington (1887–1895). Gatch served as OAC's president for ten years, stepping down in July 1907. During his tenure, the college experienced steady growth in enrollment and added several buildings to its campus infrastructure. (1908 *Orange* yearbook)

OAC board of regents, 1901. The board consisted of (from left) William E. Yates, John D. Olwell, W. P. Keady, B. G. Leedy (Master of the State Grange), James K. Weatherford (president of the board), B. F. Irvine (treasurer of the board), F.I. Dunbar (Secretary of State), John D. Daly (secretary of the board), J. M. Church, T. T. Greer (governor of Oregon), and John T. Apperson. The board posed outside of the Administration Building (Benton Hall) for the photograph. (P25:1212)

Portrait of James K. Weatherford, ca. 1900. Weatherford (1848–1935) graduated from Corvallis College in 1872. He was admitted to the Oregon Bar in 1876, and founded a successful law firm in Albany in 1875 that exists to this day. Weatherford was elected to the Oregon House of Representatives in 1876 and was chosen as speaker of the house in 1878. He subsequently served three terms in the Oregon Senate. Weatherford was appointed to the college board of regents in 1886 and served until 1929—longer than any other regent. He was board president from 1901 to 1929. Weatherford Hall, the men's dormitory built in 1928, was named after him. (HC 411)

E. E. WILSON

Eddy Elbridge "E. E." Wilson, born in 1869, was a member of the class of 1889, the last OAC class to graduate before the college moved to its current location. A Benton County native, he attended OAC as a preparatory student before enrolling in the college curriculum. After receiving a bachelor of science degree in 1889, he did graduate work at OAC. Wilson later enrolled in what later became the University of Oregon School of Law, then located in Portland, and graduated with a law degree in 1893. He set up a law practice in Corvallis that year. Wilson twice served on the OAC board of regents, from 1906 to 1915 and from 1924 to 1929. Except for 1906, he served as secretary of the board during his tenure as regent. Wilson's years as a regent were marked by the hiring of William Jasper Kerr as president and the resulting growth of the institution. He also was a member of the Memorial Union Board of Governors from 1925 to 1961.

Wilson served as Corvallis's city attorney (1910 to 1915 and 1917 to 1919), and as Benton County's district attorney in 1913. In 1925 Wilson became president and then board member of the First National Bank of Corvallis. He worked with the bank until 1940 when it was sold to US National Bank of Portland. Starting in 1940 he worked as the manager of Benton County Abstract Company, a firm he set up in 1918 with two other partners, until it was sold to Title & Trust Company in 1946. As an attorney who specialized in land acquisition and disposition, Wilson participated in many investment opportunities that influenced the development of Corvallis.

Wilson is well known for his service on the State Game Commission from 1935 to 1949. He served in a period when the commission's activities expanded in response to growing numbers of hunters and fishers coupled with decreasing numbers of game. He worked to promote science in policy formation and the inclusion of professional scientists on the staff during this expansion. Wilson acted as a liaison, encouraging collaboration between commission staff and Oregon State College faculty on individual research projects, as well as encouraging joint support for the Oregon Cooperative Wildlife Research Unit.

Wilson died in 1961. He never married and had no children but has been memorialized through the E. E. Wilson Wildlife Area north of Corvallis and OSU's Wilson Hall.

Cadet portrait of Eddy Elbridge Wilson, 1889. This was probably Wilson's senior portrait, taken just prior to his graduation from OAC. (HC 805)

E. E. Wilson in his office, ca. 1905. This photo is from around the time of Wilson's appointment to OAC's board of regents, and was likely taken in the Wilson house that stood near the location of today's Valley Library. The portrait on the desk is of Wilson's mother, Rose Wilson, who attended Corvallis College as a preparatory student in the late 1860s. (P101:401)

Clara Humason Waldo, ca. 1910. Like E. E. Wilson, Clara Waldo (1858–1933) was appointed to OAC's board of regents in 1905. She was the first woman appointed to a board of regents of a state institution of higher education, and served to 1919. She was the wife of Oregon Supreme Court Justice John B. Waldo. Waldo Hall, the women's dormitory constructed in 1907, was named in her honor. (HC 416)

Portrait of Juliet Greer, ca. 1908. Greer succeeded Margaret Snell as head of the Department of Domestic Science and Art in 1908, and was named the first dean as a result of President Kerr's academic reorganization of the college. She served until spring 1911. Greer was a graduate of Vassar College and spent ten years as an instructor at New York's Pratt Institute prior to coming to OAC. (HC 179)

Office and desk of Thomas Henry Crawford, 1907. Crawford served as OAC's purchasing agent and was professor of commerce. As purchasing agent he had responsibility for expending funds for all purchases made by the college. Apart from the president, the purchasing agent was one of a very few administrative positions in the college at the time. (P25:2619)

Dean of Engineering Grant Covell and engineering faculty, 1909. Covell (1862–1927), third from right in the front row, came to OAC in 1889 and established the college's mechanical engineering program, the first collegiate engineering program on the West Coast. Covell was appointed the first dean of engineering and mechanic arts by President Kerr during his 1908 reorganization of OAC's academic units. Covell remained dean until his death in 1927. Covell Hall was named for him. (P25:1996)

Ralph Dorn Hetzel, first director of Extension at OAC, 1912. Hetzel (1882–1947) came to OAC in 1908, where he taught English and political science. He became director of OAC's Extension Service when it was formally established in 1911. Hetzel later served as the president of the University of New Hampshire (1916–1926) and Penn State University (1926–1947). (HC 251)

OAC board of regents, April 1925. The board assembled outside the north entrance to the Library for this springtime photograph. Front row, from left, are Sam Kozer (Secretary of State, ex officio), James K. Weatherford (president of the board), E. E. Wilson (secretary of the board), B. F. Irvine (treasurer of the board), Walter Pierce (governor, ex officio), Mrs. W. S. Kinney, and Jefferson Myers. Back row, from left, are E. B. Aldrich, Sam H. Brown, George M. Cornwall, and Harry Bailey. Not in the photo were members J. A. Churchill (superintendent of public instruction, ex officio) and George A. Palmiter (Master of the State Grange, ex officio). (HC 1166)

New and emeritus deans, ca. 1932. Two of Oregon State's long-time deans retired in 1932, John A. Bexell (left), commerce, and Arthur Cordley (right), agriculture. Their successors were Harrison Hoyt (second from left) and William A. Schoenfeld (second from right). Bexell came to OAC in 1908 and established its School of Commerce that year. Cordley started at OAC in 1895 and was named dean of agriculture in 1908. Soon after Hoyt was appointed dean of commerce, the program was moved from OAC to the University of Oregon. Schoenfeld served as dean of agriculture until 1950. (HC 344)

Dean of Women Kate W. Jameson in academic regalia, ca. 1930. Jameson was dean of women at Oregon State from 1923 to 1941. During her tenure, Jameson added many programs to the purview of the dean's office, including the Associated Women Students, Mortar Board, and various honor societies. She also started what is now Moms and Families Weekend in 1924 and helped to establish co-operative houses for women students in 1935. The position of dean of women was established around 1900, with Ellen J. Chamberlin serving as the first dean. (HC 184)

President and Dean of Forestry George W. Peavy, 1935. Prior to coming to OAC in 1910, George Peavy (1869–1951) earned bachelors and masters degrees at the University of Michigan, the latter in forestry in 1905. After working for the US Forest Service in California, Peavy was selected to head OAC's new Department of Forestry in 1910 and was made the first dean of the School of Forestry in 1913. He served as dean until his retirement in 1940. After William Jasper Kerr was selected as the first chancellor of the State System of Higher Education in 1932, Peavy was appointed acting president; his appointment was made permanent in January 1934. Peavy led the college through the academic restructuring of the early 1930s as carried out by the State System of Higher Education, as well as declines in the college enrollment and budget brought on by the Great Depression. OSU's first doctoral degrees were awarded during Peavy's presidency. As dean of forestry, Peavy oversaw the establishment of Oregon State's research forests and guided the school to become one of the top programs in the nation. After retirement, Peavy served as mayor of Corvallis from 1947 until his death in 1951. (P1:60)

Dean of Men U. G. Dubach and Professor Frank A. Magruder outside Commerce Hall, 1936. Dubach (right) was Oregon State's first dean of men, serving from 1924 to 1927. He was a professor of political science. Magruder too was a professor of political science, best known as the author of the textbook *American Government: A Consideration of the Problems of Democracy*. It was used in collegiate political science classes for many decades. The sundial in the photo, a gift of the Chamber of Commerce and made by the college's industrial arts program, was located outside of Commerce Hall for many years. (HC 295)

President Peavy and the OSC Administrative Council, ca. 1940. The administrative council was established by the board of regents in 1908, soon after President Kerr assumed office. The council advised the president on administrative and policy issues. It consisted of the president, the academic deans, director of Extension, and other top college administrators such as the registrar and deans of men and women. This administrative council included (seated from left): E. B. Lemon, registrar; Herbert T. Vance, head of the secretarial science department; M. Ellwood Smith, dean of Lower Division; William A. Jensen, executive secretary to the president; President Peavy; Ava Milam, dean of home economics; Lucy Lewis, college librarian; Francois A. Gilfillan, dean of science; Earl L. Packard, dean and director of general research; and William A. Schoenfeld, dean of agriculture. Standing are, from left: Clair V. Langton, director of the physical education division; Charles L. Sampson, commandant of cadets; Carl W. Salser, head of personnel and placement service; Willibald Weniger, assistant dean of the graduate division and head of the physics department; E. G. Mason, assistant dean of forestry; Ernst T. Stuhr, head of the pharmacology and pharmacognosy department; Fred O. McMillan, head of the electrical engineering department; and Dan Poling, assistant dean of men. This may have been the last meeting of the administrative council prior to President Peavy's retirement. This photo appeared in the 1940 yearbook. (HC 1534)

Frank L. Ballard on his first day as president of Oregon State College, July 1, 1940. Frank Lewellyn Ballard (1891–1971) was the first president of Oregon State to have graduated from the institution, having received a BS in agriculture in 1916. The following year he was hired to work for the Extension Service at OAC as a specialist in rural organization and agricultural economics. He served as the county agent leader and vice director of the Extension Service before assuming OSC's presidency. Ill health forced Ballard to step down from the presidency in the fall of 1941. He worked as the editor of Extension publications until 1945 and then served as associate director of the Extension Service at Oregon State until retiring in 1961. Throughout his career he contributed to many leading farm magazines and gained national renown as an agricultural journalist. He died in Corvallis on September 20, 1971, at age 80. (HC 133)

Student pilot August. L. Strand, 1947. Strand (1894–1980) was born in Texas but was raised in Montana. He earned a BS degree in entomology from Montana State College in 1917 and both an MS degree (1925) and a PhD (1928) from the University of Minnesota. Strand returned to Montana State College in 1931 as both a professor and the head of the entomology department; six years later he was appointed as the college's president (1937–1942). He came to OSC as president in October 1942, and saw the college through the war years and the post-war boom in enrollment and facilities. Twenty-five major buildings were constructed on the OSC campus during Strand's nineteen-year presidency. His capstone achievement was the renaming of Oregon State College to Oregon State University on March 6, 1961. During his presidency, Strand took up flying, and took his first private solo flight on September 19, 1947, twenty-nine years to the day after his first solo flight as a United States Navy sea plane pilot in World War I. After his retirement in 1961, Strand served as a Benton County commissioner from 1965 to 1968. (HC 339)

Born on January 12, 1893, in Nimmekah, Oklahoma, Francois Archibald Gilfillan earned a BS in pharmacy from Oregon Agricultural College in 1918. After serving in the Army Chemical Warfare Service, he attended Yale University and earned a doctoral degree in chemistry.

Gilfillan's career at Oregon State spanned more than fifty years as a student, professor of chemistry (1927–1939), acting president (1941–1942), and dean of science (1939–1962). During his years as dean, Gilfillan was known to many on campus and in the community as "Dean Gilfillan" or "Doc Gilfillan." In addition to his professional contributions in pharmacy and chemistry, Gilfillan spoke German, Russian, French, Italian, and Chinook; translated Latin, Greek, Chinese, and Sumerian inscriptions on clay tablets; and collected rare books and antique silver. A strong supporter of the campus library, Gilfillan and his estate made major contributions to the university's collection of rare books and fine bindings.

In the 1950s Gilfillan succeeded in bringing the study of oceanography to the college and continued to promote the expansion of science curricula and programs. Gilfillan was key to the development of the Junior Engineers' and Scientists' Summer Institute (JESSI)—a two-week program offered at Oregon State from 1956 through the 1970s for high school students interested in science and engineering. Developed at OSC in conjunction with Scientists of Tomorrow (Portland), these institutes were offered at colleges and universities throughout the United States. Gilfillan also contributed to the founding of the Oregon Museum of Science and Industry (OMSI) in Portland.

Gilfillan retired as dean of science in 1962 but maintained his close ties with the university, teaching German for another six years. He remained in Corvallis until his death in April 1983 at age ninety.

Dean Gilfillan and a student examining an electron microscope, October 4, 1956. (P82:92 #2173)

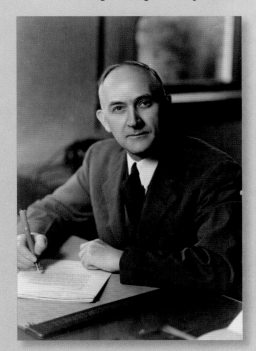

Francois Gilfillan as acting president, 1941. Gilfillan served as acting president from September 1941 to October 1942, after Frank Ballard stepped down as president due to ill health and before A. L. Strand came to OSC as president. As president, Gilfillan endured the outbreak of World War II, and the resulting removal of Japanese American students from the college. (P84:111)

Dean Ava Milam being honored by home economics international students, May 31, 1950. Milam (1884–1976; center, in dark dress) served as dean of home economics from 1917 to 1950. She came to OAC in 1911 after receiving her bachelors and masters degrees from the University of Chicago. From 1911 to 1916 Milam was professor and head of the Department of Foods and Nutrition. She took several extended trips to Pacific Rim countries, including China in 1922 to establish a home economics department at Yenching University and in 1931 to work as a home economics consultant at several universities. She developed strong ties in many countries, which resulted in a large number of international students coming to Oregon State to study home economics. After retiring as dean in 1950, Milam was a home economics advisor to Syria and Iraq for the United Nations Food and Agriculture Organization (FAO). She married J. C. Clark (class of 1904) in 1952 and received OSU's Distinguished Service Award in 1966. (P82:36 #249)

Dean of Administration E. B. Lemon at ROTC review, ca. 1950. Lemon (1889–1979) had a nearly lifelong association with Oregon State. He received a business degree from OAC in 1911 and was a part-time instructor in accounting from 1911 to 1943. He served as the college registrar from 1922 to 1943 and was appointed the college's first dean of administration that year. He served as dean until 1959. After retirement he remained active at OSU through work with the Alumni Association and the OSU Foundation. He received OSU's Distinguished Service Award in 1968. The Alumni Association established its E. B. Lemon Distinguished Alumni Award in 1981 in tribute to Lemon's extraordinary contributions to OSU. (MSS—Lora Lemon)

Gordon Gilkey demonstrating a printmaking technique, 1951. Gilkey (1912–2000) came to Oregon State in 1947 as chair of the art department. Gilkey was a strong proponent of the liberal arts and sciences at OSU, and in 1959 he was named the first dean of the School of Social Sciences and Humanities, a position he held until his retirement in 1976. Gilkey was the first MFA graduate in printmaking from the University of Oregon (1939). During World War II he played a key role in the recovery of Nazi propaganda art. He was a renowned printmaker; after his retirement from OSU, he donated his print collection to the Portland Art Museum and established its Vivian and Gordon Gilkey Center for Graphic Arts. OSU presented Gilkey with an honorary degree in June 2000. Gilkey Hall is named for him. (P82:4 #1086)

President James H. Jensen (left) and Governor Tom McCall at OSU's centennial celebration parade, 1968. Jensen (1906–1993) succeeded Strand as president, serving from August 1961 to June 1969. Prior to OSU, Jensen had been provost at Iowa State University for eight years. McCall was governor of Oregon from 1967 to 1975. Soon after his term as governor concluded, he was named the first holder of OSU's Tom McCall Chair in Public Affairs. McCall taught journalism and political science classes for one term. In 1982, the Governor McCall Lectureship in Public Affairs was created with funds from the McCall Chair. Many distinguished speakers have come to OSU as a result of the lectureship, including David Broder, William Raspberry, and Barbara Roberts. (P82:528 #17a)

Dean of Women Jo Anne Trow, ca. 1967. Trow, the first woman appointed to a vice presidential position at OSU, served as vice president for student affairs from 1983 to 1993. In 1993 she was named vice provost for student affairs, a position she held until her retirement in 1995. Trow came to OSU in 1965 as assistant dean of women, and the next year was appointed dean of women—she was the last person to serve in that position at OSU. From 1969 through 1983 she served as associate dean of students. (P57:4277)

Dean of Research Roy A. Young (center) in the computer center, ca. 1968. Young (1921–2013) served OSU in many capacities during his long career with He came to OSC in in 1948 as an assistant professor of plant pathology. He was selected chair of the Department of Botany and Plant Pathology in 1958 and served in that capacity until 1966, when he was appointed as OSU's first dean of research with campus-wide responsibility for research coordination. Young served as acting president of OSU from June 1969, after the departure of James Jensen, until July 1970, when Robert MacVicar arrived. From 1970 to 1976 Young served as vice president for research and graduate studies–OSU's first vice presidential position. In 1976 he was appointed chancellor of the University of Nebraska at Lincoln. He returned to OSU in 1986 as the part-time director of the Office of Natural Resources Policy and served until 1990. (Courtesy Benton County Historical Society #20090863690103-3)

Alumni Association director C. H. "Scram" Graham and students, 1972. Graham served as director from 1961 to 1978; he was a member of OSC's Board of Intercollegiate Athletics from 1955 to 1958. He received a BS in electrical engineering from Oregon State in 1935. (P151:1133)

President MacVicar and Black Student Union president Bobby Hill at the opening of OSU's Black Cultural Center, June 1975. Hill and MacVicar cut the ribbon to officially open the center. Behind them is Professor Betty Griffin, chair of the Black Cultural Center Advisory Board. MacVicar (1918–1998) served as OSU's president from 1970 to 1984. He came to OSU after having served as Southern Illinois University's vice president for academic affairs (1964–1968) and chancellor (1968–1970). MacVicar spent much of his career at Oklahoma State University, serving as faculty member in agricultural chemistry (1946–1964) and as vice president for academic affairs (1957–1964). (P57:5270)

President John V. Byrne with honorary doctorate recipients James DePriest (right) and Jan Karski (left), June 10, 1990. Byrne served as Oregon State's president from 1984 to 1995. He came to OSU in 1960 as one of the first faculty members in oceanography. He served as department chair, dean of oceanography, and vice president for research and graduate studies during his tenure at OSU. Prior to his selection as president, from 1981 to 1984, Byrne served as director of the National Oceanic and Atmospheric Administration. DePriest was the music director of the Oregon Symphony from 1980 to 2003, and Karski was a leader in the Polish underground during World War II. Byrne, DePriest, and Karski posed on the north balcony of the Memorial Union for this photograph taken by *Oregon Stater* editor George Edmonston on commencement day in 1990. (P195, Accession 98:84)

Dean Roy Arnold, July 1987. Arnold received a master's degree from Oregon State in 1965 and a PhD in food science and technology in 1967. He returned to OSU in 1987 as dean of the College of Agricultural Sciences. In 1991 Arnold was appointed OSU's provost and executive vice president, a position he held until 2000. He then served as the College of Agricultural Sciences' executive associate dean until his retirement in 2003. He also served as interim CEO of the Cascades Campus in 2001. Arnold served as a regent of the Honors College from 2009 to 2011, and OSU's Agricultural Research Foundation's Leadership Award is named in his honor. He was twice a recipient of OSU's Beaver Champion Award, in 1997 and 2006. (P98, slide #17765)

OSU President Paul Risser and Gladys Valley at the groundbreaking for the Valley Library expansion, May 1996. Risser served as OSU president from 1996 to 2002. He focused on student recruitment and retention and on marketing the university. During his tenure, enrollment increased from 13,836 students in the fall of 1996 to 18,789 in the fall of 2002. He left OSU to become chancellor of the Oklahoma University System in November 2002; he had served as a faculty member of the University of Oklahoma from 1967 to 1981. Risser was also president of Miami University of Ohio from 1993 to 1996. He died in 2014. Gladys Valley was a 1933 graduate of Oregon State. She and her husband, Wayne, who attended OSC in the late 1930s, established the Valley Foundation in 1977. The foundation has supported the construction of several OSU buildings, including the Valley Library, the Valley Football Center, and the Gladys Valley Gymnastics Center. Gladys Valley died in 1998. (P83, Accession 2004:052)

Dr. Larry Roper talking to a student on the MU quad, May 1997. Roper was appointed OSU's vice provost for student affairs in 1995 and served in that capacity until 2014. He also served as interim dean of the College of Liberal Arts in 2007–08 and taught classes in the College of Education and Ethnic Studies Department. (P94, Accession 2004:036)

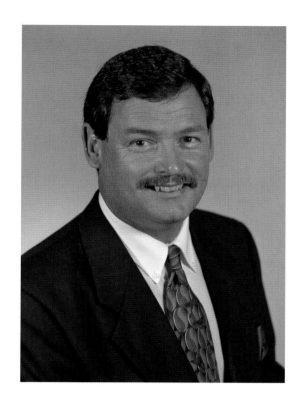

Dr. Tammy Bray, dean of the College of Public Health and Human Sciences, at the launch of the Hallie Ford Center for Healthy Children and Families, September 9, 2009. Bray came to OSU in 2002 as dean of the College of Health and Human Sciences. She oversaw the transformation of the college with its accreditation as the first public health school in Oregon. She is also executive dean of the division of health sciences, professor of nutrition and biochemistry, and a principal investigator with the Linus Pauling Institute. (Photo by Theresa Hogue, courtesy of OSU News and Research Communications)

Portrait of Tim White, July 1996. White came to OSU in 1996 to serve as the dean of the College of Health and Human Science. He served in that capacity until 2000, when he was appointed provost and executive vice president. Upon President Risser's departure from OSU in 2002, White was named interim president, and he served until Ed Ray assumed the presidency in 2003. He left OSU in 2004 to become the president of the University of Idaho, and later served as chancellor of the University of California, Riverside (2008–2012) and chancellor of the California State University system. (P119, Accession 2007:038)

President Ed Ray delivering the State of the University address to the OSU Faculty Senate, October 11, 2012. Ray was appointed president of OSU in the summer of 2003. He had been a faculty member at Ohio State University since 1970 and served as provost and executive vice president of that institution from 1998 to 2003. Ray's tenure as president has been marked by significant growth in student population, expansion of the campus infrastructure, large increases in federally sponsored research, and a $1 billion-plus capital campaign. (Photo by Theresa Hogue, courtesy of OSU News and Research Communications)

Dr. Orcilia Forbes, ca. 2013. Forbes came to OSU in 1998 as vice president of university advancement, a position she held until retiring in 2004. She also served as the OSU Foundation's interim president from 2002 to 2003. Forbes was a member of the State Board of Higher Education from July 2012 to July 2014. In 2013 she was named to OSU's new board of trustees. (Photo courtesy of OSU News and Research Communications)

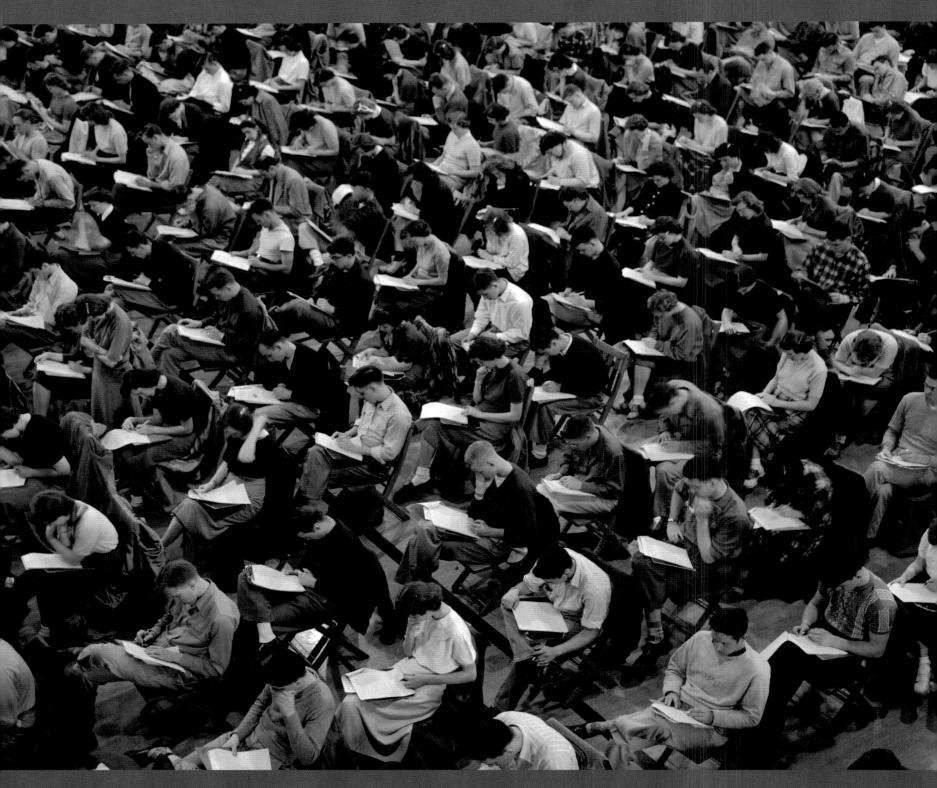

Final exams in the Memorial Union Ballroom, ca. 1950. During the years right after World War II, final exams were often given in areas that could accommodate large groups of students at a time, such as the MU Ballroom. Other locations included the gymnasiums in the Men's Gymnasium (Langton Hall) and the Women's Building. Photo by Richard Gilkey. (P252:PUM-64)

Academics at OSU
Promoting a Liberal and Practical Education

5

At the time of its designation as the state's land-grant college in 1868, the collegiate-level curriculum offered by Corvallis College was similar to that offered by other colleges in the region. It emphasized mathematics, classical languages (Greek and Latin), sciences (physiology, chemistry, and botany), and composition and rhetoric. The 1868–69 college catalog offered a "Scientific Course" (in place of "Ancient Languages") and additional courses in music and art for women. Degrees offered were bachelor of science, bachelor of arts, and master of arts.[1] The college also offered primary and preparatory department courses; for many years preparatory department students made up the majority of enrollees at the institution.

The college's acceptance of the state's land-grant designation obligated it to offer courses that met the requirements of the 1862 Morrill Act. Foremost were courses related to agriculture, as well as mechanical arts and military instruction. The 1869–70 catalog outlined the first "agricultural course" offered by the college. Following the maxim that "chemistry is the cornerstone of Scientific Agriculture," the course consisted of several chemistry-related and other science classes already being taught, such as Geology of Oregon. The mechanical arts curriculum was limited in the 1870s—the 1872–73 catalog stated that the engineering course "cannot be fully organized yet for want of funds." Students could take relevant mathematics and physics courses.

In 1883 the college established a department of agriculture and in September appointed Edgar Grimm (class of 1880) as its first professor of agriculture. Grimm provided a detailed account of the courses, which included agricultural chemistry, stock and stock breeding, fruit culture, and botany, in the 1882–84 biennial report. He also lamented the

lack of ground on the experimental farm that could be used for experiments and practical instruction (just two acres).[2] Grimm stated in the report that "the school room and the farm must be brought nearer together if theory and practice are to go hand in hand."

Early agricultural instruction was not limited to the college's students. In late 1888 and early 1889 the college conducted its first farmers' institutes.[3] Held in Corvallis, Salem, Roseburg, and Hillsboro, they were intended to be a "medium for the interchange of ideas, information and instruction between the farmers and the college."[4] College faculty, members of the board of regents, and others presented sessions such as "grasses and meadows," "the dairy cow and butter making," "bee culture," "hygiene," and "co-operation among farmers." All sessions began with music. A four-week farmers' short course was offered on campus for the first time in 1894 as another means of providing Oregon's farmers with practical knowledge. The early farmers' institutes and short courses helped to lay the groundwork for what would become, in 1911, OAC's Extension Service, which today provides a wide array of educational opportunities, including 4-H programs in most Oregon counties.

The college's curriculum greatly expanded with the hiring of two new faculty members in 1889. Margaret C. Snell, who was trained as a medical doctor, was appointed as the college's first professor of household economy and hygiene. OAC became the fourth land-grant college to establish a home economics program. Grant A. Covell was appointed the first professor of engineering. That year the board of regents reorganized the curriculum into five courses, or tracks. The agriculture and household economy courses were three-year programs, and the mechanical, scientific, and literary courses were four-year programs. Agriculture and household economy were made four-year courses in 1894.

New programs of study were established over the next dozen years. A pharmacy program was added in 1898 after druggists around the state petitioned for its creation. C. M. McKellips was the first instructor in pharmacy. A four-year curriculum in mining was established in the chemistry department in 1900, followed by literary commerce[5] in 1901 and forestry in 1906. Botany professor E. R. Lake headed the new forestry program. The addition of forestry brought the total number of programs of study offered by OAC to eight.

President William Jasper Kerr, who assumed office in 1907, reorganized OAC's academic programs in 1908. He created, and placed under the leadership of academic deans, professional schools in agriculture, commerce, engineering and mechanic arts, and domestic science and art. That year Kerr also appointed the college's first professionally trained librarian, Ida A. Kidder. In 1918 her efforts to secure a new college library finally met with success. Kerr created other schools throughout the 1910s—forestry (1913), mines (1913), pharmacy (1917), and vocational education (1918). The division of service departments was established in 1918 to provide basic instruction in subjects that did not offer majors, but were nonetheless core to the curriculum.

Kerr's expansion of OAC's curriculum in the first few years of his presidency was viewed as a potential threat by the University of Oregon. In response, the State Board of Higher Curricula was established in 1909 to determine the allocation and development of curricula at OAC and the UO. The board had limited success over the next twenty years.

During the 1920s, OAC's academic programs underwent review and accreditation. One- and two-year programs in various disciplines were eliminated in 1923. The Northwest Association of Secondary and Higher Schools accredited OAC in 1924, and in 1926 the college was placed on the Association of American Universities accredited list.

After its creation in 1929, as part of a restructuring of Oregon's public higher education administration, the State Board of Higher Education implemented a survey of Oregon's public higher education in 1930. The survey was conducted by the federal Office of Education, which made its report in 1931. The report found that Oregon's higher education expenditures were much higher than those of many states. The report recommended a massive restructuring of academic programs at all the colleges and the University of Oregon to streamline the curriculum and eliminate duplication. The results for all the institutions were considered harsh and still mark Oregon's public higher education today. Oregon State received the School of Science, but lost the School of Commerce. The School of Mines was discontinued. Humanities and social science courses at OSC were limited to freshman- and sophomore-level classes and consolidated into a new lower division. Landscape architecture became a joint program between Oregon State and the University of Oregon. Some of these changes were temporary—by 1945 OSC regained its former commerce curriculum in a new School of Business and Technology. But the social sciences and humanities at OSC would be limited to lower-level courses for many years.

Academics at Oregon State in the 1940s were affected by World War II. In 1943 and 1944, OSC hosted hundreds of soldiers who arrived on campus for training under the Army Specialized Training Program (see chapter 10). After the war, new ROTC programs affiliated with the Navy and Air Force were established in 1946 and 1949, respectively. In contrast to the war years, the 1950s were years of growth and expansion for the college's academic programs. Physical education became a major in 1950, and in 1951 the pharmacy curriculum became a five-year program, one of the first in the United States. OSC established a joint degree program in education with the Oregon College of Education (now Western Oregon University). An oceanography program had its genesis in 1954 with funds from the Office of Naval Research.[6] It achieved departmental status in 1959.

A major step forward in Oregon State's ability to provide and "promote the liberal and practical education" called for in the 1862 Morrill Act was the 1959 establishment of the School of Humanities and Social Sciences, which was able to grant degrees in each of those divisions. The creation of this school was a key factor in Oregon State's achievement of university designation in March 1961. In 1965, English was the first subject area within the School of Humanities and Social Sciences to offer a baccalaureate degree. The next year art, history, economics, political science, and speech were approved to offer undergraduate degrees. By

1970, undergraduate degree programs were also available in anthropology, technical journalism, music, philosophy, psychology, religious studies, modern languages, sociology, Russian studies, and American studies. The school also offered a major in liberal studies. The first liberal studies graduate degrees were not approved until 1988—scientific and technical communication (MA and MS) and economics (MA, MS, and PhD).

Two departments achieved school status in the 1970s—oceanography (1972) and veterinary medicine (1975). In 1973 the School of Science was re-designated as the College of Science, and the School of Humanities and Social Sciences became the College of Liberal Arts. The next year the Division of Health and Physical Education became the School of Health and Physical Education. In 1983 all of the remaining schools, except for education, became colleges.

In 1982 the School of Education took the joint degree program it had created with Western Oregon State College in 1953 a step further and created a School of Education jointly administered by the two institutions—the only school of its kind in the nation. The school also created a "teacher warranty program" in 1986, though by the early 1990s joint administration of the school was eliminated, with each institution administering separate schools of education. Another significant change was the 1988 approval of a baccalaureate core, which set certain curriculum and graduation requirements for undergraduate students.

Voter approval of a statewide property tax reduction measure in 1990 resulted in a major retrenchment of academics at OSU in the early 1990s. The ballot measure caused significant reductions in funding to public higher education. OSU responded to those cuts by eliminating or consolidating numerous programs, departments, and colleges. The departments of journalism, religious studies, and general science, as well as the program in hotel, restaurant, and tourism management, were eliminated. The College of Home Economics and the College of Education were combined.

The library was renovated and expanded between 1996 and 1999, resulting in a state-of-the art academic library facility. Growth of enrollment since the late 1990s has resulted in larger classes, especially in survey courses. At the same time, there have been significant advances in the use of technology in the classroom. In the 2000s, OSU partnered with several community colleges in Oregon to create dual enrollment programs, which allowed students to take lower cost community college classes and then transfer, without reapplying, to OSU.

OSU has been fortunate to have had numerous excellent teachers throughout its history. President Gatch was considered one of the Pacific Northwest's foremost educators when he assumed OAC's presidency in 1897. John B. Horner was a versatile instructor who taught English, history, political science, and Latin courses during his years at Oregon State. He also facilitated the consolidation of the college's various collections into what became the Horner Museum. Francois Gilfillan was as comfortable teaching Russian as he was chemistry. More recently, faculty such as Sujaya Rao and Kevin Ahern have been examples of excellent teaching at OSU. Rao has received recognition from the Entomological Society of America for her innovative teaching methods and programs. Ahern's "metabolic melodies," songs used as instructional aids, make his biochemistry classes very popular, and he is an award-winning undergraduate student advisor.

Since 1908 OSU has had a strong open enrollment program known as Summer Session, which was popular with Oregonians across the state. Many Summer Session students were teachers working on an advanced degree or wanting to gain new skills. Faculty from other institutions were often brought in to teach specialized courses. Today OSU's summer term is split into multiple sessions that range in length from one to eleven weeks.

The farmers' institutes of the late nineteenth century were the beginning of OSU's commitment to serve all Oregonians. The institutes and short courses helped lead to the creation of the Extension Service. Ecampus, OSU's distance education program, has its roots in the 1930s when educational courses were broadcast over radio station KOAC. Televised courses from Oregon State were first broadcast via KOAC-TV in the fall of 1957. Today more than 8,500 students take courses through Ecampus in a wide variety of degree and non-degree programs. In 2014 it was rated one of the top online programs among land-grant universities.[7]

Entomology students, ca. 1890. In addition to classroom and lab work, OAC students studying entomology in 1890 were required to do fieldwork during their third year. According to the 1890–91 college catalog, "each student will, under the instructor's direction, learn how to work with insecticides, and will be required to carry on experiments to discover the best means of preventing insect ravages." (HC 905)

Margaret Snell's sewing class, ca. 1890. Snell, who came to OAC in 1889, taught the college's first classes in household economy and hygiene, which later became home economics. As her students worked on their sewing projects, Snell (standing by the door) would often read to them. Snell's classroom was located on the north side of the third floor of what is now Benton Hall. (P25:1274)

Machine shop, 1891. The shop was located in the 1889 section of the original Mechanical Hall. This shop, along with the woodworking and blacksmith shops, served as the laboratory for students studying mechanics and mechanical engineering. In the machine shop, students were required to learn the use of tools through a series of exercises, and then work on building and repairing machinery. This photo appeared in the 1891–92 college catalog. (HC 601)

PERNOT TO PHOTOJOURNALISTS: PHOTOGRAPHY INSTRUCTION AT OSU

OSU has offered photography as part of its for-credit curriculum since 1891, making it one of the first colleges or universities in the western United States to do so. It was added as an optional course of study in a student's junior and senior years. The college's 1893 annual report stated that "photography is important to the student for its educational value in applying his knowledge of chemistry and physics, while for its esthetic culture it is invaluable."

The report also stated that since establishment, eighteen hundred photographs of college work (and scenery) had been created, as well as microphotographs for identifying plant diseases.

A local photographer, Emil Pernot, was hired to teach the first classes in photography, as well as classes in freehand drawing. Pernot taught photography for about five years and later used his interest in and skill with microphotography to help establish the college's bacteriology department (now microbiology) in 1899.

The 1894 *Hayseed*, forerunner to the *Beaver* yearbook, described the photography coursework at the time:

> Field work and portraiture are taken up in connection with classroom studies. The student is taught to operate his own camera, expose the plates, develop the negative, make the prints and in fact put out the finished pictures.

In the twentieth century, photography has been taught through the physics, journalism, and art departments. The first photojournalism classes were offered in 1964. Many OSU graduates have become regionally or nationally renowned photographers: Chris Johns (class of 1974) won awards as a photojournalist and is currently the editor-in-chief of *National Geographic* magazine. David Gilkey is an award-winning photographer and videographer for National Public Radio.

Portrait of Emile F. Pernot, ca. 1890. Pernot and his brother Eugene started a photography business in Corvallis around 1889, and this image was likely taken in their studio. Emile Pernot taught the first photography classes at OAC in 1891, helped establish the Bacteriology Department in 1899, and later served as the state bacteriologist. (P220:11)

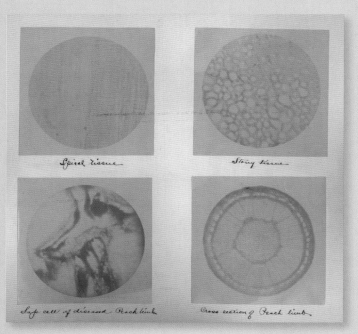

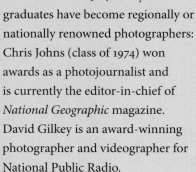

Microphotographs of plant sections, taken by Emile Pernot, ca. 1895. (P230)

94

OAC photography class, ca. 1892. Photography classes proved to be very popular with both male and female students. This photo includes John Fulton (standing, left), who took many 1890s era photographs of the college, a few of which appear in this book. (P96:96)

Portrait of Richard Gilkey, ca. 1951. Gilkey attended OSC from 1948 to 1953, receiving a BS in science education (1951) and an MS in education (1953). As a student, he took photographs for the *Beaver* yearbook and *Oregon Stater*; he was shooting *Stater* cover photos as a sophomore. While at OSC, Gilkey also worked as a stringer photographer for Portland's *Oregon Journal* newspaper. He went on to a long career with the Portland Public Schools and is the father of award-winning photographer and OSU alumnus David Gilkey. (HC 1474)

Photography

Several courses in photography, both technical and non-technical, are offered by the Physics Department for this term. See Mr. Garman or Mr. Yunker, room 101 or 202 Apperson Hall.

Photography class announcement, ca. 1925. John Garman (1896–1989) was an OAC alumnus (class of 1922) and longtime physics faculty member who taught photography classes from 1924 to 1966. In 1969 he assisted with the transfer of photography from physics to the art department. He also helped to establish the college's photographic services in the 1920s and authored two textbooks on photography technique: *Introductory Photography* (1940; revised 1957) and *Commercial Photography* (1953). Both texts were sold through the college bookstore. (P96:68)

George Coote teaching a grafting class, ca. 1893. Coote, standing on the right, taught a variety of horticulture classes and also managed the college grounds. This image was used in the 1892–93 college catalog. (P25:1309)

Women's physical culture class, ca. 1896. These women were photographed just outside the east entrance of the first Mechanical Hall, working with clubs as part of their physical culture (physical education) training. A section of one of the floors in the Mechanical Hall was used as a gymnasium. The 1896–97 college catalog stated that the system of physical culture used at OAC "strengthens the nerve centers and vital organs; and at the same time develops grace and muscular strength." (P25:1202)

Students and instructors in the bacteriology lab, ca. 1912. Professor of bacteriology Theodore Beckwith is standing at the back of the lab, which was located in Science Hall (Furman Hall). The 1912–13 catalog stated that the "relationships of the comparatively new science of Bacteriology to everyday life in the various industries have increased so largely in numbers and intimacy that it is necessary for any student properly equipped in Dairying, Agriculture, Agronomy, Pharmacy, Domestic Science, etc., to have a working knowledge of the subject." (P25:1321)

Forestry students in the field, spring 1910. All four members of OAC's first forestry graduating class in 1910 are pictured here—Jack Pernot, Harold Gill, T. J. Starker and Sinclair A. Wilson. Starker is standing, right. (HC 849)

Commencement exercises in the new Armory, June 14, 1910. Commencement was held in the armory from 1910 through 1914. Starting in 1915, the newly completed Men's Gymnasium hosted the ceremony. (P96:222)

Students in the chemistry lab, ca. 1914. Students fondly called the Science Building (Furman Hall) the "Chem Shack." Just a few years after this photograph was taken, Linus Pauling would be doing some of his first chemistry lab work at OAC in this same room. (P96:148)

Camp cookery class, ca. 1918. OAC's home economics curriculum in cooking was designed to give women experience and opportunities in a variety of settings. This was "a course designed to give advanced students of Home Economics training in application of principles of cookery to conditions found in the camp," such as logging camps. (P47:13)

Students in the library reading room, ca. 1915. Prior to the construction of what is now Kidder Hall in 1918, the college library was located in the Administration Building (Benton Hall). The reading room was located in the center section of the second floor, which today is the music rehearsal hall. The college catalog described the reading room as being supplied with about five hundred "leading magazines and newspapers," as well as encyclopedias, dictionaries, and standard reference works in various fields of study. The curriculum in 1915 included a half credit course, Library Practice, that was a requirement of all degree programs. (HC 75)

OAC women participating in an auto mechanics class, 1918. (HC 491)

Beekeeping class, ca. 1920. OAC offered two types of beekeeping courses. One was a regular part of the entomology curriculum. The other was an eight-week short course "designed to meet the needs of the man now engaged in beekeeping who does not have sufficient time to take advantage of one of the regular courses offered by the College." Like many short courses, it was taught in the winter. (HC 948)

Students in the School of Commerce lab, ca. 1920. In 1920, 652 men and women were enrolled in the School of Commerce, which was located on the second and third floors of the north (agronomy) wing of Agriculture Hall. The school was composed of four departments—business administration, economics and sociology, political science, and office training and stenography. The 1920–21 catalog stated that "modern accounting and office machinery of various types . . . is available for student practice." (HC 882)

Home economics students outside the Withycombe Home Management House, ca. 1920.
Home management, or practice, houses began at OAC's School of Home Economics in 1916.
A six-week residency was required of all home economics students, and starting in 1926 this
included care of infants and toddlers who lived in the houses. The program continued into the
1960s. The Withycombe House was located on Monroe Street just to the west of what is now
Graf Hall. Photo by Ball Studio, Corvallis. (P25:1590)

4-H Summer School general assembly in the Y-Hut auditorium, 1922. For many summers starting in 1914, youth from 4-H clubs across Oregon would come to the Oregon State campus to participate in a variety of 4-H related activities and interaction with their peers. A 1930 4-H brochure described the Summer School as being "so organized that they [the attendees] may profit by their association with one another, learn better methods in agriculture and home economics, and return this valuable information and experience to other boys and girls in their communities who are unable to attend." The school undoubtedly served as a recruiting tool for Oregon State for many years, which it continues to do today as a four-day 4-H Summer Conference. (P146:6)

Mining students demonstrating gas mask equipment, ca. 1925. Mines courses began at OAC in 1900, and in 1913 a School of Mines was authorized. This photo is likely of mining engineering students, whose major was "intended to equip the student with thorough knowledge of the basic principles of the art of mining which are essential in development of mineral properties, design and construction of mine plants, and management of mines." (HC 85)

If the ghost of Knute Rockne ever makes a complete tour of all his old football haunts, the legendary Notre Dame coach could find himself in the middle of a pickup basketball game in Dixon Recreation Center on the Oregon State campus. Rockne—perhaps the most famous football coach of all time—visited Oregon State for five summers in the late 1920s to teach his system to other coaches on old Bell Field, which is now the site of OSU's student fitness complex.

Rockne was at the height of his career when he taught in the Oregon Agricultural College Summer Session between 1925 and 1930. Rockne had been a pupil of M. H. "Dad" Butler in the Midwest before Butler went on to develop some powerful Beaver track and field teams in the 1910s and 1920s. Rockne also was acquainted with OAC football coach Paul Schissler, whose team from tiny Lombard College had stayed within fourteen points of Rockne's Irish in a 1923 game. (In 1924, Schissler

M. H. "Dad" Butler, Knute Rockne, and Paul Schissler, ca. 1926. Rockne and Schissler first met when Schissler's Lombard College football team played Notre Dame in a close game in 1923. Schissler coached football at Oregon State from 1925–1932. Butler, OAC's track and field coach from 1920 to 1927, had been Rockne's high school track and field coach in Chicago. (HC 1528)

moved on to OAC. In his nine years in Corvallis, his teams went 48-30-2 and consistently pulled Beaver football into the national spotlight.)

The April 1925 edition of the *OAC Alumnus* reported Rockne had been engaged for the Summer Session's Coaching School, noting: "No football coach has occupied the limelight longer, no coach has more consistently progressed with the constant changes in football." Rockne arrived in Corvallis on June 22 and was the guest of honor at a dinner given by the city's service clubs. His courses drew over one hundred coaches, and, according to the *Alumnus*, "in personality and driving power Rockne exerted a dynamic influence, not only upon the men in his classes but upon all men in the community that came in contact with him."

By 1927, Rockne was having Schissler assist him in the other courses he offered around the country in the summer. Rockne kept returning to OAC each June, and each time his national profile had grown larger. In 1928, Summer Session director M. Ellwood Smith wrote of Rockne's impending visit:

> There are other coaches, but there is no other Rockne . . . he has turned out winning teams until the South Bend football laboratory is looked upon by coaches and critics as the experimentation football center of the world which may be counted on to reveal possibilities and defects in new rules and new plays as they develop. Through his syndicated articles he reaches the breakfast tables of the entire nation and through his summer schools for coaches he has reached progressive coaches and directors in a professional way.

If Rockne made a favorable impression on Oregon State, then Oregon State also made a favorable impression upon Rockne. In an interview with the *Alumnus* in 1928, he said, "What do I think of the campus? I think it is a splendid one. And say, you know, these new buildings are surely going to put it on the map. I can notice a vast improvement just in the four years that I have been coming here to teach at the summer session. The change has not all been in the physical campus construction either. Your athletics have been building up steadily."

Over the years, the relationship between Rockne and Schissler had grown warm enough that Rockne was apparently willing to grant the Beavers a visit from the Fighting Irish. In June 1931 Schissler informed Notre Dame athletic director Jesse Harper that Rockne (who had died earlier that year) had promised, in writing, a home game against Notre Dame in 1933. In his history of Notre Dame football, *Shake Down The Thunder*, author Murray Sperber writes that

> Oregon State had already announced the game to an ecstatic local press and public, thus the West Coast school could not understand why the N.D. faculty athletic board had not yet approved the contest . . . It soon emerged that Rockne had made the promise without consulting the board, probably hoping that he could bluster the faculty men into accepting the game or making them the fall guys in an N.D. refusal . . . in the end, the board refused to sanction the West Coast trip and the Fighting Irish never played Oregon State.

Seven decades later, the two teams once led by Schissler and Rockne finally met.[8]

Knute Rockne instructing in Bell Field during his coaching school, ca. 1927. Rockne's coaching school was popular with high school coaches throughout the region. (Courtesy OSU Athletic Communications)

OAC Summer Session poster, 1927. Rockne was prominently featured on this poster. Like Rockne, many of Oregon State's Summer Session instructors were visiting faculty from other institutions and governmental agencies. (HC 828)

OAC Summer Session faculty and students, 1926. Summer session participants gathered in front of the Administration Building (Benton Hall) for this group photo. Notre Dame football coach Knute Rockne first participated as a summer session faculty member at Oregon State in 1926. He is pictured on the front row, just behind the summer session sign on the right and holding a boater hat. (P176:283)

Pharmacy students in the model drugstore, ca. 1927. One of the courses required of seniors studying pharmacy was "Model Drug Store Practice." The Pharmacy Building, completed in 1924, included a model drugstore used as a teaching lab. According to the 1926–27 catalog, it contained "Stedman's rubberoid flooring, 32 feet of mahogany English wall cases, 18 feet of plate glass marble base show-cases, a 10-foot wrapping counter, a 10-foot mahogany prescription case, 25 feet of cross partition, Coty display case, a cash register, an intercommunicating telephone, Watermen Pen case, and similar displays." (HC 902)

Cast of OAC's production of *The Mikado,* March 1927. Gilbert & Sullivan's *The Mikado* has been performed at Oregon State on several occasions, including in 1909 and 1916 prior to the 1927 production. Theatre productions at Oregon State date back to at least the early 1890s. In the early 1920s, the theatre program became more formalized when Elizabeth Barnes was hired to coordinate it in 1922. She also taught drama interpretation courses. Barnes retired in 1945. (HC 489)

Women's field hockey class, ca. 1929. Oregon State offered a wide variety of physical education classes to women. During the 1929–30 academic year, women could choose from hockey, field ball, baseball, basketball, volleyball, track and field, swimming, archery, tennis, riding, gymnastics, and dance. (P17:762)

Graduation portrait of Chuang Kwai Lui. Lui, who was from Hong Kong, and earned a doctorate in physics in 1941, was the first woman to receive a PhD at Oregon State. She also received an MS from OSC in 1937. (HC 2580)

Civilian pilot training, 1941. In the late 1930s and early 1940s, Oregon State College offered pilot training as part of its curriculum. The program, authorized by the Civilian Pilot Training Act of 1939, was directed by Benjamin F. Ruffner, professor of aeronautical engineering. It consisted of primary and advanced ground school instruction and flying lessons at the Albany airport. (HC 968)

Art exhibit invitation, 1942. Oregon State's art program in the 1930s and 1940s was robust, despite being limited to freshman and sophomore level classes. Activities included an annual exhibit held in May. Since the late 1930s the lobby area of Fairbanks Hall (Kidder Hall in 1942) has served as gallery space for student and faculty exhibitions and works on loan. (MC—Art Dept.)

Modern dance class taught by Betty Lynd Thompson, January 1951. The Women's Building included a dance studio room for dance instruction. Betty Lynd Thompson taught all dance classes at Oregon State from 1927 to 1945. After 1945 she concentrated on her major interest, creative dance. Dance students gave several recitals a year. Thompson retired from teaching in 1972. (Physical education was first offered as a major in 1950.) (P82:87 #543)

Russian language instruction, ca. 1942. Dean of Science Francois Gilfillan (left) introduced Russian language study into OSC's foreign languages curriculum in the early 1940s and taught Russian classes as part of the Army Specialized Training Program curriculum during World War II. (HC 935)

State Police School, July 1952. Summer Session offerings at Oregon State included specialized courses, such as this one for members of the Oregon State Police. (P82:98 #1314)

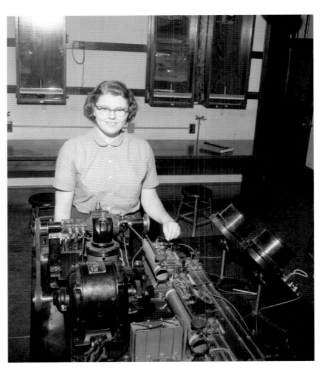

Engineering student Phyllis Aldrich, May 1954. Female engineering students were uncommon at OSU into the 1950s. Today women make up approximately 17 percent of the enrollment in the College of Engineering. (P82:34 #1633)

Dr. Wendell Slabaugh teaching chemistry class via television, fall of 1957. OSU's strong distance-education program can trace its roots back to this television broadcast. Slabaugh was a popular chemistry professor and taught OSU's first class via KOAC television. (P82:92 #2217)

Extension 4-H Club agent Julius Binder works with Jefferson County 4-H horse project members, ca. 1961. Twenty-one 4-H club members were preparing for a five-day trail ride into the Cascades. Oregon's 4-H program traces its roots to 1904, when the first boy's industrial club was established in Dayton. In 1913 the state legislature appropriated funds for establishing boy's and girl's industrial clubs throughout Oregon. These clubs engaged in projects such as vegetable growing, poultry and pig raising, sewing, canning, and woodworking. Oregon's industrial clubs were merged into a national network after the passage of the Smith-Lever Act in 1914, which formally established the Extension Service in each state. By 1924 the industrial clubs became known as the 4-H Youth Leadership Program and adopted the familiar cloverleaf emblem. Thousands of Oregon youth participate in 4-H today. (P146:2279)

University Librarian William Carlson with library staff and pages, preparing to move to the new library, September 5, 1963. Carlson served as university librarian from 1945 to 1965. He began advocating for a new library in the early 1950s, and the Oregon legislature approved the building in 1961. On September 5, 1963, Carlson led a procession of library staff and students, each carrying a few volumes, into the new building, where the books were placed on the shelves in call number order. (HC 1932)

OSU Farrier School, ca. 1965. Although a mostly lost art by the mid-twentieth century, blacksmithing at OSU continued through its farrier school program, taught in the 1960s by Lee McDaniel. This vocational, non-credit training was offered through the animal science department from the mid-1950s through 1978, when Linn-Benton Community College assumed responsibility for the program. (Courtesy Benton County Historical Society, #19910170176)

Marine Science Center faculty instructing teachers on the use of intertidal areas as outdoor labs, 1968. (P3:5187)

University Theatre production of *Macbeth*, 1971. Shakespeare has long been a staple of OSU's theatre program. *Macbeth* has been performed on multiple occasions, including the 1949 season and the summer of 2010. (P3:3984)

Experimental College student Jo McCullough demonstrating her harmonica skills, ca. 1988. The Experimental College was established in 1968 as part of the "free university movement" to provide the OSU community with opportunities for self-enrichment and experimentation in a casual setting with no grades. Classes were wide-ranging, including foreign language conversational skills, skiing, home-buying, and whale-watching. The harmonica class was one of the most popular. The program ended in the 1990s. This photo appeared in the 1989 yearbook. (P3, 1989 *Beaver Yearbook*)

Student in a pharmacy lab, ca. 1990. The College of Pharmacy was just a few years away from its centennial in 1998 when this photograph was taken. The college began offering a doctor of pharmacy degree in 2000 as its sole professional degree. This change fostered closer ties between the college and the Oregon Health & Science University, a collaboration that had begun in 1988. (P94, Accession 97:100)

Archaeology Field School near Galice, Oregon, August 1992. For many years OSU has offered a summer archaeology field school. This field school took place on the Rogue River. Other field school sites have included the Champoeg State Heritage Area near Newburg and the Fort Hoskins County Park in western Benton County. (P57, Accession 2006:046)

College of Business computer lab, ca. 1995. Beginning in the late 1980s, computer labs became an integral part of OSU's educational infrastructure. In 1995, OSU had four labs with a total of 293 computers of various types. The College of Business lab contained 89 Leading Edge and Hewlett-Packard Vectra computers. Other computer labs were located in in the Computer Science Building, Milne Computer Center, and the Kerr Library. (P57, Accession 2006:046)

Science lab at Cascades Hall, OSU-Cascades campus, September 2002. This photo was taken during the dedication ceremony for Cascades Hall. Photo by the author. (P16:1355)

Richard Nafshun explains some chemistry basics for a short video available to his distance-education students, January 28, 2009. Victor Yee from Ecampus films a number of different segments for Nafshun, which are posted for his class, as well as being available through OSU iTunes U. (Photo by Theresa Hogue, courtesy of OSU News and Research Communications)

Experiment Station entomology lab, ca. 1925. The 1925–26 college catalog described entomology research as including the toxicity of insecticides, discovery of new and cheaper insecticides, propagation of beneficial insects, various studies of orchard pests, and study of forest insects. The laboratories, located on the third floor of Agriculture Hall, were described in the catalog as "equipped for teaching general Entomology and fairly well equipped for advanced research work." (P55:15)

Producers of Knowledge
Research Through the Decades at OSU

Corvallis College's acceptance of the provisions of the Morrill Act in 1868 set in motion the events that would lead to Oregon State University becoming a major research university.

The purchase of the college farm in 1871 provided an opportunity for agriculture students to engage in basic applied research. The college's 1872 annual report indicates that most of the work done on the college farm was preparatory—fencing, ditch digging, and preparing the grounds for future crops. The 1872–74 biennial report was much more substantive. President Benjamin Arnold described wheat and oats trials on the farm, grown with applications of different fertilizers. Arnold also included the college's first research report—it pertained to white soil from the college farm and marl from the Yaquina Bay area.[1]

Basic applied agricultural research continued at the college farm for the next ten years. In the college's 1884 annual report, E. E. Grimm, professor of agriculture and chemistry, reported on a wide variety of trials, despite only having two acres to plant on. He indicated that the agriculture students "furnished seeds of various kinds of wheat, oats, barley, and potatoes from their various counties and planted them on the experimental grounds." They also planted fifty-eight experimental plots of grasses and clovers, as Grimm felt that "the cultivation of the grass and forage plants in general should demand our special attention" due to the lack of permanent pastures.

The passage of the federal Hatch Act of 1887 and its subsequent implementation had a profound effect on agricultural research at most land-grant institutions. The $15,000 annual appropriation for the establishment of an experiment station in 1889[2] formalized agricultural research at OAC. The funds enabled the college to appoint an experiment station director (Grimm) and hire a station chemist and horticulturalist. The experiment station issued its first bulletin in October 1888. Authored by Grimm, it outlined the station's research plan, which included the study of soils on the college farm and around the state; grain, grass, and other crop cultivation varieties and methods; orchard fruit varieties; and insect pests and noxious weeds.

The purchase of additional farmland west of campus in 1889 enabled agricultural research to expand quickly. The college's 1893 annual report described the planting of a new experimental orchard in 1891, which included eighty-seven varieties of apples, fifty-seven varieties of grapes, three varieties of filberts, forty-four varieties of gooseberries, and nine varieties of blackberries. Additionally, the farm's variety trials for 1891 included fifty-five varieties of tomatoes, twenty-seven varieties of cabbage, and twenty-five varieties of strawberries.

OAC's agricultural research plan was not limited to the Willamette Valley. In 1901 a branch experiment station was established at Union, near LaGrande, to research livestock (cattle), grain production, and forage/pasture grasses. (OAC research in that region had begun in the late 1890s.) Other branch experiment stations quickly followed, including Hermiston (1909), which focused on irrigated and dryland grains, irrigated crops, and poultry production; Talent (1911), which studied fruit production, especially pears; and J. J. Astor (1913), near Astoria, which conducted research on forage, cash crops, and dairy management.

In addition to the establishment of several branch experiment stations, agricultural research at OAC gained a foothold in other areas in the early twentieth century. James Dryden came to the college in 1907 and developed a nationally renowned poultry-breeding program, collaborating with commercial poultry operations such as the Hanson Leghorn Farm in Corvallis. The poultry program bred the first chicken to produce three hundred eggs in a year. Ernest Wiegand, hired in 1919 to develop a horticultural products program, soon developed a close working relationship with Oregon's food processing industry. He and his assistant, Thomas Onsdorff, are known for developing a new method—still used today—of brining cherries for maraschinos in the mid-1920s.

Research funding for agriculture received a boost in 1906, when the Adams Act was approved by Congress. It increased the annual appropriation to the experiment stations stipulated by the Hatch Act to $30,000. The Smith-Lever Act, which created a national extension program in 1914, provided funding for OAC's Extension Service, established in 1911. The Extension Service disseminated the college's research to Oregon farmers through practical publications, workshops, short courses, and broadcasts over radio station KOAC. Additional agricultural research funding came in 1925 with the passage of the federal Purnell Act. It provided funds for agricultural marketing investigations. It also funded some of the first home economics research at OAC, which previously had been limited, consisting mostly of basic lab work in areas such as cooking and textiles. The new funding enabled the School of Home Economics to engage in deeper and broader studies, such as the standard of living on Oregon farms and farming communities. Maud Wilson was hired to carry out the school's research agenda.

Forestry-related research began in the mid-1920s with the acquisition of 341 acres just north of Corvallis for a research forest. (Prior to this, forestry students used City of Corvallis watershed lands on the east slope of Marys Peak for demonstration purposes.) Eighty acres of the initial acquisition were designated as an arboretum and subsequently named for longtime forestry dean George Peavy. A state seedling nursery was established at the arboretum in 1925, and in 1928 a "post farm" was created for the study

of logs for use as fence posts and telephone poles. In the 1920s California businesswoman Mary McDonald had been assisted by OAC's School of Forestry in eliminating an invasive weed from her timberlands. As a show of gratitude, she provided funding to expand the research forest's acreage, which grew to approximately 3,000 acres at the time of her death in 1935. Funds from her estate were used to further expand the forest, named McDonald Forest in her honor, to 6,000 acres. The acquisition of former Camp Adair lands in the late 1940s nearly doubled the size of the forest; today the McDonald-Dunn Forest consists of more than 11,000 acres that are used for a wide range of forestry research.

Research in the School of Engineering was formalized in 1914 when the school partnered with the Extension Service to create the Experimental Engineering Department. Located in Mechanical Hall (Kearney Hall), the department featured a materials testing lab, a cement testing lab, a steam lab, and a gas engine and hydraulic lab. All departments in the Schools of Engineering and Forestry had access to the labs. The department and its labs moved to the new Engineering Laboratory Building (Graf Hall) when it was completed in 1920. An Engineering Experiment Station was established by the college's board of regents in 1927 to "stimulate engineering education through research" by completing investigations for industries, utilities, governmental agencies, professional engineers, and engineering teachers, and publishing the results.

Early pharmacy research primarily focused on drug purity. The Oregon State Board of Pharmacy established the State Drug Laboratory at OAC in 1927. Its purpose was to ensure the purity of drugs dispensed by Oregon pharmacies and to "prevent dishonest practice and gross adulteration of medicinal substances sold by individuals other than pharmacists." Other pharmacological research at that time included the study of medicinal properties of plants native to the Pacific Northwest, improved manufacture of pharmaceuticals, and the stability and preservation of drugs.

Despite the severe impact of the Great Depression on Oregon State, many long-term agricultural research projects began in the 1930s. Studies of hops production, breeding, and diseases began around 1930, when downy mildew struck Oregon's hops industry.[3] Subsequent research continues to make a major contribution to Oregon's robust microbrewing industry. Fiber flax research, which had begun at OAC in the 1910s, expanded in the 1930s and continued well into the 1950s. Beef cattle and poultry disease studies began and lasted for more than twenty-five years. Oregon's growing seafood industry was aided by the new Seafood Lab, established in Astoria in 1940. Likewise, the timber industry was aided by the creation of the Forest Products Lab, which sought to find new uses for wood products. Oregon State research also contributed to the war effort, such as the Food Technology Department's food dehydration studies, funded by the US War Department, and development of labor-saving devices and equipment for the farm and home.

Although most of Oregon State's research in the first half of the twentieth century was applied and focused on science and engineering, several faculty made research contributions in the social sciences and humanities. John B. Horner, who arrived at OAC in 1891, taught English until 1901 and history until 1933. He authored several Oregon history books, including *Oregon: Her History, Her Great Men, Her Literature* (1919), *A Short History of Oregon* (1924), and *Days and Deeds in the Oregon Country* (1929). Horner created a college museum in 1925 by combining several historical and natural history collections. The museum, named for Horner after his death in 1933, closed in 1995 and became part of the Benton County Historical Society in 2008. Political scientist Frank Magruder came to OAC in 1917, the first year he published his textbook, *American Government: A Consideration of the Problems of Democracy*. Subsequent editions were published into the 1990s, making it one of the longest-enduring textbooks of the twentieth century.

Oregon State's research activities expanded greatly in the 1950s and into the 1960s, with new sources of federal funding, such as the National Science Foundation (NSF),[4] available to colleges and universities. Nuclear engineering traces its roots to a 1948 announcement that the college was building a cyclotron, which was completed in the mid-1950s. Electrical engineering acquired an AGN-201 nuclear reactor in 1958 and had it online the next year. It was subsequently moved to the new Radiation Center, completed in 1964. A more substantive reactor, the TRIGA Mark II,

dedicated in 1967, was built using a $300,000 NSF grant. Computer science also had a start in the 1950s, with the first courses offered through the mathematics and mechanical engineering departments. Today computer science is a major teaching and research program in the School of Electrical Engineering and Computer Science.

Oregon State's oceanographic program exemplifies the rapid expansion of research at OSU during the 1950s and 1960s. The program got its start in 1954 with a grant from the Office of Naval Research (ONR). Additional ONR funding enabled OSC to establish a graduate program in 1958, gain departmental status in 1959, purchase its first research vessel, the eighty-foot *Acona*, in 1961,[5] and construct a new building on campus (now Burt Hall), completed in 1964. Additional marine research facilities were completed in Newport in 1965. In 1971 OSU's stature as a leading oceanographic institution was enhanced when it became one of the first four universities to achieve Sea Grant College status. The mission of the Sea Grant program was to develop "an understanding and appreciation of how to live with the ocean and how to manage the coastal zone."

The growth of OSU's research programs in the 1950s and 1960s necessitated institution-wide coordination. The university administration created the Research Office in 1965 to provide that coordination, in response to the steady increase in research funding available in the post–World War II years. Roy Young was the first dean of research. Today the Research Office is led by the vice president for research. The office coordinates more than $250 million annually in external research funding and advances "the success of the entire OSU research enterprise by facilitating the rigorous pursuit of discovery, scholarship, and innovation while maintaining the highest professional and ethical standards." The Research Office also provides administrative oversight for eighteen of OSU's research centers and institutes.

Many of OSU's current research projects have been in place for years. Likewise, food preservation research began even before the establishment of the horticultural products program[6] in 1919. Other areas of research have seen a recent revival. OSU's dairy science program was robust for several decades starting in the early twentieth century, but declined in the 1970s. Recently, however, dairy research has gained new importance through the fermentation science program's emphasis on artisanal cheeses, such as its Beaver Classic™ cheese. The fermentation science program also provides significant research support to Oregon's rapidly growing wine, craft beer, and craft cider industries.

A research institute with a direct connection to OSU's past is the Linus Pauling Institute. It was co-founded in 1973 in Palo Alto, California, by OSU alumnus and two-time Nobel Prize winner Linus Pauling (class of 1922) to study the role of vitamins and other essential micronutrients in human health. The institute moved to OSU in 1996, and today, supported by state, federal, private, and university funds, still studies the role of vitamins and micronutrients, as well as chemicals from plants, in aging, immunity, and chronic diseases. Its goal is to understand how these dietary elements affect the onset and prevention of human diseases.

Research at OSU is not limited to faculty and graduate students. Since 2000, more emphasis has been placed on developing opportunities for undergraduates to conduct original research as a part of their regular academic curriculum. The Undergraduate Research, Scholarship, and the Arts program, sponsored by the Research Office, coordinates undergraduate research opportunities across the university. An annual showcase allows top students from each college to present posters on their original research.

Today, OSU is just one of two land, sea, space, and sun grant institutions. It maintains three signature research centers and twenty-eight other research centers and institutes. Additional research is carried on outside of those centers in all of the colleges. OSU's three primary areas of research—Advancing the Science of Sustainable Earth Ecosystems, Improving Human Health and Wellness, and Promoting Economic Growth and Social Progress— "represent OSU's greatest opportunity to lead in solving complex societal problems, and to creating superior learning opportunities for students."

College greenhouses, ca. 1892. Along with the purchase of an additional 119 acres in 1889 for the college farm, facilities were expanded, including more and larger greenhouses. Standing on the right is George Coote, instructor in horticulture. The 1890–91 college catalog stated that the greenhouses "enable this department [horticulture] to offer unexcelled advantages in the study of floriculture, also the propagation and culture of plants, and decoration of ornamental grounds." (MSS-McAlister)

Chemical laboratory weighing room, ca. 1893. The Station Building constructed in 1892 also included a chemical lab in the basement. Chemicals used for various agricultural research purposes were weighed in this part of the lab. (HC 934)

OAC display at the Alaska-Yukon-Pacific Exposition in Seattle, 1909. The college exhibited its research and student work at several world's fairs, such as the Lewis and Clark Centennial Exposition in Portland in 1905 and the Panama Pacific International Exposition in San Francisco in 1915. (P25:3059)

Lady McDuff, ca. 1913. OAC's poultry program was nationally renowned in in the early twentieth century; it was under the direction of professor James Dryden from 1907 to 1922. Much of the program's research centered on breeding chickens for egg production. Of special note was one chicken named Lady McDuff, a White Leghorn that set a production record of 303 eggs in 1913. Dryden was elected to the National Agricultural Hall of Fame posthumously in 1991—the only poultry scientist so honored. (P111:1369)

Branch Experiment Station superintendents with dean of agriculture A. B. Cordley, ca. 1915. Pictured with Cordley (third from left), who also served as director of the Experiment Station, are: Harry A. Lindgren (Astor Branch Station), Ralph W. Allen (Umatilla Branch Station), David E. Stephens (Sherman Branch Station), Leroy Breithaupt (Harney Branch Station), and Frank C. Reimer (Southern Oregon Branch Station). Not present were Robert Withycombe (Union Branch Station) and John R. Winston (Hood River Branch Station). (HC 1537)

Gathering at the Harney Valley Branch Experiment Station, ca. 1915. This branch experiment station was established in 1911 and closed in 1954. Its research focused on cattle and rangeland grazing and alfalfa and grass production. (P25:1197)

On December 7, 1922, Oregon Agricultural College was granted a license to begin broadcasting radio station KFDJ, which had been put together as a lab experiment by physics professor Jacob Jordan. The station's first broadcast from the third floor of Apperson Hall was on January 23, 1923. By December 1925, the station's call letters had been changed to KOAC, its power had been boosted from 50 to 500 watts, and the Extension Service utilized the station for broadcasting several programs, with Wallace Kadderly serving as program director.

Early programming included lectures, music, student variety programs, reports of athletic events, and the annual commencement exercise. New studios were established in the new Physics Building (now Covell Hall) in 1928. Jordan oversaw the technical operations of the station until 1932, when Grant Feikert was named chief engineer. Kadderly served as program director until 1932 and as station manager through 1933. When the new State System of Higher Education was established, KOAC became the system's radio station, under the purview of the General Extension Division. Additional studios were ultimately established in Eugene, Salem, and Portland. Power was increased to 5000 watts in 1942. James Morris served as program director from 1945–1963.

KOAC-TV was established in 1957 and began broadcasting in November of that year from studios in Gill Coliseum. In its early years the TV station was used to broadcast courses to State System campuses around the state. The Extension Service used the television station in the same manner that it had used KOAC radio for the past fifty-plus years, producing programs such as *Extension 7*, later called *Oregon at Work*, which ran from 1959 to 1975.

In 1981 the State System of Higher Education divested its radio and television stations, including both KOAC-AM and KOAC-TV. These stations became part of Oregon Public Broadcasting (OPB), and administrative, TV studio, and production functions were moved to Portland. OPB maintained a radio studio on the OSU campus until 2010, and Corvallis transmitters and frequencies for both KOAC radio and TV are still used.

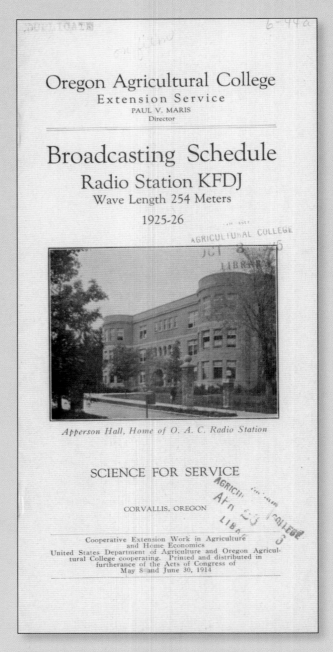

KFDJ broadcasting schedule published by the Extension Service, 1925. KFDJ, which changed its call letters to KOAC later in 1925, broadcast from Apperson Hall (Kearney Hall) from 1922 to 1928. (MC–KOAC)

Farmer listening to KOAC radio broadcast, ca. 1930. Much of the programming broadcast on KOAC was developed by the Extension Service, which used radio to share information on agriculture, home economics, and other subjects—information often based on research done at Oregon State. (HC 899)

Zeita Feike Rodenwold, director of women's programs for KOAC radio, doing a broadcast, 1930. Rodenwold's duties included coordinating the Extension Service's home economics radio programs, which included lectures on household administration, finance, art, and physical education for women. Rodenwold hosted a show called *Aunt Sammy,* which consisted of chats on homemaking based on scripts produced in Washington, DC ("Aunt Sammy" was a takeoff of Uncle Sam). Rodenwold was affiliated with KOAC for more than twenty years. (HC 378)

KOAC radio car, ca. 1958. William Smith and Lester Mock, KOAC producers, are using the station's portable tape recorder to bring special event broadcasts to the KOAC radio audience. (HC 598)

Horticultural products show, ca. 1925. For many years OAC showed off its horticultural research through shows such as these, which were often held at the Men's Gymnasium (now Langton Hall). (HC 603)

Maud Wilson, ca. 1930. The federal Purnell Act of 1925 provided funds for home economics research at the nation's land-grant schools. Maud Wilson came to OAC in 1925 as the first research faculty member of the School of Home Economics. She later served as head of home economics for the experiment station. Wilson's area of specialty was housing design, especially the design of kitchens to improve work efficiency. (HC 417)

School of Forestry post farm, ca. 1930. Forestry faculty member T. J. Starker (pictured) established this research project in 1928 at the Peavy Arboretum in order to determine the durability of different wood species. Starker was a member of OAC's first forestry class in 1910 and served as a faculty member from 1922 to 1942. (HC 1008)

College museum collections, ca. 1930. The college museum was established in 1925 by history professor John B. Horner, who brought together several of the college's historical and natural history collections. The museum had several homes, including the basement of the library (shown here), the lower level of the old gymnasium/armory, and the basement of Gill Coliseum. In 1936 the museum was renamed the Horner Museum of the Oregon Country in John Horner's memory. Its eclectic collections were a favorite for many visitors, including hundreds of schoolchildren who made field trips to the museum each year. The museum closed in 1995 for budgetary reasons. In 2008 the museum collection was donated and transferred to the Benton County Historical Society & Museum. The Horner Collection is now a major component of that organization's collections and educational program. (HC 1157)

Hops seedlings in greenhouse beds, spring of 1932. Hops research at Oregon State began in the early 1890s. In the early 1930s the research became more intensive as a fungal disease, downy mildew, invaded Oregon's hop yards. OSC's research focused on disease resistance through breeding and fungicides that could combat the disease. In the 1970s, OSU released several disease-resistant varieties of hops, including Cascade, that are among the mainstays of today's craft brewing industry. (RG 25–Hop Breeding Project Report, 1932)

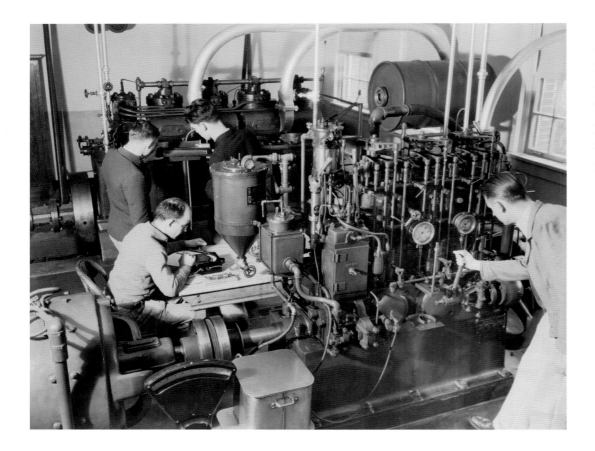

Diesel engine research in the internal combustion lab, 1935. The Engineering Laboratory (Graf Hall) included a lab for the study of internal combustion engines. The engineering experiment station's publications included research conducted in the lab, such as the analysis of exhaust gasses. (HC 899)

Chemistry professor John Fulton and a student in the chemistry glassware lab, 1941. For many years Oregon State produced the glassware it needed for scientific research. Fulton (class of 1892) was a longtime chemistry faculty member who oversaw the making of the glassware. (HC 227)

Dairy herd and barns, June 1947. Dairy research has a long history at OSU; the university has had a fully functional dairy for more than a hundred years. Milk from the herd has been used for dairy products research and to produce ice cream and cheese for sale. The barns in the photo were destroyed by fire in 1968, but were soon rebuilt. Current research centers on ruminant nutrition, reproduction, animal health and behavior, herd management, and crop/grass production. Artisanal cheese production is a research focus in food science and technology. (P82:2 #469)

George F. Waldo looking over loganberries at OSC's horticulture farm, July 1947. Waldo was an internationally renowned USDA horticulturalist based at Oregon State from 1932 to 1965. He received his BS from OAC in 1922. During his career Waldo bred and released fourteen varieties of strawberries, blackberries, and red raspberries—including the iconic Marion blackberry and Hood strawberry varieties—that have been grown commercially on the West Coast. (P120:5131)

OSU's nuclear engineering program had its genesis in the post–World War II expansion of nuclear research that was an important component of the Cold War. In 1948, OSC's physics department announced that it would be constructing a cyclotron—a particle accelerator that creates a high-energy beam used for nuclear physics experiments—to be used to train nuclear physicists, to create radio isotopes for use in research, and to research nuclear reactions.

The OSC cyclotron was funded in part by the Atomic Energy Commission (AEC), which donated fifty tons of steel salvaged from a Manhattan Project magnet through the University of California Radiation Laboratory. That lab, under the direction of cyclotron inventor Ernest O. Lawrence, machined the steel— valued at $6,000—for the OSC cyclotron's magnet. Portland General Electric, the Eugene Water Board, and the Hyster Company of Portland donated other equipment and services. The National Research Council of New York provided a $5,000 grant to support the project.

The fifty-ton steel magnet was delivered to the Corvallis airport by railroad flat car in November 1948. The forty-foot by sixty-foot aluminum "Butler" building housing the cyclotron including a concrete block containment structure with walls thirty to forty-eight inches thick, was completed in 1952. The building was located just south of where Magruder Hall is today, north of Oak Creek off Thirtieth Street.

Almost all of the labor required to construct the cyclotron and its containment building was provided by OSC faculty, staff, and students. In 1948 more than thirty students volunteered to help with the cyclotron's development. Edwin A. Yunker, who became chair of the physics department in 1949, was head of the OSC cyclotron committee. Other faculty involved in its operations were James J. Brady, Richard Dempster, David Nicodemus, and William Varner.

The cyclotron, which started operations in about 1956, was capable of producing a beam of deuterons of 6,500,000 electron volts. By 1957 five OSC graduate students had written theses based on the OSC cyclotron design and operation. In 1957 OSC received an additional $17,500 from the AEC for purchasing accessories and instruments.

Installation of the magnet for OSC's new cyclotron, summer of 1950. The fifty-ton magnet, machined at the University of California, had arrived in Corvallis in November 1948. (P82:92 #924)

Professors James J. Brady and Edwin A. Yunker with OSC's cyclotron, ca. 1955. Yunker was chair of OSC's physics department and headed the college's cyclotron committee. Brady was a physics faculty member from 1937 to 1959. (P82:136)

Ernest H. Wiegand in his lab with jars of cherries, ca. 1950. Wiegand, who came to OAC in 1919, developed the modern process for creating maraschino cherries in 1924 using Oregon's Royal Anne sweet cherries. Wiegand added a small amount of calcium salts in the brining process, as well as almond flavoring to simulate the taste of the pits of the mascara cherry, the central European variety used in making maraschino cherries. Wiegand was head of what is now the Department of Food Science and Technology until his retirement in 1953. During his years at Oregon State he developed a program that created new and improved technologies for processing and preserving foods of many types, especially the fruits and vegetables grown in abundance in Oregon. (P46:91)

Professor Charles O. Heath and others working with the engineering lab "nutcracker" to test conductors for the Bonneville Power Administration, August 1951. The Engineering Laboratory (Graf Hall) contained equipment to conduct high-pressure durability tests on structural materials for companies and other organizations, such as the federal BPA. Heath, an associate professor of engineering materials, came to OSC in 1946. (P82:34 #1499)

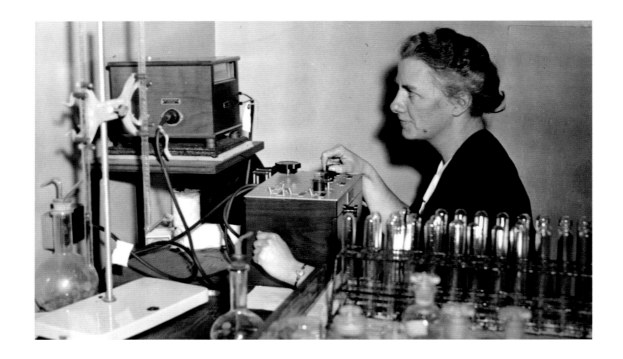

Professor Margaret Fincke conducting nutrition research, ca. 1955. Fincke came to Oregon State in 1935 after receiving her doctorate at Columbia University. She was the first home economics faculty member at OSC to hold a doctorate. Fincke became the chair of the foods and nutrition department in the School of Home Economics in 1944 and served until 1968. She authored several experiment station publications pertaining to nutrition, including a series on the nutritional status of youth in selected Oregon counties, published in the mid-1940s. Fincke received the Alumni Association's Distinguished Professor Award in 1966. (P44)

Mathematics professor Arvid Lonseth with computer, March 1957. The 1957 caption to this photo read, "'Master mathemetician' is this $60,000 electronic digital computer, used for research in mathematics and science." Oregon State's mathematics department supported some of the institution's first computer-related instruction and research in the 1950s. (P82:172)

Art Professor Wayne Taysom with his sculpture, which was displayed at Oregon's Centennial Exposition during the summer of 1959, October 1959. Taysom also created the sculpture that is on the south side of the Valley Library. (P82:4 #2345)

Meteorology research vehicle on Marys Peak, March 1960. Professors Fred Decker and Fred Jensby conducted meteorology research atop Marys Peak using this radar array on a military truck. (P82:92 #2369)

Neil Hoffman, superintendent of the Malheur Branch Experiment Station, weighing onions, November 28, 1968. Hoffman served as the branch station's first superintendent, from 1946 to 1977. Research there has been conducted on onion diseases and pests, potato varieties, sugar beet varieties and diseases, small grains irrigation of various crops, and native wildflower seed production for restoration efforts. Photograph by Robert W. Henderson, assistant director of the Agricultural Experiment Station. (P98:4171)

Horticulturalist William A. "Tex" Frazier with bush beans, ca. 1970. Frazier joined Oregon State's horticulture department in 1949; his previous position was at the University of Hawaii. At Oregon State, he worked on breeding new varieties of vegetables with his student and fellow faculty member Jim Baggett. They are known for developing a bush variety of the Blue Lake green bean, which enabled farmers to mechanically harvest this popular variety. Frazier also developed one of the first tomato varieties for the Willamette Valley, the Willamette tomato, which is still popular with home gardeners. Frazier was nicknamed "Tex" because of his Texas roots—he was born there and received his undergraduate degree from Texas A&M in 1930. (P57, Accession 95:18)

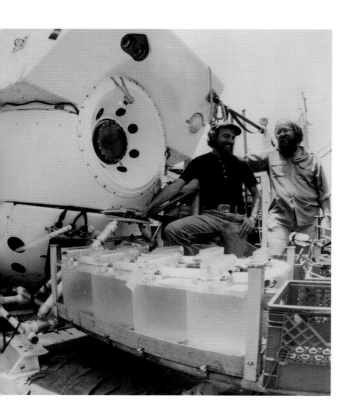

OSU researchers Jack Dymond and John Corliss talk over the use of the deep-sea sub *Alvin* (left), 1977. The two researchers used the submarine to make dives of 9,200 feet off the coast of Ecuador. The dives were featured in the October 1977 issue of *National Geographic*. The *Alvin* was also used for dives off the Oregon coast in the mid 1980s. This photograph appeared in the December 1978 *Oregon Stater*. (P57:5607)

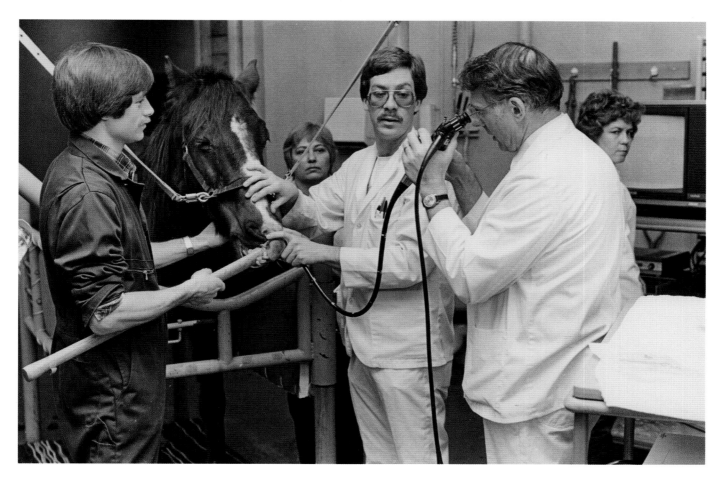

Dr. Erwin Pearson of the School of Veterinary Medicine examines a sixteen-year-old mare, Rebel's Misty, ca. 1980. With Pearson are a veterinary student and clinicians, as well as the horse's owner. The horse was the veterinary hospital's twenty-five hundredth patient. (P57:6347)

Governor Vic Atiyeh in OSU's experimental alcohol fuel car, February 1980. The car was part of the research of mechanical engineering professor John Mingle, who directed studies of alternative fuels, especially alcohols made from plant materials such as lumber mill wood waste. Mingle's students modified this 1972 Ford Pinto to run on various alcohol mixes. This photo appeared in the March 1980 *Oregon Stater*. (P57:6499)

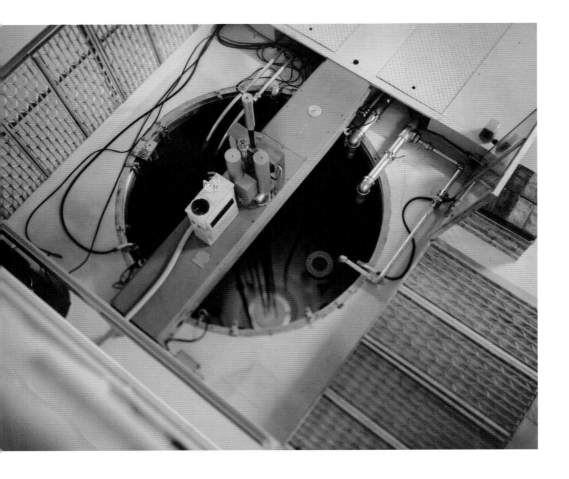

View inside OSU's nuclear reactor, ca. 1980. In 1967 OSU installed a 250-kilowatt research reactor in the Radiation Center. It was later upgraded to one-megawatt capacity. The reactor and other specialized equipment in the Radiation Center is used for instruction purposes, collaborative research with other institutions, and research contracted with the United States military, public utilities, and private research groups. It is one of two research reactors in Oregon; the other is at Reed College in Portland. (P92:1191)

Wave research facility, ca. 1982. This wave tank, constructed in 1972, was 342 feet long and served as the basis of the O. H. Hinsdale Wave Research Laboratory. Research being conducted at the time this photo was taken pertained to oil drilling in Alaska. Today the lab is one of the largest and most technically advanced centers for research and education in coastal engineering and nearshore science, especially tsunami and coastal hazard mitigation. (P57:7254)

Water sampling at Spirit Lake in the Mount St. Helens blast zone, 1982. OSU fisheries and wildlife department technician Rich Keppler took the samples as part of a project to test the lake's ability to support aquatic life after the May 18, 1980, eruption of Mount St. Helens (seen in the background). The research at the time indicated that Spirit Lake was a decade away from being able to support fish. (P57:7323)

Food scientist and enology extension specialist Barney Watson testing wine, ca. 1985. Watson was a faculty member in food science and technology for twenty-eight years. His research and teaching has greatly benefitted Oregon's burgeoning wine industry. Watson was also the winemaker for Tyee Vineyards near Corvallis from 1985 to 2005. (P57, Accession 91:156)

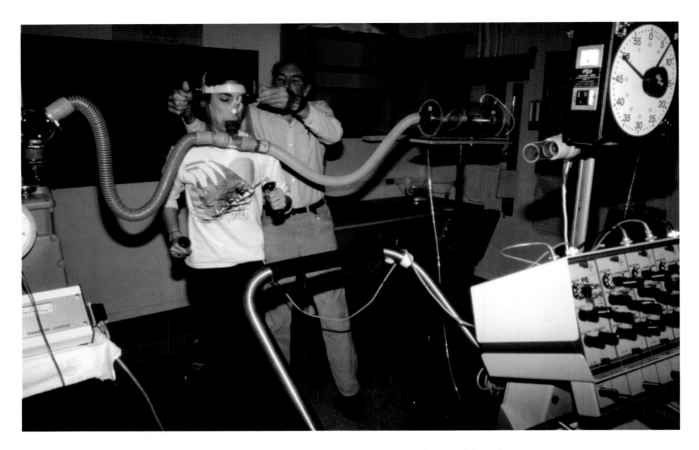

Human Performance Lab, 1987. The lab was established in 1981 in the School of Health and Physical Education. Today the lab, one of nine research labs in the College of Public Health and Human Sciences, is used for studies pertaining to exercise energy metabolism, athletic performance, and body composition. (P57, Accession 2006:046)

Linus Pauling Institute researchers, 1999. The institute relocated from Palo Alto, California, where it had been established in 1973, to OSU's Weniger Hall in 1996. In September 2011 the institute moved to state-of-the-art research facilities in the new Linus Pauling Science Center. (P57, Accession 2006:046)

Autzen House, ca. 1990. Autzen House is the home of OSU's Center for the Humanities, which was established in 1984. The center supports interdisciplinary research in the humanities through competitive fellowships and sponsors conferences, seminars, lecture series, and related events. The building was purchased in 1920 by the Gamma Phi Beta sorority and enlarged in 1936. The OSU Foundation acquired the building in 1979, and it was used by OSU as the State Climatology Office until 1989, when the Center for the Humanities occupied it. The foundation donated the building to OSU in 1994; at that time it was renamed Autzen House, in honor of 1909 alumnus Thomas Autzen. (MC–Center for the Humanities)

Robert Tanguay, an OSU researcher affiliated with the Department of Environmental and Molecular Toxicology and the Oregon Nanoscience and Microtechnologies Institute (ONAMI), checks tanks of zebra fish, May 2008. Tanguay uses zebra fish to examine the biological interactions of nanomaterials with biological systems. Embryonic zebra fish are particularly useful for studying the effects of nanomaterials on living organisms because they develop quickly, are transparent, and can be easily maintained in small amounts of water. ONAMI is one of OSU's three signature research centers. (Photo by Lynn Ketchum, courtesy of OSU Extension and Experiment Station Communications)

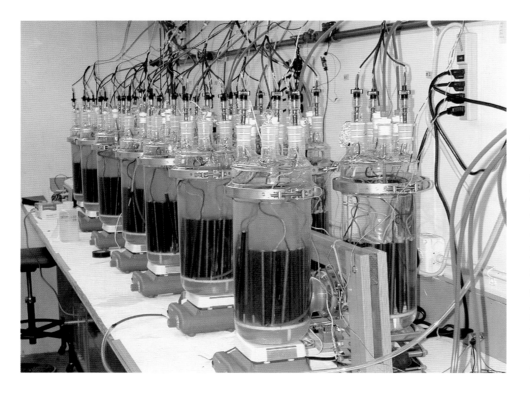

Prototype plankton fuel cells, 2009. OSU scientists successfully created fuel cells by utilizing the chemical reactions caused by decomposing plankton. Researchers in many programs across OSU have worked on sustainable energy projects in recent years. These have included harnessing the energy released by ocean waves, improving solar photovoltaic cells, biodiesel production, and utilizing wasted heat to improve energy efficiency. (Photo courtesy of OSU News and Research Communications)

Taste and aroma testing at OSU's research brewery, June 2012. Professors Tom Shellhammer (second from left) and Shaun Townsend (far right) test the taste and aroma of an experimental beer in Oregon State University's research brewery in Wiegand Hall. OSU's two-barrel research brewery, a component of the food science and technology department's pilot processing plant, has been used to produce an extensive variety of beers. The research conducted at the research brewery has supported Oregon's growing craft beer industry. Shellhammer directs the brewing science program and Townsend directs the aroma hop breeding program in the crop and soil science department. (Photo by Lynn Ketchum, courtesy of Extension and Experiment Station Communications)

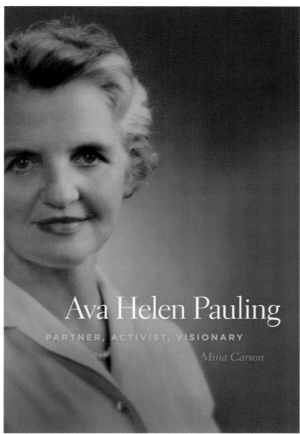

Cover of *Ava Helen Pauling: Partner, Activist, Visionary.* OSU history faculty member Mina Carson published this biography of Pauling with the OSU Press in 2013. Faculty in the College of Liberal Arts annually publish hundreds of books, articles, poems, musical compositions, and other original works. (Image courtesy of OSU Press)

Jefferson Street entrance to campus at homecoming, ca. 1917. (HC 1049)

Campus Life and Culture

College life for Corvallis College students in 1868 was likely similar to that of other colleges and academies at the time, especially those with religious affiliations. Where students boarded, unless they lived at home or with relatives nearby, was subject to faculty approval. A boarding house was available for female students. Students were expected to attend religious exercises on campus each morning and a place of worship "on the Sabbath." The college's rules prohibited obscene or profane language, the playing of cards or billiards, the frequenting of places of gambling or drinking, or the use, purchase, or possession of "any intoxicating liquors." A system of merits and demerits was in place and was "at all times subject to the examination of parents and guardians."

During the 1870s, earning one hundred demerits was cause for dismissal from the college, and any student who left the college without permission was "liable to be declared expelled." Another rule from that era forbade "all communications between ladies and gentlemen on the College premises." Regular monthly reports of grades and deportment were sent to parents. The only holidays were "one or two days at Christmas . . . at the option of the Faculty."

Many of these same rules continued into the 1880s. Although specific references to daily religious exercises and compulsory church attendance on Sundays had disappeared from the college catalog by 1889, one could still earn five demerits for missing chapel. A male student being out of uniform earned him two demerits. Absent from the 1889 catalog was the rule prohibiting communication between students of the opposite sex.

With the separation from the remaining vestiges of church control in 1888 and the move to the new campus on the college farm in 1889, campus life for OAC students (and faculty) developed a new atmosphere in the 1890s. Living accommodations for male and female students were available on campus. For the first couple of years, both sexes were housed (on different floors) in Alpha Hall, likely making it the first coed dormitory in the western United States. Removing the barrier against all contact between the sexes created opportunities for social interaction and informal events such as picnics. It opened up opportunities for amorous relationships as well; about nineteen hundred lights were installed on the roof of the Administration Building (Benton Hall) to discourage nighttime trysts on the college's front lawn. The site of numerous marriage proposals, the Trysting Tree near the Administration Building was a frequent (and not discouraged during the day) gathering place for students of the opposite sex, or for friends of both sexes, to read, study, or "hang out," in modern parlance. It remained so for many decades, well into the 1960s.

The introduction of athletics in the 1890s also contributed to the change in campus life during that decade. Football games, daylong events that often included parades, as well as meals and interaction with members of the opposing team, were well attended. Several student organizations were formed in the 1890s, including numerous literary societies (see chapter 8). Students were also encouraged to participate in "physical culture"—individual and team physical activity—not only for the health benefits but also to "acquire a training in social life destined to be of great value to them." The early encouragement of physical activity led to the development of a formal intramural program in 1916 for both men and women. Today, OSU's Recreational Sports program and its facilities, serving students, faculty, and staff alike, are considered some of the best in the nation.

A new aspect of college life for students studying agriculture in the late 1880s was the requirement to work on the college farm for five hours a week during fall and spring terms. During winter term students worked in the mechanical shop. This work was largely unpaid, though students who worked beyond the required five hours received fifteen cents per hour. By 1900 the students, although still required to work on the farm and in the shop, received compensation for that work.

Outings became a popular recreational activity. Groups of students, usually with a chaperone, traveled short distances to popular picnic spots, such as Oak Creek, northwest of Corvallis, or Marys Peak to the west. For many years a daylong excursion to the coast in late spring was a popular annual event, especially for seniors about to graduate. Students took the train west from Corvallis to Yaquina City on Yaquina Bay, and from there traveled by a small steamer to Newport. "Flunk Day" was also an opportunity for an outing; late in spring term, students, especially juniors, would cut classes for a day and travel to a favorite location in the area for a picnic.

Dormitory life was fairly regimented in the late nineteenth and early twentieth centuries, and dormitory living groups were characterized as clubs. To become a resident of Cauthorn Hall, the men's dormitory, in the 1890s, a student had to prove that he was an upstanding citizen. This meant no use of tobacco or foul language (carryovers from the nineteenth-century college rules) and that "his conduct is gentlemanly at all times." For both men and women, the college provided the basics—bed, mattress and box springs, table or desk, chair—and the student provided the rest. The 1901–02 catalog listed room and board costs at about $2.50 per week. Meals were formal occasions; students were expected to be on time and properly dressed. A 1905–06 booklet on Alpha Hall (the women's dormitory) stated that "competent ladies are employed to prepare and serve the food."

Traditions have formed an integral part of campus life at most colleges and universities, and OSU is no exception. A May Day pageant, held annually from the early twentieth century into the 1920s, involved dozens of students. One of the most enduring traditions has been homecoming, which dates back to about 1916. Specific events have changed over the years, and some, such as the bonfire and parade, have been revived at least once. Other early traditions included competitions between classes; for male students this often took the form of a tug-of-war at the millrace in south Corvallis or a pushball contest on the athletic fields. Orange and black have been OSU's school colors since 1893; in May of that year students selected orange as the school's color and then immediately adopted black as the background color.

Freshmen, or "Rooks," were especially subject to specific rules and regulations that became traditions over time. For many years, male freshmen were required to wear green "rook" caps and female freshman, green ribbons. The rules were often strictly enforced by upperclassmen. Some of the penalties would be considered hazing today. Freshmen celebrated the end of their first year by burning their caps and ribbons, a ceremony known as the "burning of the green."

Class gifts were another long-standing tradition, which started in 1901 when that year's graduating class presented a stone memorial that was placed at the Trysting Tree. The next year the class of 1902 presented the college with the "Lady of the Fountain." The class of 1920 donated "The Competitor," the bronze sculpture outside the main entrance to Langton Hall. More recently, the class of 1960, in celebration of its golden jubilee in 2010, raised and donated about $100,000 toward the construction of OSU's new south entrance.

Early athletic events had specific protocols. Men and women students sat in separate sections, and "fussing," or dating, at sporting events was prohibited. This tradition lasted into the late 1950s. All students were expected to know various cheers and songs, especially the fight song and alma mater. It also was common for large groups to see off the athletic teams at the train and bus stations as they left for out-of-town games. And major athletic victories were cause for celebration—often a parade in downtown Corvallis.

Shepard Hall was constructed as the home of the campus YMCA and YWCA organizations, but also served other organizations and was an inviting place for students to relax and study. The Memorial Union, completed in 1928, served a similar function, though on a much larger scale. The MU also provided various food services, served as the home of the bookstore for eighty-five years, provided recreational facilities, and sponsored lectures, musical events, exhibits, conferences, and other activities in its meeting rooms, ballroom, and lounges.

Formal dances were a part of campus culture from the 1890s into the 1960s. They were often sponsored by campus organizations and were held as part of a larger event, such as homecoming, or focused on a particular theme. The bands were sometimes college groups, though professional dance bands often were hired for the most significant dances. For many years, students who attended dances used dance cards to record their partners. Many of the dance cards were elaborately produced and became treasured keepsakes, often saved in scrapbooks.

Lectures and concerts have been mainstays of OSU's campus life. The 1901–02 catalog described, in addition to regular class lectures, "a course of lectures by representative men . . . delivered at convenient intervals during the year." Lecturers have ranged from Booker T. Washington (1913) to William F. Buckley (1969) to Rigoberta Menchú (2006). Today OSU has numerous lecture series that bring dozens of speakers with a broad spectrum of interests and backgrounds to campus each year.

For many years, Oregon State has been a popular concert stop for musicians and musical groups. During the 1960s and 1970s, OSU drew many internationally recognized rock, soul, folk, and jazz artists. They included Neil Diamond, the Doors, Jefferson Airplane, Peter, Paul and Mary, the 5th Dimension, Al Hirt, Donovan, Stephen Stills and Manassas, and John Denver.

Throughout the 1960s and into the 1970s, many college and university campuses across the United States experienced significant social change. Although not considered a hotbed of activism, OSU was not immune from the protests and demonstrations that marked those years. A student-faculty group opposing the war in Vietnam formed as early as 1966. OSU students and faculty participated in national Moratorium Day events on October 15, 1969, and an April 1971 peace march drew two thousand OSU students. The Armory (McAlexander Fieldhouse) was damaged in a May 1970 bombing. Students and faculty participated in a march honoring Dr. Martin Luther King Jr. after his assassination in April 1968. And OSU's African American students boycotted the university in March 1969 after football player Fred Milton was forced to shave his beard.

Commencement continues to be an important tradition and celebration at OSU, marking the end of the academic year and a new phase in life for the new graduates. Since the 1890s, it has been held in many locations on campus, including the Gymnasium and Armory (Valley Gymnastics Center), the new Armory (McAlexander Fieldhouse), the Men's Gymnasium (Langton Hall), Gill Coliseum, and, since 2001, Reser Stadium. In 2003 OSU revived its tradition of a commencement speaker; since that time speakers have included John Glenn (2004) and Michelle Obama (2012). Despite several thousand students receiving degrees at each commencement ceremony, OSU administrators hand out each student's individual diploma.

The natural beauty of Oregon and its mild climate have been selling points for Oregon State almost since its founding. The catalogs from the late 1860s stated that:

> To those who have once visited Corvallis, there is no need of mentioning that our city, in point of climate and natural beauty, is unsurpassed in the State. Corvallis is justly noted for the salubrity and healthfulness of its climate.

Today OSU touts its relative proximity to Portland, the Cascades, and the coast—"Corvallis is the perfect home base for exploring Oregon's natural wonders."

OAC students on a picnic trip to Oak Creek, 1892. Student outings such as this were a common activity. This photo was likely taken near Oak Creek along the foothills northwest of Corvallis by photography instructor Emile Pernot. Alumnus and long-time chemistry faculty member John Fulton (class of 1892) is standing near the front of the wagon. (HC 612)

OAC students posing on the steps of Alpha Hall, ca. 1890. These students may have been the first to live in Alpha Hall when it opened for the 1889–90 academic year, the first in the college's new location. Room and board in 1890 cost $2.25 per week. The male students are in their pre-1892 cadet uniforms. Some of the younger students were likely enrolled in the preparatory department. Professor John Letcher is in the center of the photo, wearing a dark suit and hat. Alpha Hall housed both men and women until Cauthorn Hall was constructed as the men's dormitory in 1892. Living groups have long been an important part of campus life. (P25:2017)

Student excursion to the coast, June 26, 1894. Annual excursions to Newport were a highly anticipated activity for many years. In the 1910s the trip became known as the "Rhododendron Excursion." Students and faculty chaperones would board the train in Corvallis, take it to its terminus at Yaquina City on Yaquina Bay, and then travel by boat to Newport. (P25:1561)

Cauthorn Hall dining room, ca. 1900. Meals were much more formal in the nineteenth and early twentieth centuries. Room and board in Cauthorn Hall in 1905 was $3.00 per week. Visitors were charged $0.15 per meal and $0.20 per night for lodging. (P25:1986)

151

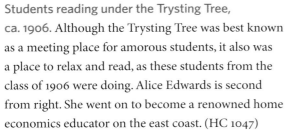

Students reading under the Trysting Tree,
ca. 1906. Although the Trysting Tree was best known
as a meeting place for amorous students, it also was
a place to relax and read, as these students from the
class of 1906 were doing. Alice Edwards is second
from right. She went on to become a renowned home
economics educator on the east coast. (HC 1047)

May Day celebration, 1909. One of the traditions at OAC in the early twentieth century was the annual spring pageant, originally called the May Day pageant, which culminated with the coronation of the May Queen. The May Queen for 1909, Marie Cathey, is in the center of the photo; to her left is Prince Charming, portrayed by Charles Watts. Other performers included jesters, pages, maids, queen's heralds, flower girls, and chair and canopy carriers. The 1921 pageant, a collaboration between the physical education, drama, music, and military departments, focused on Oregon history. The spring pageants were usually held on the lawn area in front of the Administration Building (visible in the background). (P17:631)

Waldo Hall dormitory room, ca. 1909. Waldo Hall, which opened in the fall of 1907, contained 115 dormitory rooms. This room is typically decorated for the era—with pennants and photographs on the wall attached to fish netting. The student was able to fit a piano in the room, which she likely shared with one or two other students. This photo appeared in the 1909–10 college catalog. (P17:847)

Work Day at OAC, May 27, 1910. Students are working on the grounds around the bandstand, which is under construction. The bandstand was a gift of the classes of 1908, 1909, 1910, and 1912. Class gifts to the college and university community have been a tradition since at least 1901. In addition to the bandstand, early class gifts included "Lady of the Fountain" (class of 1902), concrete benches (classes of 1903 and 1907) and the bronze statue in front of Langton Hall, "The Competitor" (class of 1920). (P109:9)

Alva Aitken shot-putting during the Waldo Girls versus Town Girls track and field meet, 1910. The Waldo Girls were the residents of Waldo Hall, and the Town Girls were OAC female students who live in co-ops, boarding houses, private residences, or at home. This competition was a precursor to OSU's intramural sports program. (P116:35)

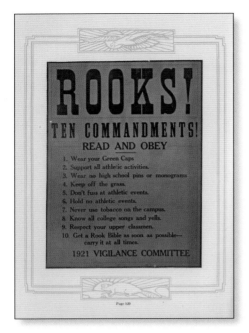

Class of 1910, June 1910. Commencement is the pinnacle of the academic year, particularly for graduating seniors. This group posed on the lawn in front of the Administration Building—women forming the apostrophe and the "1", and men forming the "0." (P116:2)

Rook Rules, 1921. For many years into the twentieth century, and well past World War II, Oregon State freshman, known as rooks, were obligated to abide by a code of rules. This set of rules, which appeared in the 1920 *Beaver* Yearbook, was typical. The *Student Handbook and Rook Bible* was a small pamphlet given to all freshmen that included a variety of information about the college, its traditions, and student organizations and publications; songs and yells for sporting events; the OAC honor code; and the constitution and by-laws of the student government.

Tug-of-War, ca. 1912. Tug-of-war competitions, another common class vs. class contest in the early twentieth century, typically drew large crowds. The event was held at the millrace in south Corvallis as part of the Junior Weekend activities. (P25:1838)

OAC rooters at the Oregon Electric depot, October 21, 1914. The Oregon Electric depot, located just across the Willamette River from downtown Corvallis, was a primary disembarking location for fans and teams. These fans were likely cheering and seeing off the football team, which was about to leave for Pullman, Washington, for its October 24 game against Washington State. OAC won the game 7–0. (P190:20)

Marys River canoe fete, ca. 1915. In the 1910s and 1920s, OAC juniors, as part of the Junior Weekend activities, sponsored a canoe fete on the Marys River that featured elaborately decorated canoes and other floats. (P25:2868)

BONFIRES, BARBECUES, AND BUTTONS: HOMECOMING AT OSU

Homecoming is a long-standing tradition at OSU, dating back to at least 1916. It grew out of the annual Civil War football game rivalry. For many years, when the University of Oregon played Oregon State in Corvallis, UO was Oregon State's homecoming opponent. During the years that the UO game was played in Eugene, Washington State College was often the Beavers' homecoming opponent.

By 1921 the festivities had grown to include several events over the course of three or four days. That year's events included a soccer game between the OAC and UO freshmen (rooks); a rally, bonfire and parade; dedication of the football field in honor of former regent John R. N. Bell; and a post-game "Beaver Feed" in the Home Economics Tea Room.

Apart from the football game, the bonfire is the oldest homecoming tradition. The construction of the pyre was the responsibility of the rooks, and typically involved an elaborate pile of anything burnable. The bonfire was banned in the early 1970s due to air pollution concerns, but was revived a few years later and continues today.

The parade evolved into a noise parade by 1923; this proved controversial and was banned twice for multiple years between 1925 and 1947. It was revived in 1948, and that year's parade included a 122-decibel air raid siren. The tradition of selecting and crowning a homecoming queen began in the early 1950s, and in 1987 a king was also selected for the first time. The queen and king tradition died out a few years later.

Food has been a key element of homecoming. In addition to the "Beaver Feed" of the early celebrations, a barbecue tradition started in 1946. Class reunions gained popularity as homecoming events in the 1950s. In the 1950s and 1960s, buttons were sold to raise money for homecoming events. In recent years homecoming celebrations have included nationally known performers, fun runs, open houses, and academic fairs.

Although the number and types of homecoming activities have evolved over the past one hundred years, this annual celebration of past, current, and future Beavers is an enduring component of OSU's campus community.

Bonfire preparations southeast of Waldo Hall, ca. 1920. Each year's freshman class tried to build the largest homecoming bonfire in school history. Scrap lumber of all kinds and other burnables, including tires, made up the pyre. A bonfire is still part of OSU's homecoming tradition, though on a smaller scale. (P25:1122)

Homecoming barbecue, October 1949. For many years a barbecue was a major component of homecoming festivities. This event, including the cooking of the barbecue meat, was held in the Armory (McAlexander Fieldhouse). In the background are "rooks" serving the food to attendees. (P82:71 #688)

Homecoming noise parade, ca. 1950. Homecoming parades in the 1940s and 1950s were held in the evening and included floats with students banging pots, pans, and anything that would make noise. The parades were banned in 1925 and again in 1947, though they were revived each time. (HC 600)

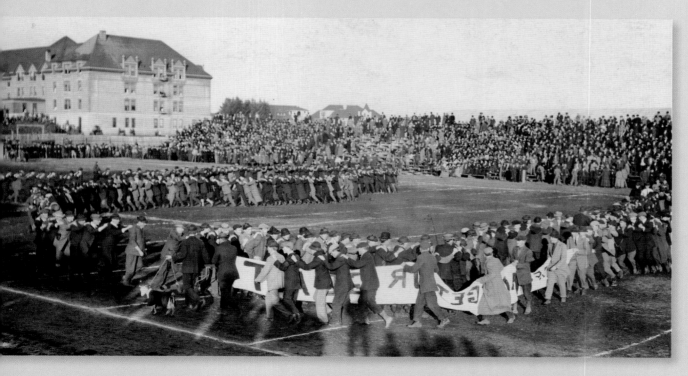

The Serpentine, ca. 1920. Fans snake around each other on the field during halftime in a popular practice at early OAC football games. Known as the "serpentine," it was often done at home games against the University of Oregon. Many colleges and universities adopted the serpentine as a halftime activity. The serpentine was done at Oregon State's first football game in 1893, but by the 1930s had largely died out. It was revived one final time in 1941; a large serpentine formed throughout the Memorial Union quad after the victory over the University of Oregon, which clinched Oregon State's first Rose Bowl berth. (HC 22)

FROM CO-OP TO BEAVER STORE: ONE HUNDRED YEARS OF OSU'S BOOKSTORE

OSU's bookstore, now known as the OSU Beaver Store, was established in 1914 as the OAC Co-operative Association. Originally housed in the building that currently serves as the OSU Women's Center, it offered students about 200 textbooks. In 1917 it moved to a new, larger location on Jefferson and Fifteenth Streets on the southeastern edge of campus, enabling it to stock other books and school-related merchandise.

For eighty-five years the Memorial Union was the primary home of the bookstore—first in the northeast corner of the original building (1928–1960) and then in the new east wing (1960–2013). Branch stores opened in Portland in 1990 and in Keizer in 2007. In 2013 the bookstore moved to new quarters near Gill Coliseum, Reser Stadium, and the Alumni Center, and renamed itself the Beaver Store.

From its founding in 1914 until 1998, the bookstore operated as a cooperative. In 1963 it changed its name from OSU Co-operative Association to OSU Bookstores, Inc. In 1998 the bookstore became a tax-exempt non-profit organization, and it has operated as such since that time. Today the Beaver Store focuses on clothing and Beaver-related accessories and no longer has a general book department, though it remains the primary outlet for the purchase of textbooks and course materials for OSU classes.

Cadets and officers in front of the OAC Co-op Association store, ca. 1920. The bookstore was located in this building on Jefferson Street from 1917 until December 1928, when it moved into the new Memorial Union. This building, located where the Kerr Administration Building is today, was demolished in 1962. (P25:2562)

OSC Co-operative Association bookstore in the Memorial Union, ca. 1932. This was the bookstore's first location in the Memorial Union after it opened in 1928. It was on the ground floor, where the Trysting Tree Lounge is located today. When the store opened in this location in early 1929, textbooks were located in the southwest corner of the store, school supplies in the northeast corner, engineering and art supplies on the south side, and stationery and candy near the east entrance. (HC 1305)

OSU Bookstore, 1960. After completion of the east and west additions to the Memorial Union in 1960, the bookstore relocated to the east addition. During its fifty-plus years in this location, the bookstore went through many facelifts. (P82:77 #2627a)

OSU Beaver Store, August 2013. The current home of the bookstore, now known as the OSU Beaver Store, is in the west side of the parking structure across from Gill Coliseum and Reser Stadium. The store moved to this location in 2013. It is still a primary source for textbooks and other educational materials for OSU classes, but carries a wider array of Beaver gear—clothing and other OSU-branded items. (Photo by Don Boucher, courtesy of OSU IMC Network)

Coeds rollerskating in front of Apperson Hall, ca. 1922. Rollerskating was one of the fads of the Roaring Twenties. Jean Bates (class of 1923) and Jean Folsom (class of 1922) took advantage of the large walkway in front of Apperson Hall (Kearney Hall) to test their skating skills. Students with skateboards can be seen in this same location today. (P25:2884)

Shepard Hall lobby, ca. 1925. Shepard Hall, constructed in 1908, was the campus headquarters for the YMCA and YWCA. It also served as a student union building—as a meeting place for student organizations and a site for other campus activities. Photograph by Ball Studio. (HC 81)

Shepard Hall swimming pool, ca. 1925. This was the first swimming pool associated with OSU. In the early 1920s it served OAC's women; the men used a new pool in Langton Hall that was completed in 1920. After the Women's Building opened in 1926 with its large pool, the Shepard Hall pool was covered over, and the space was used for storage. (HC 30)

Mothers gather for the second annual Mothers Day, May 1925. Mothers Day was established by Kate Jameson, the dean of women, in 1924. Activities for 1925 included breakfast at the dining halls and sorority houses, a luncheon sponsored by the Folk Club, an afternoon convocation featuring Oregon writer Anne Shannon Moore, the annual May Festival, and an evening reception and banquet. Around 280 mothers participated. On the right is former OAC regent Clara Waldo, who was an honored guest. The event later became known as Mothers Weekend. Today it is known as the Moms and Family Weekend and is held the first weekend in May. (HC 1039)

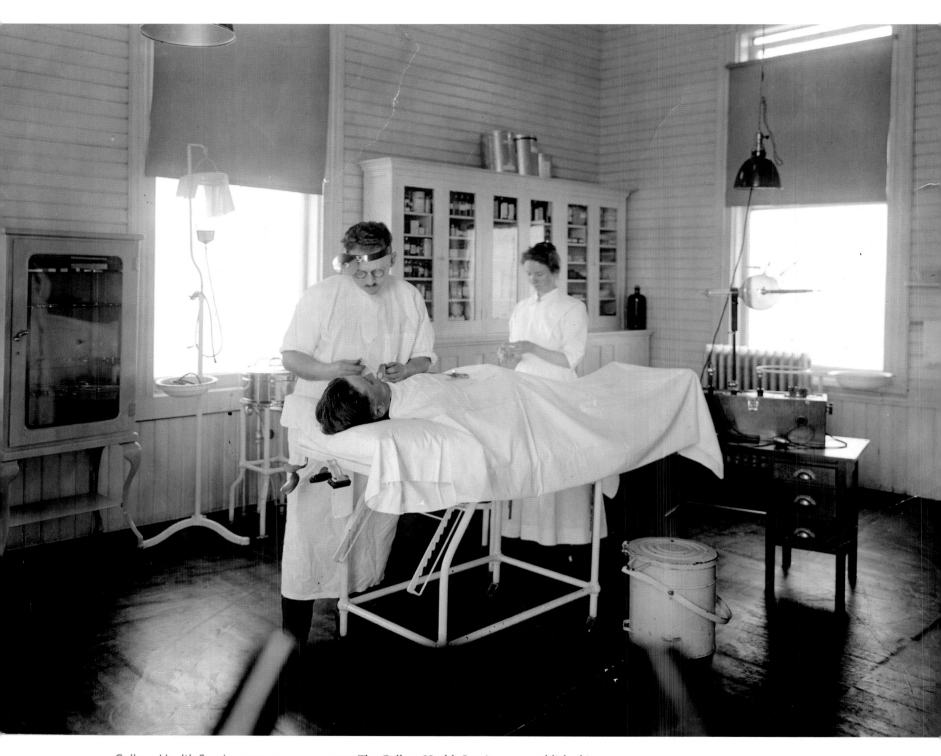

College Health Service exam room, ca. 1923. The College Health Service was established in 1916 "with the aim of promoting the health of all students." From its establishment until the opening of the new Student Health Service building (Plageman Hall) in 1936, the service maintained offices and exam rooms in the former Station Building (now the Women's Center). In 1923 the service had a staff of two full-time physicians and four nurses. It also maintained the OAC Student Hospital at Ninth and Harrison Streets. Today the OSU Student Health Services' mission is not far removed from that of 1916—to provide "campuswide comprehensive primary health care, disease prevention and treatment services, and extensive health promotion for all OSU students." (HC 79)

Margaret Snell Hall kitchen, ca. 1925. This kitchen had large food preparation areas, a large wood-fired cookstove, and the racks of dinnerware required to accommodate the 250-plus women who lived in the dormitory. (P16:993)

Demise of "Lady of the Fountain," January 21, 1929. "Lady of the Fountain," a gift of the class of 1902, was located just to the west of the present intersection of Madison and Ninth Streets. The fountain's statue was the Greek goddess Hebe, daughter of Zeus and Hera and the wife of Hercules. The statue had a difficult time during her short life of less than thirty years, suffering many pranks attributable to rival University of Oregon students. Among her indignities were being smeared with green and yellow paint, twice being kidnapped, and in January 1929, being smashed beyond repair. The fountain basin was often used for ritual "dunkings" of rooks. (HC 564)

168

Ol' John shining customers' shoes, 1937. John Finley Hinds, known as "Ol' John," was a fixture in the Memorial Union in the 1930s and 1940s and was very popular within the campus community. From 1930 to 1946, he ran a shoeshine parlor that also sold a variety of dry goods. The parlor was covered with photos of OSC students, athletes, faculty, and activities that John had collected from various sources. When he retired in 1946, his collection was estimated to be around three thousand photos. Many of those photos are now part of the holdings of the Special Collections & Archives Research Center. (HC 537)

Concert in the Memorial Union lounge, 1930. The main lounge has served as OSU's "living room" since the building opened in November 1928. It has been used for studying, public concerts, special events, quiet contemplation, and even sleeping. The lounge today looks remarkably similar to how it looked decades ago. Photo by Howell's Studio of Corvallis. (HC 34)

Students' procession to Gill Coliseum, June 4, 1950. Commencement activities in 1950 were the first to be held in newly built Gill Coliseum. Since 1915, commencement had been held in the Men's Gymnasium (Langton Hall). Its limited seating greatly restricted the number of guests who could attend graduation exercises—and basketball games in the winter months. Commencement moved outdoors to Reser Stadium in 2001. (P82:65 #842)

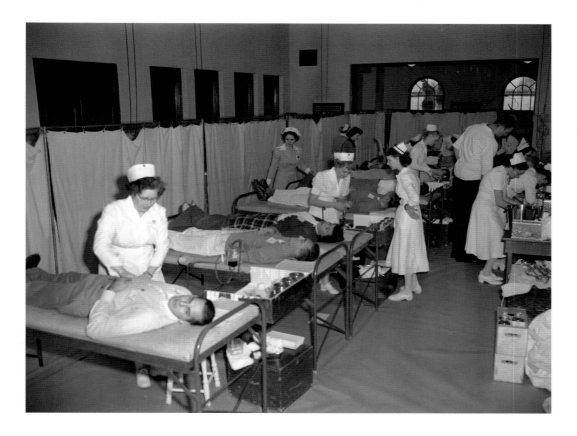

Red Cross blood drive, Women's Building, November 8, 1950. Oregon State students, faculty, and staff have demonstrated a strong culture of service and giving through support of campus blood drives, dating back to at least World War II. (P82:97 #597)

"Burning of the Green" ceremony, ca. 1955. For several decades, freshman men were required to wear green beanies, known as "rook lids," and freshman women were required to wear green ribbons. At the end of the academic year during Junior Weekend, freshmen participated in the "Burning of the Green" event where they could ceremoniously burn their lids and ribbons. By the 1950s, wearing the green tradition had been reduced to the first week of school and major events. And by the early 1960s the tradition had mostly died out. This ceremony was held in a parking lot east of Education Hall (Furman Hall). Photo by Hise Studio, Corvallis. (P17:759)

COED CHEESECAKE: THE 1959 OREGON STATE COLLEGE WRESTLING COURT *by Brittany Backen*

In 1959, OSC's new wrestling coach Dale Thomas wanted to bring the Pacific Intercollegiate Wrestling Tournament to Corvallis. The rest of the administration opposed the tournament, as it would mean more work for an undervalued sport. With little backing, Thomas decided to create a publicity stunt to promote the event.

Thomas delegated one of his star wrestlers, Ken Noteboom, to head a search committee to the find "best looking coeds" to become the 1959 Wrestling Court. Each woman would carry the title of a wrestling hold that also had a secondary, suggestive meaning. After interviewing twenty-nine students, the committee chose the final seven for the court.

Once the women were chosen, Thomas took them to a local photography studio where they posed in one-piece swimsuits with their titles on sashes. Thomas promptly sent the photographs to several media outlets. After the Corvallis *Gazette-Times* published the photographs, an angered President A. L. Strand called Thomas into his office. Strand ordered Thomas to cease contact with the press. He was notoriously conservative and he was opposed to women from his school posing for "cheesecake" photographs. The next morning another photograph was on front page of the *Daily Barometer*. President Strand's response was to issue a public edict banning the athletic department from using promotional "cheesecake" photographs.

Never one to heed authority, Thomas incorporated the edict into his publicity stunt, giving his story an element of controversy. The Oregon State Wrestling Court and the president who opposed it became international news. The story ran in newspapers from Iran to North Dakota and in national magazines such as *Life* and *Sports Illustrated*. *Life* even convinced Strand to pose with the Court in front of the Memorial Union Building. After the story was published, the women began receiving fan mail from young men. Many of the letters simply requested photographs, but others extended marriage proposals.

By 1984, the tenacious Coach Thomas had brought the wrestling department into the forefront. The twenty-fifth anniversary of the first wrestling tournament was at hand and Thomas, remembering how successful the wrestling court was the first time around, decided to bring it back. He asked one of his new wrestlers to pick a new Court and asked his former wrestler Noteboom to invite the former Court back. This time the Court received only a portion of the original publicity and none of the controversy.[1]

Ken Noteboom, star wrestler and Outstanding Senior award winner, March 1959. Noteboom played a key role, heading the committee that selected the women to be on the wrestling court. He wrestled for Oregon State from 1957 to 1959 and was one of the members of the class of 1959 designated as an Outstanding Senior. (HC 2084)

Official program of the 1984 Pac-10 Wrestling Championships. The program's cover featured both the 1959 and 1984 wrestling courts. (Courtesy of Janet Aune Essig)

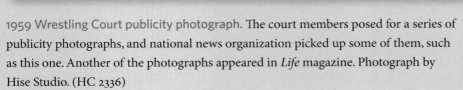

1959 Wrestling Court publicity photograph. The court members posed for a series of publicity photographs, and national news organization picked up some of them, such as this one. Another of the photographs appeared in *Life* magazine. Photograph by Hise Studio. (HC 2336)

Memorial Union bowling alley, 1960. The east and west wings of the Memorial Union, completed in 1960, added space for additional food options, the bookstore, and student recreational activities, such as bowling and billiards. The lanes are still popular with students, faculty, and staff. This was not Oregon State's first bowling venue. The Gymnasium and Armory that opened in 1898 included bowling alley lanes on the lower level. (P82:77 #2627)

Presidential candidate Richard M. Nixon campaigning at OSU, 1968. Nixon campaigned at OSU during his first successful presidential election year. He had previously visited Oregon State as vice-president in 1954. Other presidential candidates who campaigned at OSU or in Corvallis included John F. Kennedy (1960), Robert F. Kennedy (1968), and Barack Obama (2008). Hilary Clinton made a campaign stop at OSU for then President Bill Clinton's re-election in early November of 1996. Photo by Jim Cron. (P3:6256)

Civil rights leader Julian Bond speaking at OSU, 1970. Bond, who helped found the Student Nonviolent Coordinating Committee, was also a member of the Georgia House of Representatives. He was one of OSU's 1970–1971 Convocation and Lecture Series speakers. OSU has hosted many prominent guest speakers through its various lecture series. Photo by John Robbins. (P3:3614)

Vietnam War National Moratorium Day march at OSU, October 15, 1969. Hundreds of OSU students, along with students at colleges and universities across the nation, participated in National Moratorium Day events. Approximately six hundred people marched from the MU quad to Central Park west of downtown. Other events included lectures and discussion teach-ins at the MU, a debate in the MU ballroom that drew eight hundred attendees, and an evening lecture by former United States senator from Oregon and outspoken Vietnam War critic Wayne Morse. Photo by John Robbins. (P295, Accession 2013:044)

Neil Diamond performing at Gill Coliseum, February 27, 1971. OSU attracted nationally known pop and rock artists to campus in the 1960s and 1970s. Many of the concerts were held in Gill Coliseum. Diamond also performed at OSU in 1970. Photo by John Robbins. (P3:3936)

Karen Carsini of OSU's Outdoor Program tunes up skis, 1978. The Outdoor Program offered equipment rentals for outdoor activities to the OSU community, sponsored ski and rafting trips, and hosted lectures and clinics pertaining to outdoor activities. The program was located in a Quonset hut near Moreland Hall for several years. Today similar equipment and programs are available through the Dixon Recreation Center's Adventure Leadership Institute, which also offers bicycle, ski, and snowboard repair. (P3, 1978 *Beaver* yearbook)

Students assisting with the sixteenth annual Student Foundation Super Telefund, November 1988. Four hundred students participated in the telefund campaign. They made twenty thousand calls to alumni and raised $164,000. This photo appeared in the 1989 *Beaver* yearbook. (P3, 1989 *Beaver* Yearbook)

Stevens Natatorium, Dixon Recreation Center, 1992. The natatorium, completed just before this photograph was taken, was the second phase of the recreation center. Phase one opened in 1976, and phase three was completed in 2004. The natatorium was named for George Stevens, Memorial Union director from 1963 to 1990 and a strong proponent of recreational sports at OSU. (P57, Accession 2006:046)

OSU First Lady Les Risser handing out goodies at the Corvallis alumni picnic, July 2001. This picnic was held at the CH2M HILL Alumni Center. On the right side of the photo is Pete Smith (class of 1940), who managed the OSU Bookstore for many years. (P195, Accession 2005:094)

Dads Weekend rock climbing event, 2000. Like Moms and Family Weekend, Dads Weekend is also a long-standing tradition at OSU. It dates to 1934, when the OSC Dads Club set aside April 14 as a day to celebrate Beaver dads on campus. The day's events for the two hundred visiting dads and their sons and daughters included an intra-squad football game, a baseball game against Columbia University (now the University of Portland), and an evening banquet. The banquet featured music and speakers, as well as student yell leader Forrest Lindsay, who led the dads in yells and cheers "to prepare for the future football and basketball games." Dads returned that year in the fall for additional activities on homecoming weekend. For a number of years, Dads Weekend was held in the late winter, but it returned to its fall schedule in 1999. Recent Dads Weekends have offered a wide variety of events in addition to the football game, including a classic car show, golf tournament, barbecues, comedy shows featuring name acts such as Jay Leno and Jeff Foxworthy, and film showings. (P3, Accession 2005:064)

Beaver Hut sign, ca. 1970. The Beaver Hut Tavern, located on NE Second Street north of downtown, was a favorite hangout for students twenty-one and older from the 1960s into the 1980s. (P3:1806)

B. W. Johnson,   J. Fred Yates,   Miss Helen Holgate,   H. L. Holgate,   John Fulton,
2nd Bass.   2nd Tenor.   Accompanist.   1st Bass.   1st Tenor.

The Bach Quartette, ca. 1892. The quartet consisted mostly of OAC alumni men who were bachelors—hence the play on words. Members were B. W. Johnson, J. Fred Yates (class of 1885), Harry Holgate (class of 1886), and John Fulton (class of 1892). Accompanist Helen Holgate was a member of the class of 1895. This group was one of the first of many music-related organizations that have played a prominent role in OSU's history. (HC 562)

It Is All About Community
Campus Organizations at OSU

Throughout its history, Oregon State University has supported a myriad of organizations that have played vital roles in shaping the campus community. These organizations have catered to a variety of groups and interests. They have included service and honorary societies; fraternities, sororities, and other social organizations; living groups; religious and spiritually affiliated organizations; clubs associated with academic programs and professions; and recreational and sports clubs. Though most have supported OSU students, several organizations have been formed to meet the needs and interests of faculty, staff, and retirees.

Most of the earliest student organizations at OSU were literary societies. The Adelphian Literary Society, which began around 1882, was likely the first recognized student organization.[1] It disbanded in 1889, and its library was transferred to the college library. Other literary societies formed in the 1890s, most organized by gender. The societies had a social function, but their programs typically included debate, short plays and skits, recitation, and musical performances. By the 1910s, most literary societies at OAC had disbanded; some became living groups that ultimately evolved into fraternities and sororities.

OSU has a long tradition of musical organizations. It established a cadet band in late 1891—the oldest band among the present members of the Pac-12 Conference. Vocal groups also formed in the 1890s, such as the Bach Quartette pictured left. A college orchestra began in 1906; today the Corvallis-OSU Symphony is a 130-member organization composed of students, music faculty, community members, and professional musicians from western Oregon. Other music organizations were formed in the early twentieth century, such as the Mandolin Club. Today OSU's bands, choirs, orchestra, and other performance groups form a key component of the academic program in music, as well as a major source of cultural enjoyment in the OSU and local communities.

Student-created publications also had their genesis in the 1890s.[2] In 1894, a yearbook called the *Hayseed* was published by a group of engineering students. Although a one-time publication, it set the stage for subsequent yearbooks—the *Orange* (1907-1916) and *Beaver* (1916 to 2014). The *Hayseed* may have also influenced the creation of the *Barometer*—today's student-produced newspaper. It began in 1896 as a monthly literary and news magazine published by the literary societies. Ten years later it had evolved into a newspaper format, published semi-weekly, and it became a daily in 1923. Today the *Barometer* is published by the Orange Media Network (formerly Student Media), which also publishes the art and literary magazine *Prism* and manages KBVR radio and television. The final edition of the *Beaver* was published in 2014, and it turned into the online, crowd-sourced *Beaver's Digest*, published three times a year. Other student publications over the years included *Orange Owl*, a humor magazine in the 1920s, and the *Oregon State Tech Record*, an engineering magazine published from 1924 to 1959.

A number of "alternative" or independent publications—those not officially sanctioned by OSU—appeared throughout the twentieth century and up to the present. From 1961 to 1966 a group published the *Gad-Fly*, a mimeographed sheet that claimed it existed to "fight against moral and intellectual conformity." The *Scab Sheet*, formed initially in 1969 in response to the dismissal of football player Fred Milton from the team for wearing facial hair, existed for fourteen issues. The publication also protested the Vietnam War. More recently, *The Liberty* appeared on campus. OSU students published it to promote "conservative, libertarian, and independent thought." The editors filed suit against OSU in 2009 for violating their right to free speech when most of its distribution racks were removed from campus.[3]

Branches of the YMCA and YWCA were established at OAC in the 1890s, making them among the first student organizations at OSU. In 1908 Shepard Hall was built to accommodate them as well as provide meeting space for other student organizations. A separate YMCA, known as the Y-Hut, was constructed in 1918 for the men participating in the Students Army Training Corps during World War I. That facility was demolished in 1927 to make way for the Memorial Union. The Y Round Table was established in 1938 to coordinate the combined activities of the YMCA and YWCA. It became the Volunteer Student Services in 1995.

OSC cadet band decal, ca. 1935. (MC-Bands)

Other faith-related student organizations that have been part of the OSU community include Westminster House (United Campus Ministries), established in the early 1930s; Luther House (Lutheran Campus Ministry), established in 1926; Newman Catholic Campus Ministry, established 1917; Muslim Student Association at OSU, established in 1980; and Hillel OSU, established 1946.

In the early years of the twentieth century, several student clubs formed around specific academic disciplines. These included the Agricultural Club, Lewelling Club (horticulture), the Pharmaceutical Association, the Household Science Club (later Margaret Snell Club), Commercial Club (commerce), and Vorwaerts (German language). Around this same time, special-interest student clubs were established, such as the Camera Club and the Dramatic Club (later Mask and Dagger).

Honor societies had their start in the 1910s; some of the earliest were Delta Theta Sigma (agriculture), Sphinx (students with senior class standing), Sigma Tau (engineering), and Alpha Kappa Psi (commerce). Several geography-based clubs were started in the 1910s, bringing together students from specific cities or locations. These included the Portland Club, the California Club, and the Eastern Oregon Club.

Many service-related student organizations were established in the 1930s and 1940s. The Talons (founded in 1933) and Thanes (founded in 1937) were service honorary societies for sophomore women and men, respectively. Both were successors to earlier organizations. Mortar Board, a service honorary for senior women, also was established in 1933, and Blue Key, a service honorary for senior men, began in 1934.

OSU's strong Greek system had its genesis in the mid-1910s. The first sorority, Alpha Omega, was organized in 1914 and became the Chi chapter of Alpha Chi Omega in 1915. Other living groups affiliated with national fraternities and sororities to become local chapters. By 1920, OAC had nineteen fraternities and eleven sororities.[4] Today those numbers are twenty-four fraternities and twenty sororities, with more than 2,800 students participating in OSU's Greek community.

Many early living groups did not become affiliated with Greek organizations. These were cooperative residences, such as the Campus Club, and served as social and service organizations similar to the Greek system.[5] Most residence halls started their own organizations, often for governance purposes and to organize for intramural sports.

OSU has had many faculty and staff-related organizations, particularly in the past hundred years. One of the oldest is the OSU Folk Club, begun in 1908 as the College Folk Club. It is a social and service organization composed of faculty women and faculty wives. The club established a thrift shop in 1949, and the proceeds from its sales go toward OSU student scholarships and grants to nonprofit organizations in Benton County. Another enduring faculty organization is the Triad Club, established in 1926 as a faculty men's club to foster "fellowship, cooperation and service." Today it is open to all OSU faculty and staff and meets for a weekly lunch program that includes presentations on research, current events, university governance, and other OSU programs.

OSU's Alumni Association was established on February 3, 1873, less than three years after the college graduated its first class. OSU's oldest non-academic organization, its purpose is to promote the university and engage alumni and friends of OSU. Through the years, it has sponsored class reunions, alumni picnics around the state, homecoming events, lecture series, scholarships, tailgaters, and other activities. It has published an alumni magazine since 1915.

Today OSU hosts hundreds of recognized student organizations coordinated through Student Affairs. Faculty, staff, retirees, and alumni participate in dozens of service, social, and learning organizations. These organizations create a unique sense of community for all of OSU.

Utopian Literary Society, 1905. Literary societies were among the earliest student organizations at Oregon State, dating back to the 1880s. OAC had ten societies in 1905—five each for men and women students. The 1905–06 college catalog describes the societies as having "a semi-fraternal nature, offering to their members social as well as literary advantages. The exercises consist principally of essays, declamations, debates and music." The Utopian Literary Society was formed in 1900. Its objective was to "cultivate those traits of character that tend to make ideal young women; to develop the literacy and social qualities of its members; and to promote a spirit of helpful friendship." (P25:1572)

OAC Mandolin Club, 1908. In addition to the orchestra, cadet band, and various singing groups, OAC offered students opportunities for other student musicians, such as these mandolin players. A photo similar to this was used in the 1909 *Orange* yearbook. (P25:3105)

Oxford Club members showing their best side, 1913. Established in 1911, the Oxford Club was an early male living group established to promote the "highest ideals of integrity and brotherhood." In February 1918, it became the Oregon Alpha chapter of the Sigma Phi Epsilon fraternity. (P158:23)

Margaret Snell Club, 1911. Many of OAC's early clubs were organized around academic disciplines, such as the Margaret Snell Club, which represented domestic science and art. Established in 1908 (the year Margaret Snell retired from OAC), its purpose was to "promote an interest in domestic science and to assist in the social functions of the college." Anyone who was affiliated with the domestic science department was eligible for membership. By 1913 the Home Economics Club had replaced the Margaret Snell Club. The club members posed outside of Waldo Hall for this photograph. (MSS-Ferguson)

OAC Orchestra, ca. 1916. The orchestra, directed at the time by Edward Hellier-Collens, performed its annual concert in the sanctuary of Corvallis's First Presbyterian Church. The orchestra was established in 1906, and from the start included members of the community in addition to OAC students and faculty. During the 1910s and 1920s, the orchestra teamed with the Glee and Madrigal Clubs to perform light operas, such as Gilbert & Sullivan's *The Mikado* and *Pirates of Penzance*. (HC 1016)

College Folk Club members celebrating Washington's birthday, ca. 1915. Known as the OSU Folk Club today, the College Folk Club was established in 1908 as a social and service club for OAC's faculty wives and female faculty members. This photo was taken by Ball Studio in Corvallis. (HC 1205)

Cosmopolitan Club, ca. 1918. OAC's Cosmopolitan Club, established in 1911, was the first campus organization for international students and the first to promote diversity. The club was "a vital factor in uniting and holding together foreign as well as American students of this institution by the common bonds of humanity." The 1919 *Beaver* yearbook, in which this photo appears, stated that as the Great War was bringing people of many nations closer together, OAC's Cosmopolitan Club was "breaking down this racial feeling . . . and working for the common good of humanity." College librarian Ida Kidder is sitting in the center of the front row; to her left is professor of bacteriology Theodore D. Beckwith. (HC 845)

First installation of Phi Kappa Phi members at OAC, June 1924. Phi Kappa Phi is a national, all-discipline honorary society established in 1897 to recognize academic achievement for the top 10 percent of a college's senior class. OSU's chapter of Phi Kappa Phi was established in 1924 and was the society's thirty-eighth chapter to be chartered. It was preceded by the Forum Society, established at OAC in 1914; many Forum members were initiated into Phi Kappa Phi. In addition to initiation ceremonies, Phi Kappa Phi has assisted in organizing forum discussions and sponsoring lectures at OSU, such as the Biology Colloquia series. In 1965 OSU hosted the society's twenty-fifth national convention. This photo shows the first class of Phi Kappa Phi initiates at OAC, which included current students, alumni, and faculty, posed outside the library. Initiates included James K. Weatherford (class of 1872), longtime member of the board of regents; William Jasper Kerr, OAC president; and John Fulton (class of 1892), chemistry faculty member. After the initiation ceremony in the library, a banquet for the inductees was held in the Home Economics Tea Room. (HC 1178)

Beaver yearbook staff hard at work, ca. 1927. Although this photo is obviously staged, producing a yearbook involved considerable work on the part of many staff members. In 1927 the yearbook office was located on the second floor of Shepard Hall. Today the Orange Media Network offices are located in the Student Experience Center, east of the Memorial Union. The network consists of the *Daily Barometer*, KBVR-FV and TV, *Prism* magazine, and *Beaver's Digest*, which replaced the *Beaver* yearbook. (HC 2512)

Orange Owl, 1928. *Orange Owl* was a student-produced humor magazine published at OAC between 1920 and 1928 by the Hammer and Coffin Society. It was discontinued in 1928 by the college's Administrative Council and Student Interest Committee after its humor became too ribald for the late 1920s. The handwritten note at the top of the magazine reads "Edited by the girls only!" (PUB10-13c)

Barometer staff at the copy table, 1930. OSU's student newspaper, the *Barometer,* was established in 1896 as a monthly literary magazine and in 1906 shifted to a weekly newspaper. It became a daily in 1922. Today the *Daily Barometer* is a part of OSU Student Media, along with *Beaver's Digest* (successor to the *Beaver* yearbook) and KBVR radio and TV. Many *Barometer* editors have gone on to distinguished careers in journalism. (HC 823)

Newman Club members pose outside of St. Mary's Catholic Church, ca. 1929. After the separation in 1888 of the State Agricultural College from the Methodist Episcopal Church, South, religion continued to play a major role in the OAC campus community. The YMCA and YWCA established a presence in the 1890s, and the Newman Club was established in 1917. Today there are more than twenty religious and spiritual student organizations at OSU. (P17:621)

Triad Club members, 1935. The Triad Club is one of Oregon State's oldest continuing faculty/staff organizations. It was established in 1926 as an all-male club to further "fellowship, cooperation, and service" among the school's departments and offices, students, and citizens of Corvallis. The club holds weekly luncheon meetings that feature guest speakers and presentations. Triad first admitted women in 1978. The members posed for this photo outside the Hotel Corvallis. (HC 1156)

Rally Squad at homecoming, fall 1941. The squad is posing with a large, carved wood beaver on a float on the sidelines in Bell Field. This incarnation of OSU's mascot may have been the first to be called "Benny." Because the 1942 Rose Bowl was played in North Carolina instead of Pasadena, California, this rally squad was not able to go to the bowl game. Pictured are Jeanne Hetherington, Joy Hoerner, Mary Lou Blish, Esther Weibel, Vera Hollenbeck, and Pat Clark. Hetherington (front row, left) went on to a successful, but short, Hollywood career under the screen name of Jean Heather. (HC 2587)

Associated Women Students officers for 1943–44. The Associated Women Students (AWS) organization was established in 1924 to further the educational, social, and cultural aims of women. It served as an umbrella group for women's living groups, honorary societies, and clubs. AWS sponsored a variety of activities, such as war bond and stamp fundraising drives during World War II. The dean of women served as the organization's advisor and liaison to the college's administration. The AWS became inactive in June 1970. (HC 1476)

Blue Key members, 1943. Oregon State's Blue Key chapter was established in 1934 to honor male students with strong academic backgrounds and who demonstrated "superior leadership and unselfish commitment to others." Faculty included in this photo are E. B. Lemon, dean of administration (middle row, left); U. G. Dubach, dean of men (middle row, third from right); and Dan Poling, assistant dean of men (front row, second from left). (HC 86)

OSC Mountain Club members climbing Mount Rainier, 1950. The OSC Mountain Club was established in 1947 to promote and sponsor skiing and mountain-climbing activities. In addition to outings, it also organized instruction classes, films, and lectures. One of the founders of the club was Willi Unsoeld, who in 1963 became one of the first Americans to scale Mount Everest. The outdoor activities of the Mountain Club became the basis for the OSU Outdoor Program, established about 1971; by 1975, the Mountain Club had disbanded. This photograph, taken by Mountain Club member Paul Hosmer, was used on the cover of the December 1950 *Oregon Stater*. (P17:1527)

Oregon State College debate team meets the Cambridge University debate team, April 1951. Debate has had a strong presence at Oregon State since the 1890s, when debate competitions were held between the literary societies and occasionally against other colleges and universities in the region. OSC's debaters for this competition were Bill Zimmerman, right, and Bill Maxwell, second from right. H. E. Childs, center, OSC professor of English, served as moderator. In 1949, Maxwell took first place in the junior men's oratory division of the Northwest Invitational Forensics Tournament at Linfield College. During his senior year in November 1951, he won first place at the Senior Men's Oratorical Contest of the Western Speech Association at Fresno State College. Maxwell also served as Associated Students of Oregon State College vice-president for 1950–51 and was a member of the Y Round Table and Delta Sigma Rho, the forensics honor society. (P82:95 #113)

Fraternity members doing cleanup work at First Presbyterian Church, 1953. Service has been an important component of OSU's fraternities and sororities for many decades. These fraternity members were sprucing up the grounds of this church, just a few blocks from campus. (P82:67 #1316)

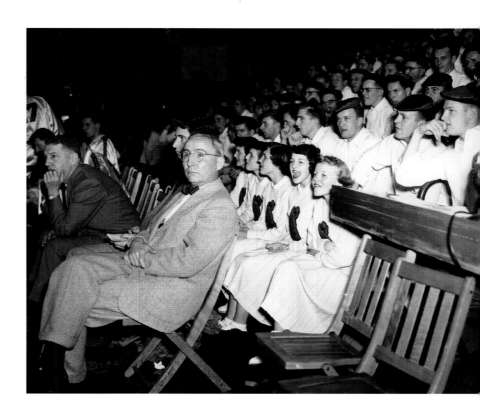

Rally Girls and Tailflappers at a basketball game, ca. 1954. During the 1950s and into the 1960s, a group of junior and senior men known as the Tailflappers were a common sight at athletic events. The group was created in 1953 to revive and promote school spirit and good sportsmanship, and their trademarks were white corduroy pants, white shirts with tails out, and black and orange "rooters" caps. Both the Tailflappers and the Rally Squad sat just behind the Beaver bench. At the end of the bench in the left foreground is team physician Waldo Ball; to his right is coach A. T. "Slats" Gill. (P17:1526)

Hui-O-Hawaii Club members promoting their luau, fall 1957. The club members posted on the main steps inside the Memorial Union. The Hui-O-Hawaii Club was established in January 1952 to "foster the spirit and friendliness of Hawaii and its customs." The group's first luau was held during spring term 1952. Oregon State has had strong connections with Hawaii for many decades. (P17:3037)

Formal dance, 1958. For many decades starting in the late 1920s, formal dances in the Memorial Union ballroom were a regular occurrence. Most dances were sponsored by student organizations, such as sororities and fraternities, the Homecoming Committee, ROTC (which sponsored an annual Military Ball), and clubs, such as the Forestry Club. Providing the music for this dance was the Billy May Orchestra, led by Frankie Lester (at the microphone). Lester was a well-known big band vocalist in the 1950s. Trumpeter Billy May was a longtime arranger for many famous vocalists, such as Frank Sinatra, Ella Fitzgerald, and Peggy Lee. (P151:405)

Sorority Rush Week, fall of 1960. Student Jean Saubert (plaid skirt) and other OSC women visit a sorority. Rush week has been a longtime tradition for OSU's Greek organizations. A common part of the rush process in the 1950s and 1960s was the "walk-in." A sorority's pledges would sneak into the sorority house at night, where they would surprise their "big sisters" with loud noise, followed by a party and gifts. (P17:2514)

Forestry Club members participating in the Spring Thaw, May 1963. The Forestry Club was established in 1906, around the same time that OAC's forestry program was created. In its early years, the club sponsored hikes, timber cruising field trips, and dances. The latter evolved into the annual Fernhopper's Banquet. For many years the club published its own yearbook, *The Annual Cruise*. The club built its first cabin at Peavy Arboretum in 1925, and a second in 1950 after the first one burned. Today the club participates in logging sports events, sponsors field trips, and raises money through firewood sales. (HC 849)

Robert Walls directing the Choralaires in the Memorial Union Lounge, ca. 1959.
The Choralaires were OSU's premier vocal ensemble for many years. Founded by
music department chair Robert Walls in 1950, the group performed throughout
Oregon and internationally, including trips to Europe in 1971 and 1973. (HC 1017)

GET INVOLVED! THE ASSOCIATED STUDENTS OF OREGON STATE UNIVERSITY

The origins of student government at OSU are rooted in an 1897 campaign to fund the football team through the establishment of incidental fees. Although the Board of Regents rejected this initial move toward the systematic funding of student activities, a student conference three years later proposed a constitution and by-laws for the establishment of a student governmental body with the power to institute and regulate student fees. This proposal was approved by a vote of the student body and faculty in 1900 and resulted in the formation of OAC's first student government, the Student Assembly.

The assembly consisted of all enrolled students, governed by two bodies: the executive committee—composed of a president elected from the senior class, a vice president from each of the senior, junior, and sophomore classes, and a secretary—and the board of control, which consisted of the executive committee, three faculty members chosen by the college president, and an alumnus appointed by the Alumni Association. The assembly established a voluntary student body fee, which became mandatory for all enrolled students by 1909. Final approval of budgets and appointments was subject to the board of control and a general manager who oversaw many aspects of the board. During the 1920s, the board of control was replaced by several new student committees, such as the Student Affairs Committee and the Committee on Student Interests, established in large part to decentralize authority over student affairs.

In 1948, the Associated Students of Oregon State College (as it was known by this time) established a senate body vested with the power to introduce legislation, approve the ASOSC budget, make changes to the constitution and statutes, and recall any elected or appointed member of student government. The creation of the senate represented a major shift in policy for the ASOSC—decision-making power over student activities now resided with students elected by their peers rather than a board or committee. The constitution set the voting membership of the senate at one senator for each 500 students enrolled in the college's eleven schools, and each school was guaranteed representation by at least one senator. The first senate consisted of twenty-eight members. Although the president and other members of the executive branch were part of the senate, they did not have the power to vote for or introduce legislation.

In 1966, a judicial branch consisting of the student traffic court and the ASOSU justice commission was added to student government. The commission was vested with the power to review the constitutionality of all legislation introduced by the senate and served as the body for hearing grievances from ASOSU members about possible student election violations and legislation passed by the senate that was potentially incompatible with the ASOSU constitution and statutes. Sometime in the 1980s, the commission was renamed the ASOSU Judicial Board.

ASOSU created the position of student advocate in 1986 to assist student government in working with student organizations, long-term strategizing, legal research, and other special projects. In 1994, ASOSU adopted a bicameral senate structure that gave graduate students voting status in their own senate body equal to their undergraduate counterparts. Membership in the graduate senate was set at one representative per hundred graduate students enrolled at OSU. Today ASOSU consists of the executive, legislative, and judicial branches, as well as numerous task forces. Elections are typically held in mid-April.

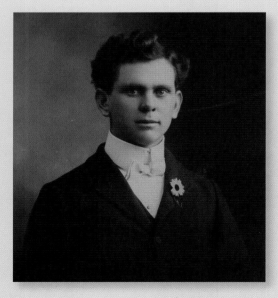

Portrait of Charles Horner, first president of the Student Assembly, ca. 1901. Horner graduated in 1901 with a BS in agriculture. (P161:1)

George Abed being sworn in as ASOSU president, 1961. Abed (class of 1962) was the first international student to serve as president of ASOSU. After graduating from OSU, he received a PhD in economics from the University of California, Berkeley. He was a longtime official with the International Monetary Fund and served as director of its Middle Eastern department from July 2002 to December 2003. He later served as the chairman of the Palestine Monetary Authority and, most recently, as a senior counselor and director for Africa and the Middle East at the Institute of International Finance. (HC 1535)

Former ASOSU president April Waddy speaking at the Valley Library groundbreaking ceremony, May 1996. Waddy was elected president of ASOSU in the spring of 1994 and served until the spring of 1995. In 1993 she coordinated a successful effort that pledged $1 million to the Valley Library campaign between that year and 2007. Waddy also served as a student member of the State Board of Higher Education from June 1995 to June 1997 and as coordinator of the Lonnie B. Harris Black Cultural Center. She was a 1996 winner of OSU's Frances Dancy Hooks Award, given to OSU students in recognition of their efforts in coalition building among diverse groups and individuals. She graduated from OSU in June 1996. (P83, Accession 2007:089)

EUGENE OKINO AND SIGMA CHI   *by Todd Moore*

With exemplary high school credentials in both academics and extra-curricular activities, and a promising start to his studies as an electrical engineering major at OSU, Eugene Okino (class of 1969) would have a been a deserving candidate for membership in any organization on campus. The undergraduate brothers of the Beta Pi chapter of Sigma Chi fraternity agreed, voting unanimously to pledge Okino late in the winter term of 1966. Upon completion of his pledging requirements later that spring, the Beta Pi chapter submitted his pledge initiation report to their regional director. Recognizing Okino's surname as Asian, and cognizant of recent controversies surrounding the initiation of non-white members at other Sigma Chi chapters, the regional director asked the Beta Pi chapter president to write a letter to all chapter alumni seeking comments before he forwarded the initiation reports to national fraternity headquarters for approval. That decision, and the ensuing letter, started an antidiscrimination controversy that put Sigma Chi fraternity at odds with OSU and endangered the continued existence of the Beta Pi chapter.

The letter concerning Okino's initiation returned one negative response from an alumnus residing in San Diego, California. Noting exclusionary practices he had encountered on a recent trip to Tokyo, the alumnus concluded that "there is nothing wrong with our adhering to our own kind in a social situation as close as Sigma Chi." He threatened to vote to suspend the chapter if a vote on the matter was held. As an active alumnus, his objection fell under Statute VIII, Section 1(c) and (f) of the Sigma Chi Constitution and Statutes, which allowed a single alumnus to block the initiation of a pledge with a negative vote. Due to his objection, the Beta Pi chapter faced a difficult decision. If they initiated Okino in spite of the objection, they risked losing their charter for disregarding a national fraternity statute. If Beta Pi did not initiate Okino, they would be in violation of the Oregon State Board of Higher Education's 1961 directive forbidding discriminatory membership practices by campus organizations.

Steadfast in their commitment to Okino but caught between their fraternity and their university, Beta Pi chapter suspended all initiations until the matter was resolved. However, progress seemed to stall until university president James Jensen commissioned a committee to review Sigma Chi's compliance

Freshman portrait of Eugene Okino, 1966. Despite the controversy surrounding his membership in Sigma Chi, Okino was finally initiated into the fraternity in March 1967. He graduated in 1969 with a degree in engineering. This photograph appeared in the 1966 *Beaver* yearbook.

with OSU policies. Responding quickly, the leadership of the Beta Pi chapter sent out notification to all alumni, including the objecting alumnus, that a direct vote on the matter of Okino's initiation would be held in Corvallis on November 21, 1966, a mere ten days after the university committee was commissioned. The alumnus who objected was not among the eight alumni in attendance along with the active membership, and so there no votes cast in opposition to the initiation of Okino.

The university review committee would come to conclude that while Sigma Chi fraternity was not explicitly discriminatory, its policies allowed for discriminatory actions to occur, as they had in Okino's case. The committee recommended that Okino be initiated as quickly as possible or there would be grounds for the university to withdraw recognition of the Beta Pi chapter. As university and chapter processes had finally aligned, Eugene Okino was initiated along with his pledge class on March 5, 1967, nearly five months after the originally scheduled initiation.

Similar controversies had split undergraduate chapters from national fraternities, crippled fraternity systems, and caused the closure of less resilient chapters nationwide, but the Beta Pi chapter of Sigma Chi fraternity showed that obligation to fraternity, university, and diversity are not mutually exclusive. They also proved that controversy can be a catalyst for improving policies. At the same time, OSU was able to firmly position itself as an advocate for the end of discriminatory practices as it pressured Sigma Chi fraternity and other national organizations to change their statutes or risk having chapters removed from campus.[6]

Sigma Chi members at the Inter-fraternity Sing, May 3, 1966. The Sing began in 1936 as a part of the college's homecoming festivities and was held in the Memorial Union Lounge. In 1951 it was opened up to include sororities, moved to Gill Coliseum, and held in the spring as part of Moms Weekend. (P35:346)

Mortar Board members, ca. 1968. Mortar Board is a national honorary society founded in 1918 for senior college women. Oregon State's chapter was established in 1933, and the organization was opened to men in 1975. The organization's ideals—service, scholarship, and leadership—are represented in the Greek letters, Pi Sigma Alpha. This photo was used in the 1969 *Beaver* yearbook. (P57:1663)

Cover of the *Scab Sheet*, March 5, 1969. The *Scab Sheet* was an alternative student publication that was published in the spring of 1969. It was formed, in part, to protest football coach Dee Andros (caricatured on the cover) dismissing player Fred Milton for wearing facial hair. Milton, who was African American, countered that it was part of his racial identity. The publication also included anti-Vietnam War content. (MC–Scab Sheet)

Talons and Thanes, 1969. Both organizations were service honorary societies for sophomores—Talons for women and Thanes for men. The organizations were created in the 1930s (Talons in 1933 and Thanes in 1937) from previously established groups. Their original focus was to ensure that freshman students upheld OSC's traditions. Over time, both organizations focused more on service, and in the late 1960s their constitutions were changed to reflect their service emphasis. (P3, 1969 *Beaver*)

One of OSU's longest enduring student organizations has been its band program, which is more than 120 years old. It was established in 1891. The instruments for the band "were secured partly by private contributions and partly through the assistance of the Board of Regents," according to the 1892–93 college catalog.

In 1905, Harry "Cap" Beard (class of 1899), who had led the band from 1897 to 1899 as a cadet, was appointed bandmaster. Beard, who also taught English and later mathematics, directed Oregon State's bands until retiring in 1945. Beard coordinated spring-break concert tours for the band for many years, which typically included performances in several cities in a region of the state. Beard was a highly regarded director and developed the band program into one of the finest on the west coast. A number of his students went on to play professionally.

For its first forty years, the cadet band was an all-male organization. Women were allowed to join for a few years in the early 1930s, though that accommodation was short lived. A coed band was formed a few years later; it disbanded after the cadet band was permanently opened to female students in 1946.

After Cap Beard's retirement, Delbert Moore directed the band until 1949, when Ted Mesang became director. Mesang, an accomplished march composer—he composed and published more than 250 musical works—served as director of bands and taught music education courses until his death in October 1967.

James Douglass took over as director of bands in 1968. He had been a soloist with the Navy Band early in his career. Douglass expanded the band program, marching as many as 200 musicians. His top concert band, the symphonic band, regularly performed for the Oregon Music Educators Association annual conference and traveled internationally, performing concert tours in Japan, Taiwan, and Costa Rica.

In the early 1990s, the marching band was temporarily eliminated due to budget cuts caused by the 1990 passage of Ballot Measure 5 (see chapter 1). Students, alumni, and community members formed a reconstituted band for a few years until an official student marching band could be formed again. From the early 1990s until about 2013, the marching band and pep band were under the authority, in part, of

OAC cadet band in front of Cauthorn Hall (Fairbanks Hall), ca. 1892. This is one of the earliest photos of OSU's band, which was established in late 1890. (HC 1015)

Intercollegiate Athletics and a separate director of athletic bands.

Today more than 450 OSU students participate in the band program, performing in the marching band, pep band, several concert bands, and a jazz band. The concert and jazz bands perform each term during the academic year. The gymnastics band, founded in the late 1980s to perform at home gymnastics meets, was the first of its kind in the nation. The band includes OSU students, alumni, faculty, and community members. Similarly, OSU's alumni band performs at selected football games in the fall, at basketball games during term breaks, and at special events.

OAC cadet band performs on radio station KFDJ, January 25, 1923, days after the station was licensed. The sixty-member band performed in the physics lab in Apperson Hall (Kearney Hall), where the radio station was located. The band was led by Harry L. Beard, cadet band director from 1905 to 1945 and professor at Oregon State. Beard was a member of OAC's class of 1899 and played cornet in the cadet band. (P95:284)

Cadet band member Eileen Morency Eason, 1932. Eason broke the gender barrier by becoming the first female member of the cadet band. However, by 1935, the band returned to its male-only status. Coeds formed their own band in 1937; this band merged with the cadet band in 1946. The basketball pep band did not allow women members until 1973. (HC 2958)

OSU Band marching at Disneyland, ca. January 1965. The band accompanied the football team to the Los Angeles area for the 1965 Rose Bowl. In addition to participating in the Rose Parade and the football game activities, the band marched in this parade in Disneyland. Band director Ted Mesang, front row center, leads the band. (P104, Accession 99:020)

OSU band in formation, ca. 1970. The band is in its "OSU" formation during halftime of an Oregon State football game in Parker Stadium. James Douglass was the director of bands at this time; he served as director from 1968 to 1999. (P3:5248)

Women's Center, April 1976. The 1892 Station Building has served many purposes throughout its history, but it has served as the Women's Center the longest. Established in 1973, OSU's Women's Center has offered learning experiences to "help women transform themselves and society." In addition to regular staff, for many years the center has had an advisory board of students, faculty, staff, and community members to help guide its mission. (P57, Accession 91:156)

Dance competition participants in the Native American Club's first powwow, October 29, 1977. The first powwow was held in the Memorial Union ballroom. The event was later moved to Gill Coliseum as it gained in popularity and drew more participants and spectators. Today the annual Klatowa Eena (Go Beavers) Powwow, sponsored by the Native American Student Association of OSU, is a two-day event held in May that draws thousands of participants and spectators from around the Pacific Northwest. (P57:5455)

KBVR DJs, Spring 1995. KBVR is OSU's student-managed, community radio station. It was established in 1967 and originally located in Shepard Hall. For several years it broadcast from Snell Hall, and in 2014 it moved into new facilities in the Student Experience Center. KBVR, which is part of OSU Student Media, provides a variety of programming, including news, sports, and talks shows. Music covers many genres. Students work as DJs, talk show hosts, sportscasters, and in a variety of technical support positions. In 2014 KBVR won several awards in the Intercollegiate Broadcasting System competition, including best college radio station (university with more than ten thousand students). (P57, Accession 2006:046)

Beaver cheerleaders performing at a basketball game in Gill Coliseum, winter of 2002. By 2002, OSU's cheerleaders had become known for routines that combined traditional cheer with tumbling and gymnastics routines. OSU's 2002 cheerleader squad won first place at the United Spirit Association's national competition in Las Vegas. OSU re-examined its cheerleading program in 2006, eliminating high-risk stunts and focusing more on cheering. (P3)

Staff of the Lonnie B. Harris Black Cultural Center for 2002–03. First opened in April 1975, a new center was built in 2014, on the site of the earlier facility. Lonnie B. Harris was the first director of OSU's Educational Opportunities Program. (RG244)

Members of the OSU Retirement Association (OSURA) talk to other University Day participants, September 23, 2010. The OSURA formed in the summer of 2001, promotes "continuing collegial ties among OSU retirees, and between retirees and the OSU community, by providing opportunities for social interaction and support, ongoing intellectual growth, and service to the University." The association sponsors tours, lectures, service projects that support OSU, retirement planning programs, and social events for its members. (Photo by Theresa Hogue, courtesy of OSU News and Research Communications)

Rover over football, April 28, 2010. OSU's nationally recognized Robotics Club took its "Mars Rover" to the final spring football practice, where they drove it over more than thirty-two football team members and coaches. OSU's rover was a hybrid of the actual Mars Rover and excavating equipment. The club won the 2008 University Mars Rover Challenge. (Photo by Theresa Hogue, courtesy of OSU News and Research Communications)

Front entrance to the Eena Haws Longhouse, May 9, 2013. The longhouse was the first of four new cultural centers on campus. "Eena Haws" is Chinook for "Beaver House." (Photo by Theresa Hogue, courtesy of OSU News and Research Communications)

Centro Cultural César Chavez (CCCC), April 1, 2014. The new home of the CCCC, the second of four cultural centers to be completed, was dedicated on April 7, 2014. Speakers included Dr. Luz Maciel Villarroel, who discussed helping to establish OSU's first Chicano center in the 1970s. (Photo by Theresa Hogue, courtesy of OSU News and Research Communications)

OSU Pride Center during the 2014 Pride Week, May 2014. The Pride Center is one of the more recently established of OSU's seven cultural resource centers. The center provides programs and support services for lesbian, gay, bisexual, transgender, queer, questioning, intersex, and asexual members of the OSU community. The organization was established in 2001 as the Queer Resource Center, and changed its name to the Pride Center in 2004. For several years OSU has been ranked as one of the top LGBT-friendly campuses in the United States. (Photo courtesy of the Pride Center)

First OAC athletes, May 1893. According to the 1938 *Orange and Black* pictorial history, "OAC's first athletic team held an inter-collegiate outdoor and indoor contest on May 4, 1893, at Brownsville," Oregon. The athletes were, from left (standing): Ed Abernathy, Arthur Wood, Harry Leonard, Wallace Harrison, Charles Owsley, Lewis Oren, Willard Smith, William Keady, Perry Baisley, G.W. Palmer, A. T. Buxton, James R. Cooley, John Herron, Brady Burnett, and Percival Nash. Seated, from left: Charles Chandler, Ed Emmett, and Fred Caples. A few of the athletes were preparatory department students. (HC 24)

A Culture of Excellence
Student Athletes at OSU

Oregon State University's formal participation in intercollegiate athletics dates back to at least the early 1890s and the administration of President John Bloss. The May 1893 event pictured above was the college's first documented intercollegiate competition. The first team sport was football, which began in November 1893. Track and field's first intercollegiate meets took place in the mid-1890s, and women's basketball formed in 1898. Baseball was played sporadically at the intercollegiate level in the 1890s and after the turn of the twentieth century, but not on a yearly basis until 1907.

Athletics were initially overseen by a student athletics council, established in the late 1890s, though a faculty committee provided general supervision of all athletic activities. The board of regents banned athletics during the 1900–01 academic year. W. O. Trine, appointed physical director in about 1903, supervised the training and physical conditioning of all athletes and also served on the faculty committee that supervised athletics. In those capacities he served as Oregon State's first director of athletics.

Early facilities for sporting events were sparse, though functional. Part of what is now lower campus, just to the east of Furman Hall, was used for baseball, football, and track and field. Basketball games played by both the men and women were held in the gymnasium, completed in 1898. A more permanent baseball diamond was created in 1907, just to the south of Waldo Hall; OSU teams have played baseball in that location ever since. In 1999 the facility was named Goss Stadium at Coleman Field; it received major expansions that year, in 2009, and in 2015. Football and track and field moved from Lower Campus to a field where McAlexander Fieldhouse is today, and then

in 1913 to what later became Bell Field on the current site of Dixon Recreation Center. Football moved to its current site in 1953 with the opening of Parker Stadium, which was renamed Reser Stadium in June 1999 and greatly enlarged and upgraded over the next six years. Men's basketball had a new home with the opening of the Men's Gymnasium (Langton Hall) in 1915; the sport moved to the brand new Gill Coliseum in late 1949. A new basketball practice facility for the men's and women's teams opened in 2013. The Merritt Truax Indoor Center opened in 2001. It is used primarily for football, although other OSU teams use the facility. It also is used for pregame festivities and special events.

Other intercollegiate sports were created in the first few decades of the twentieth century, including wrestling (1909). Several minor sports began in the 1920s, including tennis, swimming, polo, crew, and golf. Many of these sports grew out of intramural competition and later became varsity-level sports.

OSU has had a strong tradition of women's sports since the 1898 women's basketball team. Several women's sports competed at the intercollegiate level before the passage of Title IX in 1972. That federal legislation formalized women's intercollegiate sports at colleges and universities, and provided a modicum of equity, although disparities remain at many colleges and universities in funding for women's athletics and opportunities for female athletes. OSU became a charter member of the Association of Intercollegiate Athletics for Women (AIAW) in 1972 and established a women's intercollegiate athletics department in 1973. In January 1974 the department's first budget—$40,000—was approved. Pat Ingram served as the first women's athletic director until 1975. The department merged with the men's intercollegiate athletics department in 1983.

For major men's sports, Oregon State has been a member of a conference since the 1910s, except for a few years in the 1960s. It was a member of the Northwest Intercollegiate Association from 1902 to 1914, until it joined the Pacific Coast Conference (PCC) in 1915. OSU played as an independent from 1959 to 1964. It joined the Pacific-8 (Pac-8) conference in 1964, which became the Pac-10 conference in 1978 with the addition of Arizona and Arizona State and the Pac-12 in 2012, when Colorado and Utah joined.

OSU has enjoyed success in many major sports, including NCAA championships in men's cross country (1961) and baseball (2006 and 2007). In the decades before World War II, football teams had considerable success against opponents in the eastern United States, and the 1941 team participated in the only Rose Bowl game that was not played in Pasadena. Men's basketball teams have made several NCAA and NIT tournament appearances, including NCAA final four appearances in 1949 and 1963. Women's basketball twice won the WNIT in the early 1980s. In addition to baseball, OSU's wrestling, men's rowing, and gymnastics teams are consistently nationally ranked, and several OSU wrestlers, gymnasts, and track and field athletes have won individual national championships.

The University of Oregon has been OSU's closest rival since the two teams first met on the football field in the fall of 1894. Games between the two schools are known as the "Civil War," a term that came into common usage in the late 1930s. The schools have had heated rivalries in many sports beyond football, including basketball (men's and women's), women's soccer, and baseball. OSU's track and field men's teams rivaled the UO's powerful teams in the late 1960s and early 1970s.

OSU athletics has a reputation of being a relatively clean program. NCAA violations and sanctions have been few and far between—a testament to the coaches, athletic administrators, and high quality athletes recruited over the years.

For more than one hundred years, many Beaver athletes have been part of national teams for the United States and other countries in the Olympics, Pan American Games, and other world championship tournaments, dating back to Forrest Smithson's gold medal in track in the 1908 Olympic games. (See the appendix for a complete list

Classic Benny Beaver decal, ca. 1965

of Beaver Olympians.) Several have also played professionally or became successful coaches at the high school, college, and professional levels. And OSU athletes in many sports are recognized each year for their academic achievements by the Pac-12 Conference and other organizations.

OSU's student athletes have played a significant role in the development of the university and are an integral part of Beaver Nation's culture and identity.

FOOTBALL

OSU's first football team formed in late 1893 and played its first game against Albany College, winning 62–0. Like many other college teams of the day, that first team included alumni and non-students. The coach of the first team, Will Bloss, also played quarterback.[1] The early teams generally met with success. One of the best was the 1907 team, which compiled a 6–0 record and did not allow a single point to be scored against it.

Almost all of OAC's early games were played against teams in Oregon and Washington. In 1915 the team played its first game in the Midwest, winning 20–0 against highly favored Michigan Agricultural College. For the next twenty years Oregon State enjoyed some success against more favored intersectional opponents, including road game wins over New York University (1928) and Fordham (1933), and winning at home against West Virginia in 1930.

From the mid-1920s through the 1960s OSU's football program was relatively competitive, compiling twenty-six winning seasons and playing in six bowl games.[2] From 1971 through 1998, the team fell on hard times, enduring twenty-eight straight losing seasons and winning only sixty-five games. The string was broken when Dennis Erickson, in his first year with the Beavers, compiled a 7–5 record in 1999. The next year he coached the Beavers to an 11–1 record, a win over Notre Dame in the Fiesta Bowl, and a no. 4 national ranking. Erickson coached through the 2002 season, compiling an overall record of 31–17.

Paul J. Schissler coached at Oregon State from 1924 through 1932, leaving with a 48–30-2 record. Schissler went on to coach professionally, and he is credited with helping to integrate the NFL in the 1940s and creating the Pro Bowl in 1951. He was succeeded by Lon Stiner in 1933, who coached fourteen seasons through 1948.[3] Stiner led Oregon State to the 1942 Rose Bowl and a 20–16 win over favored Duke—the only year that game has not been played in Pasadena. Stiner's 1933 squad also tied two-time defending national champions USC 0–0—while using only eleven players over the course of the game. Stiner's overall record was 74–49–17. Tommy Prothro coached at Oregon State University from 1955 to 1964 and led the Beavers to 63 wins and three bowl games, including two Rose Bowl appearances and a 6–0 win over Villanova in the 1962 Liberty Bowl. He coached All-American Terry Baker, who won the 1962 Heisman Trophy. Dee Andros succeeded Prothro. Andros's teams played well in his first several years. His 1967 squad became known as the "Giant Killers," as they beat or tied the number-one or number- two ranked teams three times, including a 3–0 victory over number one USC. Stiner, Prothro, and Andros have been inducted into OSU's Sports Hall of Fame.

Mike Riley coached twice at OSU, in 1997 and 1998, and from 2003 to 2014. Although his 1997 and 1998 teams did not have winning records, he is credited with laying the groundwork for Dennis Erickson's success. Riley's teams had winning records eight out of eleven seasons and finished the season ranked in the national top twenty-five in four seasons. Eight teams played in bowl games. Riley left OSU for the University of Nebraska in late 2014. Gary Andersen, the coach at Wisconsin, was hired to replace Riley.

Herm Abraham was Oregon State's first All-American, winning honors in 1916. Since that time sixty-two Beaver players have been named All-Americans seventy-seven times. In addition to Terry Baker's 1962 Heisman Trophy, other players who have won national awards include Mike Hass, winner of the 2005 Biletnikoff Award as the nation's best receiver; Alex Serna, winner of the 2005 Lou Groza Award as the nation's top placekicker; and Brandin Cooks, winner of the 2013 Biletnikoff Award. More than one hundred Beaver football players have played in the NFL.

1937 Civil War football game ticket stub.

OAC versus Albany College, 1897. This is the earliest photograph showing the OAC football team in action. OAC played Albany College (now Lewis & Clark College) four times from 1893 to 1903, including OAC's very first intercollegiate football game in 1893, compiling a 3–1 record. OAC won this game 34–0. (P4:467)

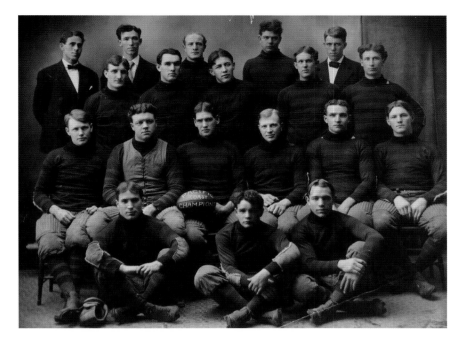

1907 football team portrait. The 1907 team achieved what few other collegiate teams ever have been able to do—it was undefeated, untied, and un-scored upon. The team was coached by Fred S. Norcross (back row, right), who had played at the University of Michigan under renowned coach Fielding Yost. Norcross coached the 1906 through 1908 teams, compiling an overall record of 14–4–3. Among the team's six victories in 1907 were wins over Willamette University (42–0), Pacific University (49–0), the University of Oregon (4–0), and west coast powerhouse St. Vincent College (10–0). OAC traveled for the first time to Los Angeles to play St. Vincent on Thanksgiving Day, and with the win, secured the Pacific Coast championship. (HC 1541)

"Ironmen" football team, 1933. The 1933 football team, coached by Lon Stiner, gained notoriety when it played nationally ranked Southern Cal to a 0–0 tie using just eleven players for the entire game. Twenty-five thousand fans saw this game, which was played in Portland's Multnomah Stadium on October 21. The players were (front row): Charles Woodrow "Woody" Joslin, Adolph Schwammel, Clyde Devine, William Tomsheck, Harry Field, Victor Curtin; (back row): Vernon Wedin, Harold Joslin, Norman "Red" Franklin, James "Pierre" Bowman, and Harold Pangle. (HC 22)

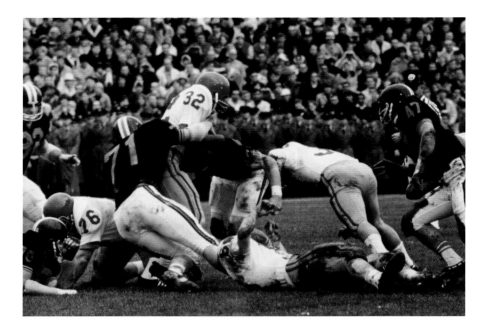

OSU's Jon Sandstrom (71) tackling Southern Cal's O.J. Simpson, November 11, 1967. OSU's 3–0 win in this game against the number-one Trojans, along with a previous win over then number-two Purdue and a tie against number-two UCLA a week earlier, earned the 1967 Beaver football team the moniker "Giant Killers." Oregon State finished the season with a record of 7–2–1 and ranked number seven in the Associated Press poll. (P3:5190a)

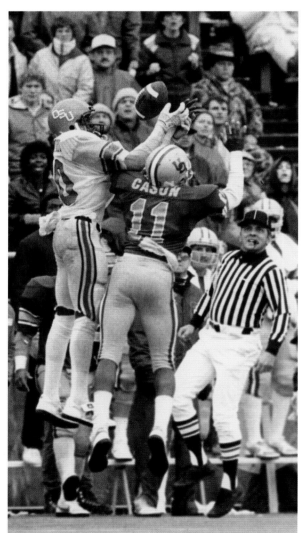

Reggie Bynum making a circus catch against the University of Oregon, November 1983. Despite Bynum's catch, the teams played to a 0–0 tie in what some dubbed the "Toilet Bowl." The game included eleven turnovers—five by the Beavers and six by the Ducks. The game was the first 0–0 tie between the teams since 1931, and the sixth in the history of the series. Despite OSU's lack of gridiron success as a team, Bynum led the nation in receiving yards per reception in 1983 at 24.2 yards. He was a ninth-round pick of the Buffalo Bills in the 1986 NFL draft. (P57:7729)

Ken Simonton scores against USC, September 30, 2000. Simonton rushed for 234 yards and three touchdowns against the number-seven Trojans in this 31–21 win for the Beavers. Simonton lead the Beavers to an 11–1 record that season, including a 41–9 win over Notre Dame in the Fiesta Bowl. Simonton is OSU's all-time leading rusher at 5,044 yards, which he accumulated in the 1998 through 2001 seasons. He played professionally in the NFL's European league and briefly in the NFL and Canadian Football League. T. J. Houshmandzadeh, right, played at OSU during the 1999 and 2000 seasons and later played professionally for many years with the Cincinnati Bengals. (P3, Accession 2005:064)

WOMEN'S BASKETBALL

Women's basketball at OAC actually got its start before organized competition began for men. The first women's game was played in 1898 (the first men's contest was in 1901). That first women's game bore little resemblance to modern-day basketball. The court was divided into three zones, each containing two players from each team. The divisions included areas for guards, centers, and forwards. A center jump was held after every basket and no player was allowed to leave her zone. Scores were low in that era—in 1914, for example, OAC beat Oregon in a 10–8 score.

By the 1930s, the philosophy about women's sports had changed. Competition, per se, was discouraged. On the other hand, mass participation via class instruction and intramurals was encouraged. That philosophy prevailed until the early 1970s, although women's basketball was organized as an extramural and club sport in the late 1950s. No school in the Northwest was quite as successful as Oregon State University. Competing against clubs from other schools, Oregon State teams went undefeated from 1959 to 1966.

Basketball became an intercollegiate sport for women in 1972, when the newly organized women's athletic department started competition as a charter member of the Association for Intercollegiate Athletics for Women (AIAW). Teams competed in the Northwest College Women's Sports Association (NCWSA), region 9 of the nine-division AIAW. Accurate records, however, were not kept in women's basketball until the 1976–77 season, when Mary Covington coached the Beavers. The women's program joined the Pac-10 Conference in the 1986–87 season and has remained a member ever since.

Since the 1976–77 season, OSU has made seven NCAA tournament appearances and nine Women's National Invitational Tournament (WNIT) appearances, winning WNIT titles in 1980 and 1982. Six players have earned All-American status since 1981. Coaches since 1977 have been Mary Covington (1977–78), Aki Hill (1979–95), Judy Spoelstra (1996–05), LaVonda Wagner (2006–10), and Scott Rueck (2010–present).

First women's basketball team, 1898. Coached by W. H. Beach (back row, left), a junior in mechanical engineering, the team played at least one game, against Chemawa. Players were Fanny Getty, second back; Dora Hodgins, second forward; Leona Smith, first back; Inez Fuller, first forward; Blanche Holden, goal thrower; Lillian Ranney, center; and Bessie Smith, captain and guard. F. W. Smith, also a junior in mechanical engineering, was the team manager. (P17:835)

Coach Aki Hill giving directions, 1980. Pictured
are players Jan Martin and Robyn Clark. Hill
coached seventeen seasons at Oregon State (1978–
79 to 1994–95), compiling a record of 274 wins
and 206 losses. In 1980 her team went 20–8 and
won the NIT championship; six of her teams had
twenty or more wins. Four of Hill's teams played
in the NCAA tournament. Both Martin and
Clark scored more than 1,000 points during their
careers at OSU. Clark is also in the OSU top ten in
career rebounds and steals. This photo appeared
in the March 1980 *Oregon Stater*. (P57:6484)

Carol Menken scoring against San Jose State, December 1979. Menken scored
34 points in the game and followed that up with a then-school-record 43 points
against Seattle University later in the season. Menken earned Kodak First Team
All-American status in 1981 and played on the Olympic gold medal winning 1984
United States women's basketball team. She played for OSU from 1979 to 1981 and
set several school records, some of which still stand. In eighty-one games played,
she is second all-time at OSU for scoring (2,243) and rebounding (901), first in
field goal percentage (.692), and leads in per game averages for both scoring (27.7)
and rebounding (12.5). Menken still holds OSU's single game scoring record, fifty-
one points against Alaska-Anchorage on February 7, 1980. (P57:6419)

Felicia Ragland playing against Loyola Marymount in the Preseason WNIT, November 2001. OSU opened its 2001–2002 season with a 65–58 win. Ragland received a Kodak All-American honorable mention honors in 2001 and 2002 and was the Pac-10 Player of the year in 2001. She led the Pac-10 in scoring in 2002 at 19.9 points per game. She was the first OSU player selected in the WNBA draft, taken as the twenty-eighth overall pick in 2002 by the Seattle Storm. This photo appeared in the 2002 *Beaver* yearbook. (P3, Accession 2005:064)

Tanja Kostic shooting a layup against Southern Cal, March 11, 1995. Kostic is one of the greatest women basketball players to have worn the Beaver uniform. She played at OSU from 1992 to 1996 and led the Beavers to three consecutive NCAA playoff appearances in 1994, 1995, and 1996. Kostic was twice named Pac-10 player of the year (1995 and 1996), was All-Conference all four years and was a consensus All-American in 1996. She was the Pac-10 player of the week on eight occasions, more than any other player. She was inducted into the OSU Athletic Hall of Fame in 2005. She is the current OSU recordholder for career points (2,349) and rebounds (1,001). After leaving OSU, Kostic played professionally in the ABL and WNBA as well as overseas. Photo by Travis Jansen. (P3, Accession 96:005)

Coach Scott Rueck advising point guard Sydney Weise, 2014. Rueck returned to OSU in 2010 to coach the women's basketball team after receiving his undergraduate degree in 1991. In 2013–14, his fourth season at OSU, he guided the Beavers to the second round of the NCAA tournament, the team's first appearance since 1996, and an overall 24–11 record. Rueck was named Pac-12 coach of the year by the league's media and ESPN. In 2011–12, Rueck's second season, the Beavers made it to the third round of the WNIT. Guard Sydney Weise's stellar play as a freshman in 2013–14 was one of the keys to the Beavers success that season. She was named to the All-Pac-12 team after making 112 three-point shots, second most in a season in conference history and best ever for a freshman. She was just the second OSU freshman to score more than five hundred points in a season. (Photo by Dave Nishitani, courtesy of OSU Athletic Communications)

A men's basketball team formed at OAC in 1901 and played its first intercollegiate game the next year. Unlike the football team, which crushed Albany College in its first game in 1893, the basketball team fared poorly in its first game, a 63–11 loss to Willamette University.

From the 1910s through the 1980s, Beaver basketball teams met with considerable success. The 1918 squad was undefeated with a 15–0 record. The 1981 squad, coached by Ralph Miller, was perhaps the best in OSU history. The team spent twenty-five weeks ranked as the top team in the country and entered the NCAA tournament with a 26–1 record. They were upset by Kansas State, 50–48, in the second round.

Two coaches account for most of OSU's wins and tournament appearances. Amory T. "Slats" Gill coached the Beavers from 1929 to 1964. His teams won 599 games, won nine conference titles, and made six NCAA tournament appearances, including the Final Four in 1949 and 1963. Ralph Miller came to OSU in 1971 and coached through 1989. He won 359 games and lost 186—a winning percentage of nearly 66 percent. His teams played in eight NCAA tournaments and made three National Invitational Tournament (NIT) appearances.

In total, Beaver basketball squads have played in sixteen NCAA tournaments, including two Final Four appearances. Four teams have played in the National Invitational Tournament, and four in the College Basketball Invitational. The 2009 squad coached by Craig Robinson[4] won the CBI tournament title.

Twenty-seven Beavers have been named All-Americans since 1916; five were named twice[5]. Since 1976, five players have been named Pac-8/10/12 player of the year, and OSU's coaches have been conference coach of the year four times. Ralph Miller was twice named National Coach of the Year. Four players have played on Olympic teams; one, Jose Ortiz, played on four teams (Puerto Rico, 1988, 1992, 1996, and 2004), and the other three won gold medals playing for the United States team. Two coaches (Gill and Miller) and one player (Gary Payton) have been named to the Naismith Memorial Basketball Hall of Fame. Twenty-four players have played in the NBA.

In addition to Gill and Miller, other OSU basketball coaches have included Bob Hager (1923–1928), Paul Valenti (1965–1970), Jimmy Anderson (1990–1995), Eddie Payne (1996–2000), Jay John (2003–2007), and Craig Robinson (2008–2014). Wayne Tinkle was named coach in 2014.

1907 men's basketball team displays its season record. This team won seventeen games and lost only one—in an end of the season series with the professional Chicago Crescents. Among the team's wins were home games against Albany College (74–0), Pacific University (73–2), and the University of Oregon (41–7). The team's schedule also included games against high schools and athletic clubs. The previous year's squad went undefeated with a 10–0 record. (HC 23)

1933 Pacific Coast Conference champions. This was the first Oregon State team to win a PCC basketball title under coach A. T. "Slats" Gill. The team was led by All-American Ed Lewis (center, wearing number twenty-five). The team went 12–4 in conference play and 21–6 overall. As the Northern Division champions, they played and defeated USC, the Southern Division winners, in a best of three games series to win the conference championship. Gill coached the Beavers for thirty-six years, compiling an overall record of 599 wins and 392 losses. OSU's team leadership award is named for Lewis. (HC 23)

Mel Counts shoots against Seattle University as Terry Baker (24) and Frank Peters (14) look on, February 1, 1963. OSU defeated the Redhawks 66–60, after losing to them in the season opener, 60–58. Counts played for OSU's varsity team from 1962 to 1964. OSU played in the NCAA tournament all three of Counts's years. The 1962 squad made to the western regional finals before falling to UCLA, and Counts led the 1963 team to a Final Four appearance. He was an All-American in 1963 and 1964, and as a senior, he averaged 26.7 points and 18.9 rebounds per game. Counts played on the gold medal-winning 1964 US Olympic team and spent twelve years in the NBA. Baker was recruited to play basketball at Oregon State but is better known for his football exploits; he won the 1962 Heisman Trophy. He also played baseball as a freshman. On the basketball court, Baker averaged 10.7 and 13.4 points per game during his junior and senior years. He was the captain of the 1963 team. Baker is the only college athlete to have ever won both the Heisman Trophy and played in an NCAA basketball tournament Final Four. (P195, Accession 89:019)

Coach Paul Valenti confers with center Ed Fredenberg, 1966. Valenti was connected with OSU athletics for more than seventy years. As an undergraduate, he played basketball at Oregon State from 1938 to 1942. He led his freshman team to a 16–0 record, and played on the 1940 and 1942 varsity teams that won PCC Northern Division titles. After serving in World War II, he returned to OSC in 1946. Valenti served as head basketball coach for the 1965 through 1970 seasons, succeeding Slats Gill, after serving as freshman coach and assistant varsity coach. His 1966 team made it to the NCAA tournament, and Valenti was named the United Press International's West Coast Coach of the Year. After stepping down as basketball coach, Valenti served as tennis coach from 1971 to 1975 and as assistant athletic director for many years. (P17:4355)

Coach Ralph Miller and the OSU bench, Far West Classic game against Indiana, 1973 Ralph Miller was one of the most successful basketball coaches in OSU and college basketball history. His OSU record was 359–186 (1971–1989), and his career collegiate record was 657–382. Miller's teams only had three losing seasons during his thirty-eight-season career. His OSU teams won four Pac-10 championships and played in the NCAA tournament eight times. Five of his teams were ranked in the top ten. Miller was National Coach of the Year in 1981 and 1982. He was inducted into the Naismith Memorial Basketball Hall of Fame (1988) and the OSU Sports Hall of Fame (1991). The Far West Classic was a holiday basketball tournament founded by Oregon State in 1956. It originally included four teams, and expanded to eight in 1959, adding the University of Oregon as a co-host. Starting in 1961, it was played in Portland's Memorial Coliseum, and in the 1970s was considered one of the top tournaments in college basketball. It moved to Portland's Rose Garden in 1995, but the tournament was dropped after 1996. OSU won the tournament twenty times during its forty-year history. (P57:6171)

OSU's Steve Ericksen blocks a shot by UCLA All-American Bill Walton, February 15, 1974. OSU defeated number-one ranked UCLA, 61–57, before 10,376 fans in Gill Coliseum. The win by the Beavers ended UCLA's conference winning streak of fifty games. This photo, taken by student photographer Chris Johns, appeared in the March 1974 *Oregon Stater*. Johns tied his camera to one of the basket supports behind the backboard in order to get the photo. (P57:4733)

Gary Payton in action against Washington, 1987. Payton, who played at OSU from 1986 to 1990 and started every game of his OSU career, was one of the greatest basketball players in OSU history. Among his honors were consensus All-American First Team (1990), Pac-12 Player of the Year (1990), *Sports Illustrated* Player of the Year (1990), Pac-12 Freshman of the Year (1987), Olympic gold medals for the United States team in the 1996 and 2000 games, and Naismith Memorial Basketball Hall of Fame (2013). He is the all-time leading scorer at OSU (2,172 points) and the Pac-12's all-time leader in assists (938) and steals (321). Professionally, he played most of his career with the Seattle Supersonics. (Photo by Dave Nishitani, courtesy of OSU Athletic Communications).

MEN'S TRACK AND FIELD, CROSS COUNTRY

OSU's history with intercollegiate competition in track and field began in June 1895 when several students participated in a collegiate field day meet at the State Fairgrounds in Salem. Other teams were from the University of Oregon, Willamette University, Pacific University, Pacific College, and the Oregon State Normal School (now Western Oregon University). OAC participated in the field day meet through at least 1900, placing third in 1896 and first in 1897. Track meets in the early twentieth century were with nearby opponents, such as the University of Oregon.

The team's first outstanding athlete was Forrest Smithson, who was a gold medal winner at the 1908 Olympics. Ten other OSU men's track and field athletes were members of Olympic teams, including 1968 high jump gold medal winner Dick Fosbury. Two held world records in their events. OSU has had sixteen individual NCAA champions and six NCAA top ten team finishes. The 1960 team took fourth place, and the 1969 team took third place, OSU's highest ranking.

W. O. Trine, OAC's physical education director, was the first regular track coach, leading the squad in 1906 and 1907. Berny Wagner, who coached track and cross country from 1966 to 1975, was the most successful, leading the team to four top ten finishes during his ten years. His dual meet record for his ten years was 49–24. Fifteen of his athletes won twenty-three All-American designations. In 1972 he was voted as a United States Track Coaches Association Coach of the Year, and was an assistant track coach for the 1976 US Olympic team.

Other coaches have included M. H. Butler (1920–1927), Grant Swan (1934–1951), Sam Bell (1959–1965), Steve Simmons (1976–1979), and Chuck McNeil (1984–1988).

Cross country became an intercollegiate sport in 1934. Under coach Sam Bell, Dale Story led the 1961 team to that year's national championship.

Both track and field and cross country were eliminated in 1988 for budgetary reasons. In recent years, football athletes have traveled with the re-established women's team to compete in selected track and field events. Football player Jordan Bishop was an All-American in the high jump in 2010.

E. W. Stimpson clears nine feet in the pole vault, May 15, 1897. This is one of the earliest photographs showing OAC track and field athletes in action. The meet took place at Oregon State's first athletic field, which was located on the south side of what today is lower campus. The Administration Building (Benton Hall) is on the left side of the photo. (HC 24)

Forrest Smithson and other runners competing in the high hurdles, 1905. Smithson (second from right) was Oregon State's first track and field star and Olympian. Smithson won the 110-meter hurdles at the 1908 Summer Olympics in London. He was also the AAU champion in the 120-yard hurdles in 1907 and 1909. (P128:1)

Lyle Dickey, Oregon State's first NCAA individual champion, 1952. Dickey won the pole vault at the NCAA Championships, clearing 13 feet, 9 inches. He won the PCC Northern Division title in 1951 and was the PCC co-champ in 1952. (P182:12)

Dale Story running at Bell Field, spring 1962. Story led the OSU cross-country team to the 1961 NCAA championship— OSU's first team national championship. He was also the individual medalist, defeating six future Olympians while running barefoot (his trademark style) in subfreezing conditions. Story also ran track as a long distance runner and earned All-American honors in the 3-mile run during the spring of 1962. This photo appeared in the April 1962 *Oregon Stater*. (P17:3834)

Cross-country track meet at Avery Park, fall of 1967. This meet, against the University of Oregon, was the first run on a new course at Corvallis's Avery Park. Although the UO edged out OSU in this meet, the Beavers went on to a tie for sixth place at the NCAA Finals. (P3:2794)

Hailu Ebba winning the 880 against the University of Washington, April 22, 1972. Ebba, one of OSU's best distance runners, ran the 880 and mile/1500 meters. He also ran for the cross-country team. Ebba was the conference champion in the mile from 1972 to 1974. He competed in the 1972 Olympics for Ethiopia and was also selected for the 1976 games. Ebba is perhaps best known for the 1500-meter race in 1972 in a meet between OSU and the University of Oregon, which pitted him against the UO's Steve Prefontaine. Today Ebba is a medical doctor at the Cedars-Sinai Center in Los Angeles, specializing in neuro and cardiothoracic anesthesiology. (P57:6207)

Track coach Berny Wagner and high jumpers Tom Woods and Joni Huntley, fall 1975. Wagner coached both OSU athletes at the Pan American games in Mexico City, where they both won gold medals. He coached at OSU from 1966 to 1975, compiling a dual meet record of 49–24. He led OSU to four top-six finishes at the NCAA Championships, where the 1969 squad finished second. Nine of his athletes won individual NCAA titles, and fifteen athletes won twenty-three All-American honors. Tom Woods was a four-time All-American in the high jump and captured the 1972 NCAA title. Huntley competed at OSU in 1975 and participated on two US Olympic teams. In the early 1970s OSU was called the "high jump capital of the world" by some sportswriters due to the success of Dick Fosbury, Woods, Huntley, and other Beaver high jumpers. (P57:5048)

WOMEN'S TRACK AND FIELD, CROSS COUNTRY

Women's intercollegiate track and field competition had its start in 1975, when OSU finished seventh at the AIAW national championship meet behind Joni Huntley's individual championships in the high and long jumps.

Will Stephens's coaching (he arrived at OSU in 1977) and athletes such as Kathy Weston and Cindy Greiner turned the women's track and field program into a national powerhouse before his death in 1982. During Stephens's tenure as coach, his athletes earned eight All-American designations and several regional championship titles. The 1979 two-mile relay team won the national championship in that event.

Eliminated in 1988 for budgetary reasons, the women's programs were reinstated in 2004, and since then the program has become competitive again, led by athletes such as Laura Carlyle. A new state-of-the-art facility, the Whyte Track and Field Center, opened in September 2012.

Coaches of the women's track and field and cross-country teams before the programs were eliminated in 1988 were Pat Ingram (1975), Mary Covington (1976), Marie Laird (1977), Will Stephens (1978–1982), Frank Morris (1983), and Chuck McNeil (1984–1988). Kelly Sullivan has coached both the women's track and field and cross-country teams since 2004.

Joni Huntley high jumping, 1975. Huntley competed for OSU in 1975. She competed for the United States team in the 1976 and 1984 Olympics and won the bronze medal in 1984. She was ranked the number-one female high jumper in the United States five times. She also served as an assistant track and field coach for OSU in 1981. (Photo courtesy of OSU Athletic Communications)

OSU women's cross country team running in Avery Park, fall 1977. The team included (from left) Kris Trom, Karen Brown, Julia Anderson, Janet Lovelace, and Jenny Bird. Lovelace placed fifth at the regionals in 1977 and twenty-sixth at the AIWA championships in 1978. (P57:5725)

OSU runner Kathy Weston, spring 1979. Weston, who had been named to the 1976 Olympic team, was a standout runner for OSU's track and field program in 1979 and 1980. Her outdoor specialties were the 400- and 800-meter runs, and she also ran on the 4 x 100 meter and 4 x 400 meter relay teams. She still owns the school records in all four events, as well as several indoor track and field records. Weston participated in the 1975 Pan American Games in Mexico City, where she took first in the 800 meters and second as a member of the 4 x 400 meter relay team. (P57:8951)

Laura Carlyle running in the Pac-12 track and field championships, May 2012. Since the revival of the OSU women's track and field program in 2004, Laura Carlyle has been one of the team's best distance runners. As of 2014, she held OSU team records in the 1,500- and 5,000-meter outdoor runs and the mile and 3,000-meter indoor runs. She was a three-time NCAA All-American: 2011, 5,000 meters (outdoor, placed twenty-fourth); 2012, mile (indoor, placed thirteenth); 2012, 1,500 meters (outdoor, placed twenty-second). (Photo courtesy of OSU Athletic Communications)

BASEBALL

Beginning in the 1890s, OAC periodically played baseball games at the intercollegiate level. But not until 1907 did baseball become a regular intercollegiate sport. Since that time it has been perhaps OSU's most successful intercollegiate sport, winning two national championships, twenty-four conference/division titles, and producing numerous All-Americans and several student-athletes who have gone on to play professionally.

For its first fifteen years, OAC's baseball teams had a new coach almost every year. Most met with success; one of the most notable was Fielder Jones, a former professional player and manager who took the 1910 team to the Northwest Collegiate Championship. In 1923 Ralph Coleman began one of the longest coaching tenures at Oregon State. From that year through 1966 he coached thirty-five seasons, winning 64 percent of his games and capturing ten conference/division titles. He coached the Beavers to their first College World Series appearance in 1952—the same year that OSC English faculty member Bernard Malamud published *The Natural*, considered by many to be the best baseball novel ever written.

Another long-serving coach was Jack Riley[6], who piloted OSU baseball from 1973 to 1994. Riley's teams won nearly 60 percent of their games and five Pac-8/10 Northern Division titles. Current coach Pat Casey has had considerable success, guiding the Beavers to three Pac-10/12 conference titles, four College World Series appearances, and two NCAA championships.

Since 1952 twenty-four Beaver players have won baseball All-American honors—five of them more than once. Pat Casey has twice earned national Coach of the Year honors. One player was a member of the United States' Olympic team. OSU consistently places multiple student-athletes on the Pac-12 All-Academic team. As of 2014, twenty-five Beavers have played in the major leagues, and scores of others have played in the minor leagues.

OSU baseball has been played in the same location since 1907. What is now Goss Stadium at Coleman Field is the oldest continuous collegiate ballpark in the United States. Since 1907 OSU has won 70 percent of its home games.

OAC indoor baseball team, 1900. Before 1907, when baseball was played consistently on the intercollegiate level at OAC, the college played baseball on an occasional basis. In 1899, the school began playing an indoor version of the game. In 1900, the indoor baseball team compiled a 3–1 record, which included wins over the University of Oregon, Albany College, and the Salem YMCA. Players included: Arthur Derby, ——Hamilton, Arthur Bier, ——Small, Ellwood Clark, Grant Elain, Raymond Henkle, Ruben Burgess, Harold Belt, and Jim Hartley. (P25:1352)

1910 baseball team. This team, which won OAC's first Northwest Championship, was coached by Fielder A. Jones (standing, right) and had a record of 13–4–1. Jones had a rich baseball pedigree, having played for Brooklyn and the Chicago White Sox in the major leagues and managed the White Sox to the 1906 World Series title over its cross-town rival, the Chicago Cubs. He started his professional career in 1891 with the Portland team in the Oregon State League. (P161:52)

Coach Ralph Coleman and pitcher Norb Wellman, 1954. Wellman pitched for the Beavers from 1952 through 1954 and was a starting pitcher on Oregon State's first College World Series team in 1952. He won one of the playoff games against Fresno State that put the Beavers in the series. Coleman was a 1918 alumnus of Oregon State and coached baseball from 1923 to 1928, 1930 to 1931, and 1938 to 1966. He compiled a career coaching record of 561 wins, 316 losses, and one tie. His teams won ten division or conference titles and played in three NCAA regional tournaments. This photo appeared on the cover of the 1954 OSC baseball press guide. (P7:73)

Wes Schulmerich playing for the Cincinnati Reds, 1934. Schulmerich was the first Beaver baseball player to play in the major leagues, breaking in with the Boston Braves in 1931. He was OAC's team captain in 1927 and led Oregon State to the Northern Division title that year. Schulmerich also played football and ran track at OAC. In addition to Boston, Schulmerich also played professionally for the Philadelphia Phillies, the Cincinnati Reds, and several minor league teams. He retired from baseball in 1941. (Photo courtesy of OSU Athletic Communications)

Jonah Nickerson pitching, 2005. Nickerson led the Beavers to the 2006 College World Series championship and was named the CWS Most Outstanding Player. He made three appearances in the 2006 CWS, allowing just four runs in just under twenty-two innings and winning two games. In the 2005 CWS, Nickerson won one game and lost one. He was a second team All-American in 2005 and 2006, and his 299 career strikeouts are an Oregon State record. (Photo courtesy of OSU Athletic Communications)

Coach Jack Riley confers with an umpire, ca. 1985. Riley coached OSU baseball from 1973 through 1994, compiling a record of 613–411–5. His teams won five Northern Division titles and made three NCAA Regional appearances. (P57, Accession 92:054)

Michael Conforto at bat, 2014. Conforto was among the best players in OSU baseball history. In three years he received more recognition than any other player, including Pac-12 Player of the Year (2013 and 2014) and All-American honors from 2012 to 2014, including consensus first team honors in 2014. He was selected by the New York Mets in the first round of the 2014 major league draft—the tenth player taken overall. (Photo by Scobel Wiggins, courtesy of OSU Athletic Communications)

GYMNASTICS

Women's gymnastics at OSU dates to 1962, when it was established as a club sport under the auspices of the Women's Recreation Association. In 1969 the club began competing at the intercollegiate level and was sanctioned as an official intercollegiate sport in 1972, competing in the Northwest Collegiate Women's Sports Association. The first athletic scholarship in gymnastics was given in 1977, and that year the program gained national prominence, winning eighteen of nineteen matches.

Gymnastics was designated as an NCAA sport in 1982, and in 1987 OSU's gymnastics team became part of the Pac-10 conference. Three years later, the program hosted the NCAA gymnastics national championship at Gill Coliseum in April 1990. Since then it has hosted the national championship meet in 1993 and 2006.

OSU's first All-American gymnast was Donna Southwick, who won her honors in 1977 on the uneven bars. Laurie Carter was OSU's first individual national champion, winning the balance beam in 1981. Joy Selig, one of OSU's most successful gymnasts, won three individual championships while at OSU (one in 1989 and two in 1990), and has won more first team All-American honors than any other OSU gymnast. Along with Selig, Chari Knight and Mandi Rodriguez have been seven-time All-Americans. Knight won All-American honors in all four events, as did Amy Durham (a five-time All-American). Makayla Stambaugh earned All-American honors all four years with the Beavers, 2010 to 2013.

Since 1975, OSU has won the NCAA regional championship ten times, and since 1987, has won the Pac-12 conference championship six times. OSU has participated in the NCAA championship meet twenty-four times since 1982; the highest finish was fourth in 1982 and 1991. OSU's gymnastics coaches have been Sylvia Moore (1967–1975), Ron Ludwig (1976–1985), Jim Turpin (1986–1997), and Tanya Chaplin (1998–present).

Sylvia Moore, 1980. Moore coached the gymnastics team from 1967 to 1975. She came to OSU as a faculty member in physical education in 1966. She served as director of women's athletics from 1975–1977 and 1980–1982. After the men's and women's intercollegiate athletics programs merged, Moore served as deputy athletic director from 1983 to 1985. When Dee Andros stepped down as athletic director in 1985, Moore was named interim director of intercollegiate athletics—she was the only woman to have held that post at OSU until July 2015, when Marianne Vydra, senior associate athletic director, was appointed interim director. (P170)

Mary Ayotte-Law competing in the floor exercise, January 1982. Ayotte-Law earned All-American status in 1981 (beam) and 1982 (floor and all-around). She was the second OSU gymnast to win a national championship, claiming the floor exercise title in 1982. Ayotte-Law also represented the United States in the 1981 World University Games in Romania, placing as the highest all-around gymnast. This photo appeared in the January 1982 *Oregon Stater*. (P57:6900)

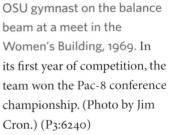

OSU gymnast on the balance beam at a meet in the Women's Building, 1969. In its first year of competition, the team won the Pac-8 conference championship. (Photo by Jim Cron.) (P3:6240)

Practice in the new Gladys Valley Gymnastics Center, fall 1992. In 1992 the gymnasium and armory building was restored and refurbished to serve as the new training facility for the women's gymnastics team. The building, which had served as the Mitchell Playhouse from the early 1950s to 1990, was repurposed to create a state-of-the-art training facility through a $700,000 grant from the Wayne and Gladys Valley Foundation. (P57, Accession 2006:046)

Chari Knight performing on the balance beam, 1993. Knight was a seven-time All-American and one of just two OSU gymnasts to earn those honors in all four events. She was also a two-time Pac-10 Gymnast of the Year, and eight times during her career at OSU she scored a perfect ten. This photo appeared in the 1993 *Beaver* yearbook. (P3, Accession 93:062)

Mandy Rodriguez completes a floor exercise routine against the University of Kentucky, March 19, 2010. Rodriguez, who competed for OSU from 2007 to 2010, was a seven-time All-American, including four first-team honors. She finished third nationally in the vault in 2010 and fifth in 2007. In 2009 Rodriguez claimed two first-team honors, on vault and the floor exercise. She was also a Pac-12 All-Conference selection all four years, including first-team honors each year from 2008 to 2010. She was also the conference's Gymnast of the Year in 2009. (Photo courtesy of OSU Athletic Communications)

WRESTLING

Wrestling at the intercollegiate level began in 1909 at OAC, and the sport has been one of the most successful at Oregon State through its ninety-four seasons.[7] OAC wrestled in two meets that first season, defeating Washington and Washington State. In 1926 the Beavers won the Amateur Athletic Union national title under coach and alumnus Robin Reed, himself an Olympic gold medalist in 1924.

At the end of the 2015 season, OSU had a cumulative dual meet record of 999 wins, 320 losses and 28 ties—third nationally in number of wins. Fifty teams have won conference titles through 2015. OSU has made regular appearances at the NCAA tournament since 1957, finishing in the top ten nineteen times and finishing at no. 2 in the nation twice (1973 and 1995).

OSU wrestlers have garnered ninety All-American designations since 1952, including twelve individual NCAA champions. John Witte was Oregon State's first All-American. Four wrestlers—Jess Lewis, Greg Strobel, Dan Hicks and Les Gutches—have won two individual titles each. Three wrestlers were named All-Americans four times—Larry Beilenberg (1974–1977), Howard Harris (1977–1980) and Babak Mohammedi (1991–1992 and 1994–1995). OSU has twice hosted the NCAA national championship meet—in 1961 and 1980. Eight wrestlers have participated in the Olympics. In 1924, Robin Reed won the gold and OAC teammate Chet Newton the silver. Reed defeated Newton in the finals.

OSU has had many outstanding wrestling coaches. Dale Thomas was the most successful and well-known. During his thirty-four seasons as coach (1957–1990), Thomas compiled a dual meet record of 616–168–13 and won twenty-two conference titles. Other coaches include James Arbuthnot (1911–1917 and 1920), with a 10–3–3 record and five conference titles; Jim Dixon (1934–1938 and 1952–1955), 23–7–4 record and one conference title; Joe Wells (1993–2006), 161–94–3 record and one conference title; and Jim Zalesky (2007–present), 111–41–2 record and six conference titles (through 2015).

Coach James Arbuthnot (right) and the 1911 OAC wrestling team. In Arbuthnot's first year as coach, the team competed in one meet at the University of Washington and was defeated by the Huskies. Arbuthnot's later teams met with considerable success, going undefeated in 1917 and 1920. His dog, seated in front, was the team's unofficial mascot. Arbuthnot also served as OAC's athletic director from 1906 to 1918. He later coached wrestling and tennis at the University of Washington. (P191:264)

OAC wrestler Robin Reed, ca. 1924. Reed came to OAC from Portland's Franklin High. Though his actual weight was close to 140 pounds, Reed often wrestled at 170 pounds. Reed won the Olympic gold at 135 pounds in Paris in 1924, pinning all his foes, including OAC teammate Chet Newton in the final. Legend has it that Reed wrestled against each of his United States teammates while sailing to Europe for the Olympics; he won every match and pinned all but the heavyweight. Reed also won two national amateur titles. Later, Reed coached the Beavers for two seasons; his teams dominated Pacific Coast competition and won the 1926 Amateur Athletic Union national championship in a meet held in Corvallis. (Text courtesy of OSU Athletic Communications' 2013 wrestling media guide.) (HC 51)

John Witte, Oregon State's first All-American wrestler, 1952. Witte finished second in the heavyweight division at the 1952 NCAA Championships as a freshman. He also played football, garnering All-American honors twice, and led the Beavers to the 1957 Rose Bowl game. (P17:935)

Jess Lewis wrestling against a University of Oregon opponent, ca. 1970. Lewis (top) was an All-American in 1968, 1969, and 1970. He won national titles in the heavyweight category in 1969 and 1970 and was a member of the 1968 Olympic team. Lewis also played football. He spent much of his career supervising the maintenance of OSU's numerous athletics facilities. (P3:1542)

Coach Dale Thomas, ca. 1970. Thomas was one of the most successful collegiate wrestling coaches. Thomas's OSU wrestling squads won 616 dual meets and twenty-two conference titles in thirty-four years. Thomas was the NCAA coach of the year in 1961 and 1970. (P57:6249)

Les Gutches (top) in action, 1994. Considered to be the best OSU wrester in modern history, Gutches won two NCAA titles and was a three-time Academic All-American. He was a member of the 1996 Olympic team and won the gold medal at the 1998 Goodwill Games. (P3, Accession 94:079)

VOLLEYBALL

Volleyball began as a women's intercollegiate sport at OSU in 1976. Nadine Nixon coached the team to a 16–14 record that year. Over the years, OSU's volleyball teams have been competitive, and many players have won all-conference designations for their play and for academics. One OSU volleyball player has been an Olympian; Selina Scoble (1996–1998) played on the Australian Olympic team in 2000. Rachel Rourke was named an All-American honorable mention in 2008. The Beavers have played in the 1983, 2001, and 2014 NCAA tournaments, making it to the "Sweet 16" round in 2014.

In addition to Nixon, who coached volleyball through 1977, other coaches include Rita Emery (1978–79), Gerry Gregory (1980–82), Jim Iams (1983–84), Tino Reyes (1985–86), Guy Enriques (1987–90), Dave Gantt (1991–92), Jeff Mozzochi (1993–98), Nancy Somera (1999–2004) and Taras "Terry" Lyskevych (2005–present).

Sandy Huntley spikes the ball, ca. 1981. Huntley, who played at OSU from 1979 to 1982, was one of OSU's first volleyball players to win post-season honors. She was named a Northwest Women's Volleyball League All-Star in 1981 and was named to the All-NORPAC second team in 1982. (P57:9153)

Shelly Smith in action, 1991. Smith played at OSU from 1991 to 1994. She was named to the All-Pac-10 Freshman Team in 1991 and to the All-Pac-10 first team in 1993. She also played basketball in 1994. (P3, Acc. 93:062)

Rowing (also known as crew) at OSU dates to 1926 when the University of California donated two regulation shells to OAC. The college started an interclass club the next year, and by 1929 was competing against other schools. The current dock facilities were first developed in 1950 when OSU purchased a large parcel of land on the east side of the Willamette River just across from downtown Corvallis. Crew became a varsity sport in 1967.

Since achieving varsity status, men's rowing has been a strong sport at OSU. The varsity 8 team has consistently finished in the top four at the Pacific Coast/Pac-10/12 championships since 1977. The 2002 varsity 8 placed a best-ever fourth at that year's Intercollegiate Rowing Association (IRA) national championships, and have placed in the IRA top twenty most years since 1995. Fourteen OSU rowers have been part of the US National Team, with three

participating in the Olympics and several winning medals in the World Championships, Pan American Games, and the Olympics.

OSU's rowers (men and women) have also garnered many academic awards, having placed multiple members on the Pac-12 All-Academic first team every year since 2002. Daniel Werner was named to the 2013 IRA All-Academic Team.

Head coaches have included J. P. Othis (1927–1931), Ed Stevens (1931–1949), Karl Drlica (1949–1985), Dave Emigh (1985–1994), Dave Reischman (1994–2002), Kjell Oswald (2002–2004), Fred Honebein (2004–2006), and Steve Todd (2006–2014). Gabe Winkler served as interim head coach for 2014–15. Oswald was named Pac-10 coach of the year in 2004 after guiding OSU to its second straight top-ten finish.

Oregon State rowing club members, ca. 1929. The club hosted its first intercollegiate meet in 1929 against the University of Washington. (P15)

237

Rowing team on the Willamette River, 1935. (HC 50)

Joey Hansen in action, ca. 2001. Hansen earned Pac-10 All-Conference first-team honors in 1999, 2000, and 2001, all three years that he rowed for Oregon State. Before coming to OSU, Hansen had never rowed. He was on the US National Team from 2001 to 2004 and was a member of the 2004 Olympic team, which won the gold medal at that year's games in Athens, Greece, in the Heavyweight 8 category. (Photo courtesy of OSU Athletic Communications)

OSU rowing team, 1976. Rob Zagunis (back row, left) led OSU to its first-ever event title at the 1975 National Intercollegiate Rowing Championships in the Varsity 4. He was the first OSU crew athlete to be named to the US National Team and was a member of the 1976 Olympic team. (P57:6311)

WOMEN'S ROWING

OSU women's rowing dates to 1952, when it was established as an intramural sport by men's coach Karl Drlica, making rowing one of the first collegiate sports programs to support women's participation. It became a club sport in 1966, and in 1970 was one of seven teams to compete at the intercollegiate level under the National Constitution for Women's Rowing. It became a recognized intercollegiate varsity sport at OSU in 1977. Since 1978, OSU's women rowers have placed four times at the NCAA Championships (ninth in 1997, thirteenth in 1999, fifteenth in 2000, and fifteenth in 2009).

Since 2001, eight women rowers have received Collegiate Rowing Coaches Association (CRCA) All-American recognition, and many more have been recognized by that organization for their academic achievements. Three rowers have been named to national teams, and one, Amy Martin, has been an Olympian.

Coaches of women's crew have been Karl Drlica (1952–1982), Dave Emigh (1983–1993), Charlie Owen (1994–2006) and Emily Ford (2006–present). Owen was the first official women's head coach; up to that time one coach served both the men's and women's programs.

Women's rowing team on the Willamette River, 1971. (P3:3888)

Julia White-Hoppe (left) at a meet, ca. 2004. White-Hoppe, who rowed for OSU from 2002 to 2004, was named a CRCA All-American in 2003 (first team) and 2004 (second team). She was also Pac-12 All-Conference first team both years, and OSU's Most Valuable Oarswoman in 2003. (Photo courtesy of OSU Athletic Communications)

Women's rowing practice, spring 1994. Team members (from left) Amy Martin, Kimberly White, Jen Lesko, and Karen Thompson practice for a seat on the women's Varsity 8. Martin was one of OSU's most successful rowers, garnering two first-team All-Pac-10 selections (1995 and 1996) and being named to the 2000 Olympic team. Martin led the Beavers to a ninth-place finish in the Varsity 8 at the 1997 NCAA Championships. She also participated in the 1997, 1998, and 1999 World Championships, earning a bronze medal in 1998 in the women's 2 and a silver medal in 1999 in the women's 8. White was named a US Rowing Association Scholar All-American in 1994. (P3, Accession 94:079)

MEN'S SOCCER

Soccer was established as a club sport for men in 1963, and became an intercollegiate sport at the NCAA level in 1988. The team played as an independent in 1988, was a member of the Northwest Colleges Soccer Conference (NCSC) from 1989 to 1991, played in the Mountain Pacific Sports Federation (MPSF) from 1992 to 1999, and joined the Pac-10 in 2000. The team's best Pac-10 finish was in 2003, when it finished second. The 2002, 2003, and 2014 teams made NCAA tournament appearances.

Three players have earned All-American honors—Alan Gordon in 2003, Danny Mwanga in 2009, and Khiry Shelton in 2014. Joe Zaher (2002) and Daniel Leach (2005) were freshman All-Americans. Zaher was also the Pac-12 freshman of the year, as were Robbie Findley (2003), Mwanga (2008), and Timmy Mueller (2014). OSU has consistently placed multiple players on the Pac-10/12 All-Academic team since it joined the conference in 2000. Twelve players were named in 2006.

Both the men's and women's soccer teams have played their home games at Lorenz Field since September 1996. Coaches have included Jimmy Conway (1988–1998), Dana Taylor (1999–2008) and Steve Simmons (2009–present). Conway was the NCSC (1990) and MPSF (1995) coach of the year.

Soccer team playing in Parker Stadium, 1970–71. This club team was coached by Tolley Lauretti. Its "A" squad played in the Oregon Intercollegiate Soccer Association. (P3:4913)

Rick Kempf moving the ball against Evergreen State, October 5, 1991. Kempf was one of OSU's first standout soccer players after the sport achieved varsity status in 1988. He played at OSU for the 1989 through 1991 seasons and again in 1993. Kempf's 17 goals and 35 total points in 1990 are OSU single season records, and his 31 career goals and 71 career points remain the second-best records at OSU. He holds the OSU career record for multi-goal games (8). Kempf was the Northwest Colleges Soccer Conference player of the year in 1990. This photo appeared in the 1992 *Beaver* yearbook. (P3, Accession 93:062)

Danny Mwanga playing against Cal, 2009. Mwanga played forward for OSU during the 2008 and 2009 seasons. He was an NSCAA and College Soccer News All-American in 2009, and in 2008 was the Pac-10 Freshman of the Year. He led OSU in goals (14) and points (30) in 2009. He was the first overall pick in the 2010 MLS SuperDraft and began playing professionally for the Philadelphia Union in March 2010. He played for the Portland Timbers in 2012. (Photo courtesy of OSU Athletic Communications)

WOMEN'S SOCCER

Women's soccer became an NCAA varsity sport at OSU in 1988, the same year that men's soccer began at the varsity level. Under coach Dave Oberbillig, OSU achieved a 13–7–1 record that first season, playing an independent schedule. The team joined the Northwest College Soccer Conference for the 1989 season and became part of the Pac-10 in 1993.

OSU women have enjoyed success on the soccer field, compiling winning records in 13 seasons and making appearances in four NCAA tournaments—in 1994 and in 2009 through 2011. The 2009 squad made it to the Sweet 16 before losing to Notre Dame, 1–0.

Two players, Val Williams (1995) and Colleen Boyd (2010) have earned All-American honors, and two others, Jodie Taylor (2004) and Jenna Richardson (2010), were named to freshman All-American first teams. Team members consistently are at the top of the conference in academics; since 1996 at least four women have been named to the Pac-10/12 All-Academic team, with a record fourteen members named in 2011.

In addition to Oberbillig (1988–1991), other women's soccer coaches include Tom Rowney (1992–1997), Steve Fennah (1998–2007), and Linus Rhode (2008–present).

Val Williams against the University of Washington, ca. 1995. Williams was OSU's first women's soccer player to be honored with All-American honors; she was third team NSCAA in 1995. She was also first team All-Pac-10 in 1995. In her two years playing for OSU, Williams set and still holds numerous single-season records, including points (47, in 1994); goals (19, in 1994); and game-winning goals (8, in 1994). (Photo courtesy of OSU Athletic Communications)

Jodie Taylor, ca. 2007. Taylor, who played for the Beavers from 2004 to 2007, is OSU's career record holder in several categories, including points (113), goals (47), game-winning goals (18), multi-goal games (10) and shots (269). She is OSU's most honored women's soccer player, having won numerous regional awards from Soccer Buzz, NSCAA, and *ESPN The Magazine*. She was a first team All-Pac-10 selection in all four of her years at OSU. (Photo courtesy of OSU Athletic Communications)

MEN'S GOLF

Golf began as a minor intercollegiate sport in the late 1920s and achieved major sport status in 1947. Except for 1963–64, the team has competed in the Pac-12 conference or its predecessors since at least the 1934–35 season.

OSU won the conference's Northern Division crown on four occasions—1950, 1966, 1967, and 1969. Bob Allard (1969), Scott Massingill (1971), and Alex Moore (2011) won conference tournament championships; Allard beat Stanford star and future pro great Tom Watson. OSU has placed nine times in the NCAA final rankings, finishing eleventh in 1958–59 and tying for twelfth in 2000–01. Six Beaver golfers have been named to All-American teams; Diego Velasquez was named to three All-American teams in 2010.

OSU has had numerous golf coaches, including Louis Baker (1948–49 to 1951–52), Jim Barratt (1952–53 to 1956–57 and 1961–62 to 1962–63), Perry Overstreet (1979–80 to 1984–85), Steve Altman (1991–92 to 1995–96), Mike Ketcham (1996–97 to 2000–01), Brian Watts (2001–02 to 2009–10) and Jon Reehorn (2010–11 to present). Overstreet was Pac-10 coach of the year in 1984.

Dick Yost, ca. 1950. The 1950 team captured the Northern Division title, led by Dick Yost who earned his second consecutive individual title. Yost also made three appearances in the NCAA tournament, highlighted by a first-round upset of future pro great Don January in 1951. (P17:891)

OSC golf team, 1930. The team had mixed success during the season, splitting matches with the University of Washington, losing both matches to the University of Oregon, and defeating a Corvallis Country Club team. The team was disqualified in the Pacific Coast Conference meet when one of the Beaver golfers picked up his ball from the course. (P17:905)

Scott Masingill putting, 1971. Masingill was a two-time NGCA All-American, named to the third team in 1971 and honorable mention in 1973. He was the PAC-8 individual champion in 1971. (P3:4956)

Diego Velasquez teeing off, ca. 2010. Velasquez, an international student from Bogotá, Colombia, enjoyed considerable success as a golfer at OSU from 2007 to 2010, starting all four years. As a senior in 2010 he garnered several first team All-American honors and won the Pac-10 Tom Hansen Conference Medal. He was also a Pac-10 All-Academic selection in 2009 and 2010. Velasquez's 2009–10 single season average of 70.31 per round is an OSU record. He led OSU to sixteenth place at the 2010 NCAA tournament, one of OSU's highest finishes in the event. After completing his eligibility, Velasquez turned pro in 2010. (Photo courtesy of OSU Athletic Communications)

WOMEN'S GOLF

OSU women began playing intercollegiate golf in 1975. Mary Covington was the team's first coach (1975–1978). Covington also served as coach of other women's sports, including basketball (1977–78), track and field (1976), and field hockey.

OSU has made the final NCAA rankings once; at the conclusion of the 1997–98 season, they were ranked sixteenth in the nation. Although OSU has had only one All-American (Kathleen Takaishi, 1998), OSU's women golfers are consistently named NGCA All-American Scholars and Pac-12 All-Academic selections.

OSU golf alumnus Risë Alexander took over coaching duties in 1990 and served until 2014. She had been the golf coach twice previously, 1978–79 and 1982–1984. Other coaches have included Forrest Gathercoal (1979–1982), Walter Kennick (1984–1988), and Sammie Chergo (2014–present).

OSU golfer Risë Alexander, June 1976. Alexander played at OSU from 1974 to 1977. She was twice an individual tournament winner, winning a three-way meet with Washington and Oregon in 1976 and a dual meet against Oregon in 1977. She was one of the longest-serving coaches at OSU. (P57:5198a)

Kathleen Takaishi drives the ball, ca. 1999. Takaishi played varsity golf at OSU from 1995 to 1996 and 1998 to 1999. She was named an All-American in 1998. (Photo by Steve Shields, courtesy of OSU Athletic Communications)

Jessi Gebhardt in action, ca. 2008. Gebhardt golfed for OSU from 2005 to 2008. She was an All-Pac-12 honorable mention in 2007. From 2006 to 2008 Gebhardt was both an NGCA All-American Scholar and Pac-10 All-Academic selection. Gebhardt turned pro in 2009, playing in the LPGA Futures Tour in 2010 and 2011, and has recently played in the Cactus and Symetra tours. (Photo courtesy of OSU Athletic Communications)

WOMEN'S SWIMMING

Women's swimming was formally established as an inter-collegiate sport in 1974, after being a club sport for many years. OAC women had competed in swimming against the University of Oregon as early as 1918. Bob Maestre was the first of several coaches to lead the women swimmers. Other coaches have included Bob Yamate (1979–1982), Julie Saunders (1990–1996), Mariusz Podkoscielny (1997–2003), and Larry Liebowitz (2004–present).

In its early years, the program competed in AIAW Region 9 and was one of the conference powers from 1979 to 1984, finishing no worse than third each year. Since 1987, OSU has competed in the Pac-12. OSU has placed eleven times at the NCAA championship meet, with 2004 being its best showing at twentieth place.

Eight swimmers have been All-Americans. Amy Van Loben Sels was the first, winning honors in the 50-yard freestyle in 1994 and 1995. Birte Steven was a seven-time All-American from 2001 to 2004, and Saori Haraguchi is OSU's most honored All-American, garnering that status ten times in five different events from 2007 to 2009. In 2008 she placed first in the 200 butterfly at the NCAA championships. OSU's 2007 swim team included four All-Americans; in addition to Haraguchi, they were Kayla Rawlings, Brittney Iverson, and Anna Crandall, all of whom competed in the 800 freestyle relay.

Birte Steven, 2004. Steven, from Hannover, Germany, swam for OSU from 2001 to 2004, earning All-American honors seven times. She qualified for the NCAA Championships all four years, placing second in the 200-meter breaststroke and third in the 100-meter breaststroke in 2004. (Photo courtesy of OSU Athletic Communications)

Saori Haraguchi, ca. 2009. Haraguchi has been OSU's most successful swimmer, earning ten All-American designations from 2007 to 2009. She holds all the OSU records in the butterfly and individual medley events and is in the top five in several others. She was the individual champion in the 200-meter butterfly at the 2008 NCAA Championships. (Photo courtesy of OSU Athletic Communications)

SOFTBALL

Like many other women's sports at OSU, softball was established as an intercollegiate sport in the mid-1970s. The program's first season was 1975, and coach Diane Thompson guided the team to an 8–6 record. Softball became a Pac-10 conference sport in 1987.

The team has played in the post-season eleven times.[8] Its first post-season appearance was in 1977, and the first NCAA appearance was in 1999, when the team was led by All-American Tarrah Beyster. In 2006 the team made its first NCAA College World Series appearance. The team plays its home games at the OSU softball complex, which opened in April 2001. In the grand opening game, OSU defeated number-one-ranked UCLA, 2–1.

Erin Capps was the program's first All-American, named to the second team in 1983. Beyster, who played from 1997–2000, has been the program's marquee player. She was an All-American all four years, including a first team designation in 2000. She was also a two-time Pac-10 All-Academic selection. During her career at OSU, Beyster posted a .381 career batting average, hit 52 home runs, recorded an NCAA record 211 walks, won 91 games as a pitcher, and had an earned run average of 1.72. Her jersey, #00, was retired in 2001 in recognition of her accomplishments. Brianne McGowan and Cambria Miranda are more recent OSU All-Americans. McGowan earned honors in 2005 (first team) and 2006 (third team), and Miranda in 2006 (first team) and 2007 (second team).

OSU's softball coaches include Diane Thompson (1975–1976), Rayne Brooks (1977), Rita Emery (1978–1980), Ellen Margolis (1981–1985), Carol Browning (1986–1988), Vickie Dugan (1989–1994), Kirk Walker (1995–2012) and Laura Berg (2013–present).

Erin Capps at bat, ca. 1983. Capps played at OSU from 1982 to 1985. She was OSU's first softball All-American, named to the second team in 1983. That year she led the Beavers to a 9–2 NorPac conference record and a 26–14 overall record. (P57:7522)

Tarrah Beyster pitching against the University of Washington, May 2, 1998. Beyster has been OSU's greatest softball player, being named an All-American all four of her years at OSU (1997 to 2000), including first team in her senior year. She is in the top five in many statistical categories at OSU, including first in complete games (104), innings pitched (949), batting average (.381), home runs (52), and runs batted in (143). (Photo by Brian Bubak, courtesy of OSU Athletic Communications)

Brianne McGowan about to deliver a pitch against the California Bears, March 2007. McGowan played for OSU from 2004 to 2007 and is considered to be the best pitcher in OSU softball history. She holds the OSU career record for wins (100), saves (13), strikeouts (852), and complete game shutouts (36). She was an All-American in 2005 (first team) and 2006 (third team). She was also the Pac-10's Pitcher of the Year in 2005 and that year led OSU to a share of the Pac-10 title. In 2006 she helped the Beavers to their first appearance in the NCAA Women's College World Series. (Photo courtesy of OSU Athletic Communications)

TENNIS

Varsity tennis dates to 1908 at Oregon State, although it had been played recreationally and between classes as early as 1890. A women's team played against the University of California Berkeley in 1914 and the University of Oregon in 1915.

Tennis became a regular sport in 1921 when professor of veterinary medicine B. T. Simms began coaching the men's team, a position he held until 1937. OSC won the 1937 PCC Northern Division title, with Claude Hockley winning the singles championship. Bill McKalip was the coach from 1938 to 1942. Irwin Harris coached the team from 1943 until 1962, developing it into a west coast powerhouse. Don Megale coached from 1962 through 1970, and his 1966 and 1967 teams were the Pac-8 Northern Division champions. Former basketball coach Paul Valenti coached the team from 1971 through the 1975 season, when the program was eliminated due to budget cuts. His 1973 team went 15–0 in dual meets.

Tennis became an intercollegiate sport for women in the mid-1970s but was eliminated in 1984. The 1982 team took second place at the conference regional tournament. Coaches were Patty Nevue (1978–1982) and Don Megale (1983–1984).

Tennis team with coach B. T. Simms, 1928. At that time the tennis courts were located in the northeast corner of the Memorial Union quad. Simms is in the center of the photograph, and team captain George Speros is on the left. The 1932 squad went 3–2, defeating Willamette University twice and Reed College once, but losing twice to the University of Oregon. The Home Economics Building (Milam Hall) is in the background. Photo by Ball Studio. (P17:989)

Mary Govaars, 1976. Govaars was a junior and the team's co-captain in 1976. She was the team's number-one-rated singles and doubles player. (P57:5094)

Greg Bryan dives into the pool, 1969. Bryan was a junior college All-American diver prior to coming to OSU. Bryan participated in the 1969 NCAA Championships. Men's intercollegiate swimming and diving began in 1922 and was eliminated in the mid-1970s. (P3:6188)

OSC polo team, 1937. Polo began at OAC in 1923; the first match was against Stanford on October 20. OAC won 10–4, but lost their next two matches. Polo was formally organized as a club sport in 1924, and Arizona and Stanford were common opponents in the sport's initial years. ROTC cavalry horses were used at first; later horses were kept and trained specifically for polo. The sport died out by World War II, though a new polo club was established in 1996. (HC 1035)

OSC boxer Don Hawkins, ca. 1942.
Don Hawkins captured the Pacific Coast middleweight championship in 1942. Oregon State's venture into boxing as an intercollegiate sport was short-lived but met with some success. With Jim Dixon as coach, it began in 1937 as a minor sport and was elevated to a varsity sport the next year. It was suspended as a sport at the end of 1942 due to the outbreak of World War II and was not resumed after the war ended. (P17:1033)

OSU field hockey team in action, 1967. Field hockey was one of the few intercollegiate sports available to women at OSU prior to the passage of Title IX. OSU women began playing intercollegiate field hockey as early as 1938, and in the mid-1970s it became a varsity sport. In this photo OSU player Linda Sims (front left) works against an unidentified opponent. During the 1967 season OSU compiled a record of eight wins, two losses, and one tie, which included two wins over the University of Oregon. Field hockey was eliminated as an intercollegiate sport in about 1978. (P3:1526)

Rugby scrum, 1969. OSU has a long and successful history of rugby as a club sport, a status it gained in 1961. OSU has won several Pacific Northwest Rugby Union Collegiate Conference championships, including seventeen between 1981 and 2005. The club is supported in part by an endowment established by Wayne and Gladys Valley in memory of their son, an OSU varsity athlete who also played rugby and was tragically killed in 1969. This photo by John Robbins appeared in the 1969 *Beaver* yearbook. (P3:6178)

OAC cadets drilling in front of Agriculture Hall (Furman Hall), 1905. Military drill was part of the cadets' daily routine. During inclement weather, cadets drilled on the main floor of the Gymnasium and Armory (upper left). (P126:12)

The West Point of the West

10

A major provision of the 1862 Morrill Act was the teaching of military tactics at all land-grant institutions, to fill the need for trained officers required by the Union Army during the Civil War. The Oregon legislature permanently adopted Corvallis College as the state's land-grant institution in 1870, and soon after he assumed the college's presidency in 1872, President Benjamin Arnold established a cadet corps. Under his leadership, all "State"[1] male students would be required to join the cadet corps and receive training in military science and tactics. Initially this consisted of daily military drill. Arnold was no stranger to the military—during the Civil War he had served in the Confederate Army under Robert E. Lee.

The US War Department appointed Captain Benjamin D. Boswell professor of military science and tactics at Corvallis College in 1873. Boswell had some difficulties with the assignment; he stated in the 1874 college biennial report that though there were sixty-four students enrolled in military science and tactics, the average daily attendance was only fifteen cadets. Boswell attributed this to three major factors:

- There is no room attached to the College suitable for drilling.
- There are no books on Military Science and Tactics to be had in this city.
- The majority of the students in my Department are the sons of farmers; hence, they are withdrawn from school during the seed time and harvest, which embraces the greater portion of the scholastic year suitable for military drill out of doors.

Boswell also recommended the "enforcement of some prescribed uniform for cadets," as that would "greatly advance the interests of the State Agricultural College."[2] Boswell served until 1876, at which time Arnold resumed the position of commandant until 1884.

By the late 1880s, the college farm served as a training and parade ground for the cadet corps. A combination armory and gymnasium was built on the campus grounds in 1898, with the lower level providing storage for firearms and munitions. The Spanish American War was the first war in which cadets from the college served. A number of them fought in the Second Regiment, Oregon Volunteer Infantry, at the Battle of Manila in August 1898.

As the college's enrollment grew, the cadet corps saw a proportional increase in its numbers, as military training was required of all male students. By the end of the first decade of the twentieth century, the 1898 armory was inadequate, and plans were made for a more substantial home for the cadet corps. The push for new facilities was spearheaded by Capt. Ulysses Grant McAlexander, who was appointed commandant at OAC in 1908. A new armory fit with President William Jasper Kerr's vision for the campus and John Olmsted's 1909 campus plan. The college called on architect John V. Bennes, who had designed several other campus buildings and was quickly establishing himself as the college's go-to architect, to design an appropriate facility. The result was a massive fortress-like building with a large covered arena—one of the largest armories in the country.

McAlexander served as commandant from 1908 to 1911 and from 1913 to 1915. He ensured that the cadet

253

corps maintained a strong public presence by regularly performing in parades and drill exhibitions. The corps spent several days at the Alaska-Yukon-Pacific Exposition in Seattle in June 1909, camping on the grounds of the University of Washington. Closer to home, the cadets marched in Rose Festival parades in Portland and parades in Corvallis. McAlexander was greatly admired by OAC students, and they dedicated the 1912 *Orange* yearbook to him. The armory that he had pushed for was dedicated to him, and in 1971 it was renamed McAlexander Fieldhouse. McAlexander later served with distinction in World War I; his actions in July 1918 at the Second Battle of the Marne in France earned him the nickname "Rock of the Marne."

According to the OAC biennial report for 1918–1920, World War I had a significant impact on OAC, like other land-grant institutions, "to such an extent as to be a dominant interest even before the declaration of war and long after the signing of the Armistice." With the United States entering the war in Europe in April 1917, the importance of OAC's military training grew. Students Army Training Corps (SATC) units were authorized at colleges and universities by the US secretary of war, utilizing the facilities, equipment, and faculty of those institutions to select and train officer candidates and provide technical and vocational training. The unit at OAC was formed in August 1918 and included officer trainees as well as draftees to be trained as toolmakers, foundrymen, machinists, auto mechanics, and radio operators. Nearly 1,600 men participated in OAC's SATC unit.[3] In all, 1,931 OAC students, alumni, and faculty served in the armed forces during World War I; 2 faculty and 62 alumni and students died while serving their country in the war, either because of military action, illness, or accidents.

In 1917 the nature of the cadet corps changed when OAC's Department of Military Sciences assumed responsibility for military training under the National Defense Act of 1916. This act expanded and standardized the training of army officers at colleges and universities and established the Reserve Officer Training Corps. ROTC was established at OAC on February 1, 1917. It was temporarily suspended in 1918 with the implementation of the SATC, but resumed shortly after the war in Europe ended. In the 1920s, OAC's ROTC program included an artillery, motor transport, signal corps, and radio training units, in addition to a traditional horse cavalry unit. OAC's ROTC program included many cadets with superb horsemanship skills; they won many awards and also formed a strong polo team in the 1920s and 1930s.

Beginning in the 1910s and over the next three decades, OAC was regularly designated a "distinguished institution" by the federal government, a designation given to land-grant colleges that maintained efficient military departments. Graduates of these institutions could receive commissions as 2nd lieutenants in the regular army without further examination (beyond the physical required of all army inductees). The designation positioned Oregon State to supply the Army with many qualified officers leading up the United States' entrance into World War II. In 1941 alone Oregon State commissioned 110 officers. Oregon State had became known as the "West Point of the West" during the 1920s because it commissioned more officers than any other non-military academy in the United States, and this trend continued into the World War II years.

In addition to the many officers commissioned through its ROTC program, Oregon State contributed to the war effort in other ways. It was selected as a host institution for a unit of the Army Specialized Training Program (ASTP) in March 1943. The ASTP provided training for high-grade technicians and specialists needed by the Army. The trainees were regular Army personnel identified as potential candidates for training in engineering, chemistry, foreign languages, and other areas. Instruction at Oregon State was provided by regular faculty; OSC dean of administration, E. B. Lemon, coordinated the college's ASTP program. The men lived in Snell (now Ballard) and Waldo halls during their time at Oregon State, resulting in women students being housed in fraternity houses and other improvised housing. The ASTP ended in December 1945; more than 3,000 soldier students participated in Oregon State's ASTP unit.

More than 8,500 Oregon State students and alumni served in the armed forces during World War II. Nearly one hundred faculty were granted leaves of absence for military service and others resigned to join the military. At least 275 Oregon Staters died in the war, and many served with distinction. Marion Carl (class of 1938) and Rex T. Barber (class of 1941) were fighter pilots who achieved "ace" status.

Barber was credited with shooting down a plane carrying Japanese Admiral Isokuru Yamamoto in 1943, an action for which he was awarded the Navy Cross. Barber later served as commander of one of the military's first fighter jet squadrons and retired in 1961 as a colonel. Carl served in the Marine Corps and became its first-ever ace, being credited with 18.5 victories. After the war, he served as a test pilot, setting speed and altitude records, and later flew combat missions in Vietnam. He retired from the Marines as a major general.[4]

The college's 1946 biennial report provided a fitting summary of Oregon Staters' service in World War II:

> An adequate account of the achievement of the many thousands of Oregon State men and women in World War II is impossible. They won honor in every zone of occupation or combat. They served in North Africa, the Aleutians, Belgium, the Bulge, Burma, Guam, India, Italy; at Bougainville, Corregidor, Iwo Jima, Leyte, Luzon, in the Marianas, the Marshalls, New Guinea, Normandy, the Solomons; at Mindanoa, Okinawa, Saipan, St. Lo, Shimusha, Tarawa.

Oregon State had many connections to Camp Adair, a massive 60,000-acre army cantonment and training facility established just north of Corvallis in 1942. Several engineering faculty served as consultants on the construction of the facility. OSC sports teams competed against teams of Camp Adair soldiers, and the college provided the camp's personnel with free tickets to OSC athletic events. Alumnus and future Oregon governor Douglas McKay, who had served in Europe during World War I, commanded the camp's artillery training unit and also served as a public information officer.

Oregon State's ROTC programs expanded in the years immediately after World War II. A Naval ROTC unit was established in 1946 and moved its armory into Quonset huts that had been part of the World War II–era Central Hall/Hudson Hall complex. An Army Air Corps training branch was also added in 1946

and graduated its first unit in March 1948. That branch became an Air Force ROTC unit in 1949; Detachment 685 is known today as the Flying Beavs.

The nature of ROTC changed across the country during the 1960s and 1970s. In 1962, participation requirements for qualified males were changed from a mandatory two years to voluntary service. Under the federal ROTC Vitalization Act of 1964, OSU established both two- and four-year programs. OSU's ROTC units were all coeducational by 1973. In the fall of 1964, a freshman became OSU's first female cadet, and a female student had been allowed to take Naval ROTC classes as early as 1958. One particularly noteworthy female ROTC alumnus is Major General Julie Bentz, a 1986 OSU graduate. She was the first female officer from the Oregon Army National Guard to achieve the rank of general and served as a presidential advisor on national security matters. She was inducted into OSU's Engineering Hall of Fame in 2012.

In response to the war in Vietnam, the Army ROTC established the Raiders, a detachment trained in counter-guerilla techniques. That group won a marksmanship trophy in competition with thirty-nine other schools, continuing OSU's long tradition of excellence in that area.

Graduates of OSU's ROTC programs have served in all of the armed conflicts in recent years, including Vietnam, Operation Desert Storm, Iraq and Afghanistan. John Holcomb, who attended OSU in the mid 1960s and died in combat in Vietnam in 1968, won the Congressional Medal of Honor posthumously for bravery. Holcomb was OSU's second medal-of-honor winner—alumnus and later Memorial Union general manager Ed Allworth received the honor in 1917.

Today, OSU is one of just thirty-three universities in the United States that offer ROTC training in all of the major branches of the military. The units focus on leadership development "so as to assume the highest responsibilities of command, citizenship and government." They continue OSU's proud tradition of being "the West Point of the West."

Oregon Agricultural College Cadet Companies A and B next to the Administration Building, 1889. This is one of the earliest photographs showing cadets on the grounds of the college farm. The cadets are in formation near the south entrance of the Administration Building (Benton Hall). The cadets wore gray uniforms and traditional nineteenth-century campaign hats; the uniform had been approved by the board of regents in October of 1888. The cadet officer in front of the company on the left is E. E. "Eddy" Wilson (class of 1889), who later became a prominent Corvallis lawyer and businessman and served for many years on the college's board of regents. (HC 85)

OAC commandant and cadet officers, 1892. The commandant (center) was likely Captain Charles E. Warren (Ret.), who served from January to July 1892. The college catalog for that year described the uniforms:

> A neat uniform of cadet grey, suitable for all occasions, is required to be worn by male students during school hours. At the reasonable price at which the College is able to obtain it by contract, it makes an extremely economical dress. The cost of the entire suit—coat, pants, vest, and cap, is about $16.

President Bloss replaced the gray uniforms with blue ones later that year. (P25:2637)

OAC cadets in box formation with rifles ready, May 1895. The cadet battalion is in the box formation on the parade grounds (lower campus today). The large building in the background is a carriage and wagon factory, a short-lived manufacturing venture. (P2:383)

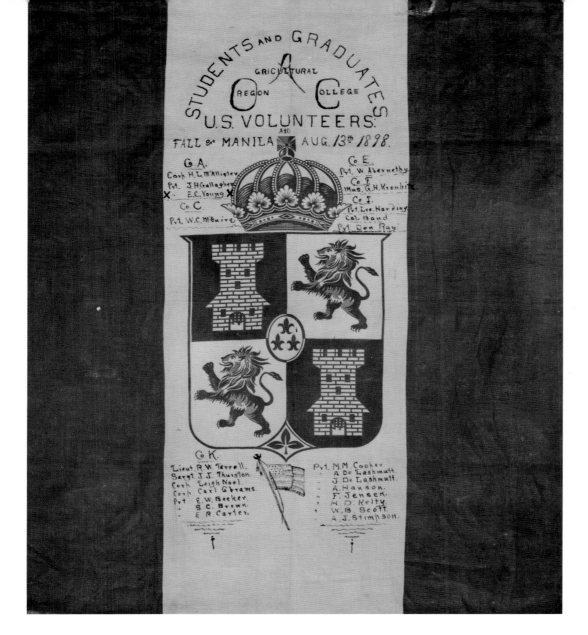

Spanish War flag with the names of OAC alumni who fought at the Battle of Manila in August 1898. The flag, which lists all of the OAC alumni who served with the 2nd Regiment, Oregon Volunteer Infantry, was presented to Oregon State by alumnus John H. Gallagher (class of 1900) in 1949. Gallagher served in Co. A., 2nd Regiment of the Oregon Volunteer Infantry. Private E. C. Young was the only OAC alumnus who died as a result of the battle. (HC 2319)

OAC cadets marching in a parade in Portland. This is most likely a parade on May 21, 1903, in honor of President Teddy Roosevelt's visit to the city. The *Morning Oregonian* newspaper described the parade as "the most noteworthy in Portland's history. Bands of music played thrilling marches and delightful measures. Soldiers trod as if for martial purposes." Seventy-five thousand people lined the streets of downtown Portland to see the president and watch the parade. The parade ended in City (Washington) Park, where Roosevelt participated in a cornerstone-laying ceremony for a statue honoring the Lewis and Clark Expedition. (P126:1)

259

OAC cadets in camp at the Alaska-Yukon-Pacific Exposition in Seattle, June 5–9, 1909.
Commandant of Cadets Ulysses Grant McAlexander arranged this trip, during which the cadets
camped on the grounds of the University of Washington and participated in drills and parades.
OAC's cadets also participated in the 1915 Panama Pacific Exposition in San Francisco. (P224)

O.A.C. Cadets
Forming the Human
O.A.C. at Portland
Rose Festival, 6/8/11.
OAC's cadet corps
regularly participated
in drills and parades
in Portland, Corvallis,
and other locations.
This photo was
taken at Portland's
Multnomah Field;
today it is known as
Providence Park.
(HC 85)

Armaments room in the new Armory, ca. 1911. The Armory could accommodate arms and munitions for up to a thousand cadets. (P16:869)

OAC men with the 3rd Oregon Infantry on the Mexican border, summer of 1916. After the outbreak of war in Europe in 1914 but before it officially became involved in that conflict, the United States dealt with the effects of armed rebellion in Mexico. The revolutionary Pancho Villa crossed into United States territory and attacked the town of Columbus, New Mexico, on March 9, 1916. In response, the United States sent a detachment of 4,800 troops under General John Pershing into Mexico to chase and capture Villa in retribution. Pershing and his troops spent the next few months tracking Villa, to no avail. Toward the end of Pershing's campaign in June 1916, President Woodrow Wilson ordered several National Guard units from around the country to protect the border and as a show of force. The 3rd Oregon Infantry was one of the units that made up the 110,000-soldier National Guard contingent on the border. (HC 1650)

THE STUDENTS ARMY TRAINING CORPS

The Students Army Training Corps (SATC), authorized nationally by the US Secretary of War during the summer of 1918, was formally established at Oregon Agricultural College on October 1, 1918. According to the US Secretary of War, the SATC was designed to "provide for the very important needs of the army for highly trained men as officers, engineers, doctors, chemists, and administrators of every kind ... Its object is to prevent the premature enlistment for active service of those men who could by extending the period of their collegiate training multiply manifold their value to the country."

The program, informally known as the "Saturday Afternoon Tea Club," consisted of two sections. Section A participants were regular collegiate students. Section B section participants, who did not meet collegiate entrance requirements, received vocational training to be toolmakers, foundry workers, machinists, auto mechanics, and radio operators.

OAC's SATC unit existed for just a few short months. The program was demobilized at OAC on December 21, 1918. Regardless, OAC's SATC trained nearly 1,600 soldiers—931 Section A participants; 105 in a naval unit; and 529 Section B participants.

SATC cadets watch a boxing match in the Armory, 1918. Recreational opportunities were an important part of the SATC program. (P25:2939)

SATC radio training, 1918. Radio training was a component of the SATC's Section B. (P2:289)

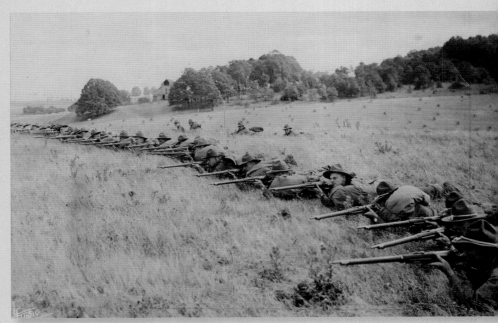

SATC field maneuvers and mock battle west of Corvallis, 1918. Today this location is part of the Bald Hill Natural Area. (HC 1050)

ULYSSES GRANT McALEXANDER, THE "ROCK OF THE MARNE"

Ulysses Grant McAlexander (1864–1936) was an 1887 West Point graduate who served at Fort Meade in the Dakota Territory and Fort Custer and Fort Missoula in Montana. He fought in Cuba during the Spanish-American War and served in the Philippines from 1900 to 1907.

In 1907 McAlexander was appointed commandant of cadets and professor of military science and tactics at Oregon Agricultural College. He served in that role from 1907 to 1911 and from 1915 to 1916. He was greatly admired by the students, and the 1912 *Orange* was dedicated to him. The armory, built in 1911, was also dedicated to him and in 1971 was renamed the McAlexander Fieldhouse.

During World War I, Colonel McAlexander commanded troops on the front lines of battle in Europe. In July 1918, he led the 38th US Infantry against German forces at the Battle of the Marne, which proved to be a turning point in the war. Although outnumbered and attacked from three sides, his troops held their position and the Germans were forced to retreat. He earned the nickname "Rock of the Marne" for his actions and was promoted to brigadier general. He was also highly decorated for his leadership during the war, including the Italian La Croce al Merito di Guerra (1919) and the French Croix de Guerre (1924).

McAlexander served in the US Army until retiring to Newport, Oregon, in 1924. Oregon State conferred an honorary doctorate on McAlexander in 1930, and he was an unsuccessful candidate in the 1934 Republican gubernatorial primary election.

Brigadier General McAlexander in France, 1918. After his success at the Battle of the Marne, McAlexander was promoted to temporary brigadier general and given command of a brigade in the 90th Infantry Division, which he led in the St. Mihiel and Meuse-Argonne operations and also commanded in occupied Germany until June 1919. US Army Signal Corps photograph. (P2:431)

Gen. McAlexander poses for a bust by renowned sculptor Pompeo Coppini, ca. 1930. The completed bust of Major General U. G. McAlexander, US Army Retired, was awarded the Grand Prize and Gold Medal at the Balogne, Italy, exhibition in 1931. Today the bust is on display in McAlexander Fieldhouse. (P17:4729)

Brigadier General Ulysses Grant McAlexander in Bernkastel-Cues, Germany, ca. 1924. McAlexander returned to Europe several times after the end of World War I and was twice presented with commendations. (P2:430)

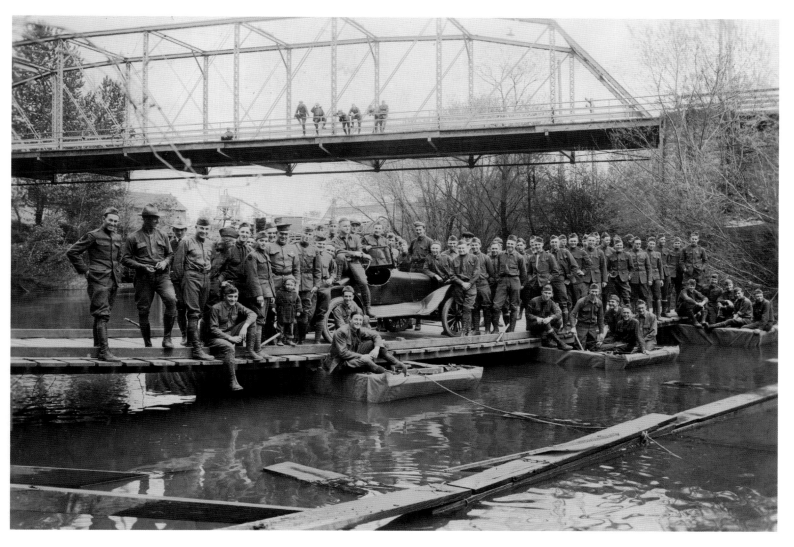

Cadets pose after constructing a temporary bridge across the Marys River, ca. 1920. The proximity of the Marys River to the OAC campus made it a suitable location for this type of military exercise. The more permanent Third Street bridge is in the background. (HC 85)

"Aggie Boy" heavy artillery piece, ca. 1920. "Aggie Boy" was the name affectionately given to a heavy artillery training piece assigned to OAC, an M1918 155mm Howitzer, a French design from World War I. The name was painted in black on its barrel. The ROTC artillery unit was established at OAC in 1919. (P2:660)

OAC ROTC cavalry company with the Armory in the background, ca. 1920. OAC's ROTC Cadet Cavalry Company B is in formation just west of the Armory. Although somewhat obsolete after World War I, horse-mounted cavalry units remained a part of the regular army into World War II. This photo appeared in the 1922 *Beaver* yearbook. (P2:250)

ROTC military motor transport unit, ca. 1924. Technological changes in warfare during World War I, such as the use of motorized transport for troops, munitions, and equipment, were reflected in the training provided to ROTC cadets. Equipment in this photo includes Dodge staff cars, FWD trucks, and Caterpillar artillery tractors. (HC 85)

OAC ROTC cadets in a sham battle on Bell Field, 1927. The cadets were exhibiting a battle scene on the athletic field during that year's military tournament. Much of the equipment used was World War I surplus. (P2:290)

Marine Corps ace Captain Marion E. Carl, 1942. Carl was a 1938 engineering graduate of Oregon State and was commissioned a lieutenant in the Army Reserve. He later joined the Marine Corps and became its first ace during World War II. Carl was credited with 18.5 kills in Pacific theater combat. He was also a record-setting test pilot after World War II and served as an air wing commander in Vietnam. The photo is inscribed "To my old friend—John." This likely refers to John Hinds, who for many years ran the Memorial Union's shoe shine parlor. (P17:403)

THE ARMY SPECIALIZED TRAINING PROGRAM

Unit 3900 of the Army Specialized Training Program was established at OSC in March 1943 with an initial contingent of 381 student soldiers. The eleven men who received certificates at OSC in September 1943 were some of the first in the nation to complete ASTP work. The ASTP had been established by the US War Department in December 1942 to:

> provide the continuous and accelerated flow of high grade technicians and specialists needed by the Army. To achieve this purpose, qualified soldiers are sent to colleges and universities selected by the War Department for terms of prescribed study in fields where the Army's own training facilities are insufficient in extent or character. These soldiers are selected on a broad, democratic basis. While in academic training they are on active duty, in uniform, under military discipline and receive regular Army pay. (1944-45 OSC Catalog)

The ASTP was divided into twelve-week terms, with the number of terms varying according to the curriculum. Most soldier students completed the ASTP curriculum in four terms or less. College credit was given for most courses taken; some ASTP students with significant prior college experience were able to complete OSC's degree requirements and participate in its graduation exercises. The program had basic and advanced phases, depending on the level of a soldier student's college education. The ASTP Basic course included basic studies in English, math, history, geology, political science, physics, physical education, and military science. The Advanced curriculum focused on three major areas—engineering, science, and foreign languages, and included specific courses of study in chemistry (including a sanitary engineering option); chemical, civil, electrical, mechanical engineering; mathematics; communications; and foreign area and language studies.

Dean of Administration E. B. Lemon coordinated the ASTP at Oregon State. Many faculty taught ASTP classes, but the primary faculty assisting Lemon were ROTC Commandant Lt. Col. Glen Webster, Dean of Science Francois Gilfillan, Assistant Dean of Engineering George Gleeson, Director of Physical Education Clair Langton, and Dean of Lower Division M. Ellwood Smith. Gilfillan also taught the ASTP's Russian language courses, the first to be taught at OSC.

During the 1943–44 academic year, enrollment ranged from 1,354 in summer 1943 to 1,260 in winter 1944. The program was curtailed nationally in the spring of 1944, with OSC's enrollment limited to 120 advanced engineering students that term. At the same time, a new program for boys seventeen and eighteen years of age was established—the Army Specialized Training Reserve Program provided college-level training to members of the Enlisted Reserve Corps who were on inactive status. This program replaced the ASTP's basic course of study.

OSC's ASTP and ASTRP provided training to 3,023 student soldiers before they ended in December 1945.

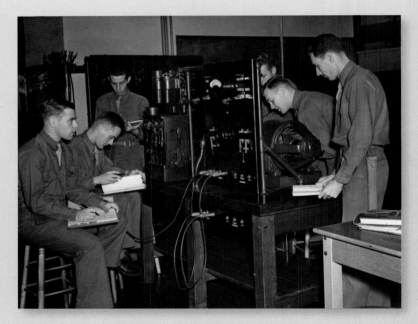

ASTP students studying electrical engineering, ca. 1943. (HC 935)

Humorous cartoon depicting the "invasion" of the ASTP at OSC, April 1943. (MSS–Maple Manor)

ASTP students at OSC relax at the college dairy bar, ca. 1945. The ice cream counter in the Dairy Building was one of the most popular spots on campus. Army students in the ASTP program discovered the place and praised the quality of the ice cream. ASTP soldier students participated in many facets of campus life, including an ASTP glee club. (HC 939)

ASTP students in physical conditioning drill on the intramural fields near the Weatherford Hall complex, ca. 1944. Physical education training was a required part of the ASTP curriculum. (HC 935)

WAC T/5 Nancy Dewey on Biak Island, 1945. Dewey, from Portland, attended Oregon State from 1939 to 1942. She left college before graduating and joined the Women's Army Corps (WAC) in 1942, soon after it was established. Dewey was one of the first Oregon Staters to join the WACs. She was stationed on Biak Island in the South Pacific in 1945, months after the island was recaptured from the Japanese in late spring 1944. Dewey was a member of the Pi Beta Phi sorority at OSC. Many Oregon State women served in the armed forces during World War II. (HC 427)

Leaders of OSC's ROTC units, October 1950. From left are Colonel Henry Demuth, Army ROTC; Captain Clyde M. Jensen, Navy ROTC; and Colonel Rex W. Beach, Air Force ROTC. (P82:90 #607)

President Strand commissioning new Navy officers, 1952. Commissioning ceremonies have a long tradition at Oregon State during commencement weekend. In 1952 the ceremony was held in Bell Field. Today officers are commissioned in Reser Stadium as part of regular commencement exercises. (P82:84 #1425)

Scabbard and Blade members, 1957–58. Scabbard and Blade is a national collegiate military honor society founded in 1904. The OAC chapter was established on April 17, 1920, and has included members from the Army and Navy ROTC detachments. For many years OSU's Scabbard and Blade society hosted an annual Military Ball. Arnold Air Society, the Air Force ROTC honor society, was formed at OSC in 1951. (HC 1163)

Protestor at OSC Armed Forces Review Day, May 24, 1960. OSU's ROTC program has not been without controversy. This protestor held a sign that read "Indoctrination is NOT Education for Democracy." Ten years later, at the height of the Vietnam War, the Armory was damaged by a bomb. (P92:1080)

Project Capsule team member in flight suit testing the simulator's inclined chair, February 1961. Junior cadet officers in OSU's Air Force ROTC detachment engaged in a project in fall 1960 to construct a full-scale model of a NASA Mercury space capsule. One of the officers served as a test subject in the capsule for an extended period. The project's purposes were to:

- give the junior AFROTC cadets a practical means of applying the leadership and management principles that they had learned in class; and
- increase the space mindedness and space education of the sophomore AFROTC cadets and the general public.

The "astronaut" selected was Donald Cram, a sophomore majoring in physics. Cram spent forty-eight hours in the capsule and, though weak when he emerged, was free of any other ill effects. A later project team constructed a model of an Apollo capsule. (MC–Project Capsule)

OSU Army ROTC Drill Team performing in Portland, ca. 1962. The Pershing Rifles' Company E-11 drill team performed at halftime during this Portland high school basketball game. They wore full dress uniform except for shoes; they donned white tennis shoes to protect the gymnasium floor. (P2:438)

OSU ROTC cadet participating in summer camp bayonet training, July 1967. Upper division ROTC cadets often spent weeks each summer at training camp. Army ROTC cadets participated in the 6th US Army Summer Camp at Fort Lewis, Washington. (US Army Photograph, P257)

Training on lower campus, ca. 1990. Just as it had been used for military drills and training in the early twentieth century, lower campus was again used for military training purposes toward the end of the century. These cadets are training in an obstacle course near the campus gates (visible on left). (P257)

Joint Service Review, spring 2003. The review has been a long-standing tradition at Oregon State. This review was held in the Memorial Union quad. (P257)

Major General Julie A. Bentz (class of 1986) sings the Army song during OSU's Army ROTC commissioning ceremony, June 14, 2013. Bentz, OSU's 2013 commencement speaker, served as an advisor to President Barack Obama on national security issues. She was the first female officer from the Oregon Army National Guard to earn the rank of general. (Photo by Theresa Hogue, courtesy of OSU News and Research Communications)

Jane Lubchenco, 1992. Except for a federal appointment, Lubchenco has been at OSU since 1977, where her research has focused on community ecology, conservation biology, biodiversity, global change, and sustainability. Lubchenco served as the director of the National Oceanic and Atmospheric Administration from 2009 to 2013, the first woman to serve in that capacity. Her awards have included MacArthur and Pew fellowships, the Nierenberg Prize for Science in the Public Interest from the Scripps Institution of Oceanography, and several honorary degrees. In 1997 she served as president of the American Association for the Advancement of Science. Lubchenco is a distinguished professor of zoology and was OSU's Wayne and Gladys Valley Professor of Marine Biology from 1995 to 2009 and from 2013 to 2014. Lubchenco's fellow faculty member and spouse, Bruce Menge, is also a distinguished professor of zoology. (P57, Accession 2006:046)

The Best of the Best
Prominent Faculty and Alumni

Since its establishment as a land-grant institution in 1868, OSU has enrolled nearly half a million students, and thousands of faculty and staff have served the institution. Throughout that history, many OSU faculty and alumni have served as leaders at the local, regional, national, and international levels. Faculty and alumni have been prominent educators, inventors, industry, military and government leaders, entertainers, and world-class athletes. Many of Oregon State's early faculty were highly versatile, often called on to teach classes outside their primary areas of expertise.

Thomas M. Gatch, who served as president of Oregon Agricultural College from 1897 to 1907, was the first in that office to hold a doctorate.[1] Gatch was already a highly regarded educator when he was selected as OAC's president. He had served as president of the Wasco Independent Academy in The Dalles, the University of Washington, and Willamette University (twice).

Many Oregon Staters have been major contributors to business and industry through their leadership and/or patents and inventions. Alumnus and forestry faculty member T. J. Starker (class of 1910) started a timber business in 1936 that is now one of Oregon's strongest family-owned timber concerns, Starker Forests, Inc. Bond and Barte Starker (classes of 1969 and 1972) are the third generation to manage the business. Loren L. "Stub" Stewart (class of 1932) and his brother Faye (class of 1938) turned Bohemia Lumber into a strong leader in Oregon's timber industry.

In the world of high tech, Douglas Engelbart (class of 1948) is credited with several contributions to computer technology, including the mouse, hypertext, and early work on graphical user interfaces. John Young (class of 1953) was president and CEO of Hewlett-Packard from 1978 to 1992.

Bob Lundeen (class of 1942) and Keith McKennon (class of 1955) both served as executives with Dow Chemical. Ralph Cheek (class of 1952) was a Kaiser Aluminum executive. Ken Austin (class of 1953) founded A-dec, one of the largest dental equipment manufacturers in the world. Al and Pat Reser (class of 1960) turned a small family potato salad business into an internationally recognized prepared food business, Reser's Fine Foods. Bernie Newcomb (class of 1965) was one of the founders of E-Trade. Timothy Leatherman (class of 1970) invented the Leatherman multipurpose tool and founded the Leatherman Tool Group in 1983.

More recently, Mike and Brian McMenamin (classes of 1973 and 1980) have been pioneers in Oregon's craft brewing industry and have built a company that includes dozens of brewpubs, restaurants, and lodging venues in Oregon and Washington. Alumnus and microbiology faculty member Dennis Hruby (class of 1973) has served as vice president and chief scientific officer of Siga Technologies, a company that specializes in solutions for treating lethal pathogens.

Several OSU alumni have made major contributions to science. Most famous is Linus Pauling, who graduated from Oregon State in 1922 and went on to a distinguished career as a scientist and peace activist, winning the 1954 Nobel Prize for Chemistry and the 1962 Nobel Peace Prize. More recently, two alumni, William Oefelein (class of 1988) and Donald Pettit (class of 1978), have gone on to work in the space program as NASA astronauts. Ann Kiessling (class of 1971) is an internationally prominent stem cell researcher.

OSU faculty and alumni have a long and proud tradition of government service in both elected and appointed offices at the local, state, and federal levels. Three Oregon Staters have served as Oregon governors. James Withycombe, the college's experiment station director from 1902 to 1914, first ran for governor (unsuccessfully) in 1906. In 1914 he ran again and was elected, and he served from 1915 until his death in 1919. Alumnus Douglas McKay (class of 1917) served in a variety of capacities—mayor of Salem (1932–1935), state senator (1935–1941; 1947–1949), governor (1949–1952), and US Secretary of the Interior (1953–1956). He also ran unsuccessfully for the US Senate in 1956 against Wayne Morse. John Hubert Hall (class of 1923) preceded McKay as governor. As speaker of the Oregon House of Representatives, Hall assumed the governorship in October 1947 after Governor Earl Snell died in a plane crash. Walter M. Pierce was a member of OAC's board of regents from 1905 to 1927; he served as governor from 1923 to 1927 and later as a US representative from Oregon.

Two other alumni had direct connections to Oregon governors. Elizabeth Hoover (class of 1901) married Jay Bowerman in 1903. He became governor in June 1910 and served until January 1911.[2] Dovie Odom Hatfield, the mother of past governor and US Senator Mark Hatfield, graduated from Oregon State in 1931 when Mark was a young child.

Lowell Stockman (class of 1922) served in the US House of Representatives from 1943 to 1953, and Darlene Hooley (class of 1962) represented Oregon's fifth congressional district as a US representative from 1997 to 2009, after having served in the Oregon legislature and as a commissioner for Clackamas County. Fred Steiwer (class of 1902) was a US senator from Oregon from 1927 to 1937. John Ensign (class of 1981) represented Nevada in the US House and Senate. Jolene Unsoeld (class of 1953) represented Washington in the US House from 1989 to 1995.

Other Oregon Staters elected to statewide office in Oregon have included Charles Crookham (attended 1941 to 1943), attorney general (1992–1993); Susan Castillo (class of 1983), Oregon superintendent of public instruction (2003–2012); and Brad Avakian (class of 1984), commissioner of the Oregon Bureau of Labor and Industries

(2008–present). Cecil Andrus, who attended Oregon State in the late 1940s, twice served as governor of Idaho (1971–1977 and 1987–1995) and as US secretary of the interior in the Carter administration (1977–1981).

Many Oregon Staters have had success in the arts and entertainment fields. One of the first to make a mark was Vance DeBar "Pinto" Colvig, who attended OAC in the early 1910s. He was an accomplished artist and musician; his drawings appear in yearbooks from the early 1910s. His major claim to fame was as the first Bozo the Clown. George Bruns (class of 1936) co-wrote the "Ballad of Davy Crockett" as the music director for Disney Studios. Jean Hetherington attended OSC in 1940 before leaving for Hollywood for a successful, if short, career as actress Jean Heather. More recently, Harley Jessup (class of 1976) is an Emmy- and Oscar-winning visual effects artist for Pixar. Mike Rich, who attended OSU in the late 1970s and early 1980s, is a screenwriter whose credits include the films *Finding Forrester, The Rookie, Invincible,* and *Secretariat.* Roosevelt Credit (class of 1990) has become a successful performer on Broadway, including Tony Award winning productions of *Show Boat* and *The Gershwins' Porgy and Bess.*

Journalism was a mainstay for many OSU alumni and others with OSU connections. B. F. Irvine, who served on both the Board of Regents of OAC and the State Board of Higher Education in the first few decades of the twentieth century, was affiliated with a number of Oregon newspapers, including the *Corvallis Times,* the *Benton Leader,* and the *Oregon Journal.* Webley Edwards (class of 1927) was a World War II news correspondent who announced both the Japanese attack on Pearl Harbor and the surrender aboard the USS *Missouri.*

Chris Anderson (class of 1972) was editor of the *Orange County Register* when it won two Pulitzer Prizes. Chris Johns (class of 1974) discovered photography while a student at OSU and became an award-winning photojournalist. He is presently editor-in-chief of *National Geographic.* Photojournalist Roger Werth (class of 1980) was part of the team of the *Longview (WA) Daily News* that won a Pulitzer Prize for its May 1980 coverage (including Werth's photos) of the eruption of Mount St. Helens. David Gilkey, who studied journalism at OSU in the mid-1980s, is also an award-winning photographer who covered the wars in Iraq and Afghanistan and is now affiliated with National Public Radio.

Alumnus and faculty member Willi Unsoeld (class of 1951) was part of the first US team to reach the summit of Mount Everest in 1963. Twenty-five years later another Oregon Stater, Stacey Allison, became the first woman from the United States to scale Mount Everest.

OSU has always had superb faculty who have excelled in teaching, research, and service. Faculty members have been recognized nationally and internationally; they have been members of the National Academy of Sciences, been elected fellows of the American Association for the Advancement of Science, and won literary awards on the state, regional, and national level. Forty-five faculty across many disciplines have been designated Distinguished Professors. Many have gone on to serve in leadership roles at OSU and/or other higher education institutions.

Dr. Margaret Comstock Snell, ca. 1889. Snell (1843–1923) came to OAC in 1889 to begin the college's program in household economy and hygiene, which was the first in the western United States. She was considered to be among the greatest of OAC's early faculty members. Snell was trained as a medical doctor at Boston University, graduating in 1886, though she formally practiced medicine for only a short period of time. She was recruited to OAC by regent Wallis Nash and his wife, Louisa. At OAC, she incorporated aspects of her medical training into the curriculum, in order to "teach people how to stay well, rather than treat them once they're sick." In 1889 she started with an enrollment of twenty-four women. When she retired from teaching in 1907, more than two hundred women were taking classes from her. Over the years, three different campus buildings have carried the name Snell Hall in her memory. (P103:28)

Portrait of professor Frederick Berchtold, 1902. Berchtold (1857–1942) was an OAC faculty member for forty-eight years, from 1884 to 1932. He joined the faculty as the college was being separated from the Methodist Episcopal Church, South in the mid 1880s, was part of the move of the campus from downtown Corvallis to the new campus on the college farm lands in 1889, and saw the college become part of the State System of Higher Education in 1929. He served as dean of faculty from 1896 to 1901 and head of the English department from 1900 to 1932. Berchtold was initially hired as professor of languages, but his early years at the college also included teaching classes in history, English literature, freehand drawing, and physics. OSC awarded him an honorary doctorate in literature in 1934. (HC 99)

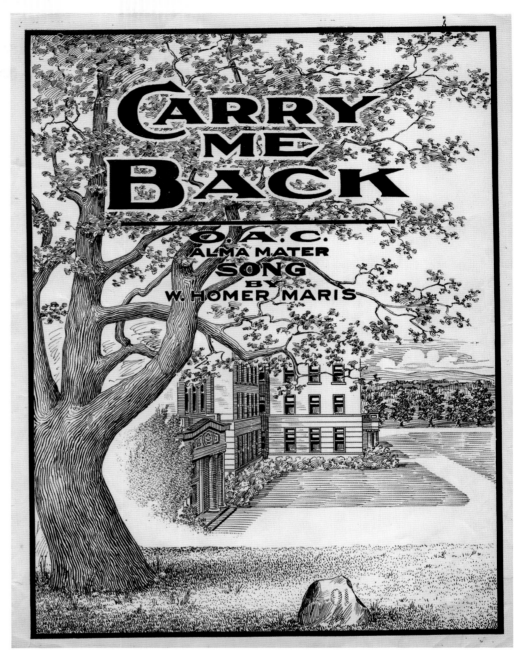

Portrait of W. Homer Maris, ca. 1920. Although Maris received his undergraduate degree from the University of Oregon, he earned an MS in agriculture from OAC in 1918, and he was clearly a Beaver at heart. In 1914, Maris began composing the song that would become the college's alma mater, *Carry Me Back*. He dedicated the piece to Ida "Mother" Kidder, OAC's much-loved college librarian. Maris died in 1933 in a bicycle accident. (HC 1888)

James Withycombe and others participating in the farming demonstration train tour of Oregon, sponsored by the Southern Pacific Railroad and Oregon Agricultural College, 1911. Withycombe, second from the left in the back row, was the associate director (1898 to 1902) and director of OAC's Agricultural Experiment Station (1902 to 1914). Prior to his work at OAC, he served as the state veterinarian from 1889 to 1898. During his tenure, Experiment Station research was greatly expanded and branch stations were established in several parts of the state. He was an advocate of cover crops and crop rotation. Withycombe was elected governor of Oregon in 1914 and worked to develop the state's flax industry. He was re-elected in 1918 and died in 1919, two months into his second term. Withycombe Hall is named for him. (MSS–Withycombe)

Thomas Autzen and alumni manager Bob Knoll, ca. 1950. Autzen was a member
of OAC's class of 1909 and graduated with a degree in electrical engineering. After
graduation he rejoined Portland Manufacturing Company, a lumber business owned
in part by his family. It became one of the nation's leading manufacturers of plywood.
Thomas Autzen formed the Autzen Foundation in the early 1950s. Bob Knoll was a 1948
graduate of OSC and served as alumni manager from 1948 to 1961. (HC 2126)

Vance DeBar "Pinto" Colvig, who was from Medford, attended OAC in the early twentieth century, leaving the school about 1911. He played E-flat soprano clarinet in the cadet band, and his distinctive cartoons were used in yearbooks in the early 1910s.

After stints as a circus performer and newspaper cartoonist, Colvig went on to a successful career as a sound effects and voice-over artist, especially for Disney Studios, where he was the voice for two of the dwarfs in *Snow White and the Seven Dwarfs* and for the "Goofy" cartoon character. He did sound effects for Jack Benny's radio show in the 1930s. Colvig was the first Bozo the Clown, recording a number of albums for Capitol Records in the 1940s and 1950s, and starring as the clown on KTTV in Los Angeles. He died in 1967.

Portrait of Pinto Colvig during his student days at OAC, ca. 1911. (HC 424)

This Pinto cartoon was featured at the beginning of the football section of the 1914 yearbook. (1914 OAC *Orange* yearbook, page 171).

Pinto Colvig signing Alumni guest book, ca. 1950. Colvig was an occasional visitor to Oregon State and always remembered his student years fondly. (HC 424)

Governor Douglas McKay and Bozo the Clown, fall 1951. Colvig transformed into Bozo the Clown to meet with McKay during OSC's fall 1951 homecoming celebration. McKay was a 1917 graduate of Oregon State, where he was freshman class president and student body president. He served as mayor of Salem (1933–35), state senator (1935–1949, including a break in service during World War II), and governor of Oregon from 1949 to 1952. He later served as Interior Secretary in the Eisenhower administration. (P17:863)

Conde B. McCullough, ca. 1916. McCullough was a member of the OAC engineering faculty from 1916 to 1919. He joined the state highway department in 1919 to head its bridge division. McCullough and his engineers, many of whom were OAC graduates, designed most of the major bridges on the Oregon coast and other bridges around Oregon. In all he helped to design more than six hundred bridges in Oregon, many of which have become architectural landmarks. He was granted an honorary doctorate by Oregon State in 1934. Twelve McCullough-designed bridges were listed on the National Register of Historic Places in 2005, including eleven on the Oregon coast. (P17:451)

College librarian Ida Kidder in the reading room of the new library, ca. 1919. Kidder (seated at the second table on the right) came to OAC as its first professionally training librarian in 1908. During her twelve years as librarian, she transformed the college library from a functional, yet inadequate, facility in the Administration Building (Benton Hall) into a first-class library with superb facilities and services that accommodated a quickly growing student and faculty population. Kidder was very popular with students, who fondly called her "Mother Kidder." After her death in 1920, her body lay in state in the library. This building was renamed Kidder Hall in her memory in 1965. (HC 75)

LINUS PAULING—OREGON STATE'S MOST FAMOUS ALUMNUS

Born in Portland, Oregon, on February 28, 1901, Linus Pauling is widely regarded as one of the most influential scientists of all time. After receiving his BS in chemical engineering from Oregon Agricultural College in 1922, Pauling attended the California Institute of Technology (Caltech), where in 1925 he received a PhD in chemistry with minors in physics and mathematics. With the help of a Guggenheim Fellowship, Pauling studied the fledgling discipline of quantum mechanics in Europe for a year and a half, becoming one of the first scientists to gain a strong understanding of the intersection of chemistry and the new physics. This crossing of disciplinary boundaries was a characteristic of Pauling's scientific work throughout his career.

After completing his fellowship, Pauling returned to Caltech to join the chemistry faculty. In 1937 he was named chairman of the department, a position he held for the next twenty years. In 1939 Pauling published *The Nature of the Chemical Bond*, which remains the most frequently cited scientific publication of the twentieth century.

In the mid-1930s, Pauling brought his knowledge of molecular structure to bear on biological molecules, particularly hemoglobin—the protein in red blood cells. By the end of the 1940s, Pauling had determined the basic structure of proteins, the alpha-helix. He further suggested that sickle-cell anemia was a molecular disease, a hypothesis that he would later confirm with a colleague, Harvey Itano. Pauling utilized his commitment to the US government during World War II to explore practical applications of his research, chiefly through his successful development of a substitute for blood plasma. In many respects, Pauling was the godfather of modern molecular biology.

Pauling's public and political activities during the 1950s made him one of the most well-known scientists of the twentieth century. His outspoken statements on the issues of loyalty oaths, nuclear bomb tests, and disarmament, as well as a host of other peace and humanitarian causes, resulted in both government and media harassment for more than a decade as well as a concomitant reputation as both a maverick and a hero.

Portrait of Linus Pauling, ca. 1918. This portrait was taken during Pauling's student days at Oregon Agricultural College. He came to OAC in 1917 and graduated in 1922. This photo was taken by Ball Studio of Corvallis. (HC 676)

In 1954, Pauling was awarded the Nobel Prize in Chemistry for his research into chemical bonding. Pauling's award marked the first time the Nobel Committee had awarded a prize for a body of work, rather than one landmark discovery. Following the Nobel ceremonies in Stockholm, Pauling and his wife, Ava Helen, embarked on a lecture tour around the world. Throughout his life, Pauling's traveling companion for the bulk of his numerous journeys was Ava Helen, to whom he was married for nearly sixty years. She also attended OAC, and they met in a chemistry class for home economics majors that he was teaching during his senior year. Only after Ava Helen's death in 1981 was Linus separated from the person he commonly referred to as "the greatest influence on my life."

In 1963, Pauling was awarded a second Nobel Prize for his efforts to achieve nuclear disarmament, which he dedicated to Ava Helen. The genesis for the 1963 award was Pauling's 1958 submission to the United Nations of a petition signed by over 9,000 international scientists advocating the cessation of nuclear testing. Notice of Pauling's receipt of the Peace Prize was given on the same day that the United States and the Soviet Union signed a treaty agreeing to halt all above-ground nuclear explosions. Linus Pauling remains the only individual to be awarded two unshared Nobel Prizes.

After leaving Caltech, Pauling's scientific career centered around medical issues. He again used his scientific knowledge to make advances in a discipline other than his original field of expertise. His research led him to develop the concept of orthomolecular medicine. Pauling also espoused the health benefits of mega-doses of vitamin C. In 1973 he founded the Institute of Orthomolecular Medicine to expedite his forward-thinking research. To this day the Institute, now known as the Linus Pauling Institute and located on the campus of Oregon State University, carries on the legacy of Pauling's work in medicine and nutrition.

Linus Pauling died on August 19, 1994.[3]

Ava Helen and Linus Pauling on the beach at Corona del Mar, California, 1924. Pauling met Ava Helen Miller in 1922 when he was teaching a chemistry class for freshman home economics majors during his senior year. They began dating in March 1922, despite the teacher/student relationship. Although they wished to marry after Pauling graduated in June 1922, they waited a year, until after his first year of graduate school at Caltech. They married on June 17, 1923, in Salem, Oregon. Their marriage lasted until Ava Helen's death in December 1981—more than fifty-eight years. (MSS-Pauling Papers, LP Photographs, 1923i.3)

Linus Pauling receiving an honorary doctorate from Oregon State Agricultural College, June 1933. Though just thirty-two years old in 1933, Pauling (center) was already beginning to make his mark as a scientist. Oregon State bestowed an honorary doctor of science degree on him, describing him in the commencement program as "now acclaimed among the distinguished scientists of our time." Chancellor William Jasper Kerr is to the right of Pauling. Others in the photo (from left): Dr. Marvin Gordon Neale, president of the University of Idaho and the commencement speaker; David C. Henny, honorary degree recipient; and Charles A. Howard, honorary degree recipient. (HC 1578)

Linus Pauling and Paul Emmett at OSC, November 1948. Pauling
was on campus to lecture to Phi Lambda Upsilon, the national
chemistry honor society. Pauling and Emmett were classmates at
OAC and lifelong friends. Like Pauling, Emmett completed his
graduate studies at Caltech. Emmett became the chair of Johns
Hopkins University's chemical engineering department in 1937.
In 1943 he joined the Manhattan Project and worked on a process
for separating Uranium-235 from Uranium-238. After ten years
at the Mellon Institute in Pittsburgh, Emmett returned to Johns
Hopkins in 1955, where he remained until retiring in 1971. He then
returned to his hometown of Portland, Oregon, where he served
as a research professor in Portland State University's chemistry
department. In 1976 he married Pauline Pauling, one of Linus
Pauling's sisters. In 1974 OSU bestowed its Distinguished Service
Award on Emmett. He died in April 1985. (HC 676)

Linus Pauling at OSU, April 18, 1986. Pauling (left) visited
OSU in April 1986 when the announcement was made that the
Ava Helen and Linus Pauling Papers were being donated to the
university's libraries. Talking with Pauling are OSU President
John Byrne and Betty and Les Buell. (P92:1316a)

Carrie Halsell graduation portrait, 1926. Halsell, who graduated in 1926 with a BS in commerce, was the first African American graduate of Oregon State. Halsell became an educator, serving as a business faculty member at Virginia State University and South Carolina State University. OSU's Halsell Hall residence hall is named in her memory. (1927 *Beaver* Yearbook, p. 40)

US Representative Lowell Stockman and his wife, Dorcas, during a visit to Hawaii, ca. 1950. Stockman (1901–1962), like Linus Pauling, was a member of OAC's class of 1922. He was from Helix in Umatilla County, and he farmed after obtaining his OAC degree. Stockman was a member of the Pendleton school board and the Oregon Liquor Control Commission prior to being elected to Congress in 1942. He represented Oregon's Second District in the US House of Representatives from 1943 to 1953. (HC 751)

RUTH NOMURA

Ruth Nomura (class of 1930) was one of Oregon State's first Nisei students. She was born in 1907 in Portland and graduated from Jefferson High School in 1924. In 1926 she won an essay contest that enabled her to visit Japan. She wrote that the trip

> ... enriched my life and gave me a deep appreciation of Japan, its people, arts and civilization. It encouraged me to study the language, flower arrangement, holiday festivals, the tea ceremony, daily customs, Japanese cooking and serving, music, arts and crafts, particularly pottery, painting and calligraphy.

While at OAC Nomura lived in Margaret Snell Hall and earned a BS in home economics. She participated in a wide range of campus activities:

- Omicron Nu, secretary: National honorary fraternity in home economics, which was established at Michigan State college in 1912 and installed at OSC in 1919
- Phi Kappa Phi: National all-college scholastic honor society, which was established at OSC in June, 1924
- Kappa Delta Pi: Education honor society
- Clara H. Waldo prize, honorable mention
- Cosmopolitan Club, vice-president: The Cosmopolitan Club was formed to promote brotherhood and place humanity above all nations

Nomura married Earl Tanbara in Portland on September 16, 1935. During World War II, they were able to avoid internment by relocating to Minneapolis, Minnesota. They helped more than one hundred Japanese Americans leave internment camps and relocate to the Twin Cities. Ruth and Earl remained in Minnesota after the war. Ruth earned a master's degree in home economics from the University of Minnesota in 1953. Her thesis advisor there wrote of Ruth:

> I have never known anyone who was so versatile and could do well so many different things—from arranging flowers to organizing programs for the YWCA; from teaching foreign foods to writing publicity material. She is a charming, gracious person.

Nomura served as the Adult Education Director and International Program Director for the St. Paul YWCA from 1942 to 1972. She was also a founding member of the St. Paul-Nagasaki Sister City Committee in 1955, later serving as its president for several years, and a charter member of the Japan America Society in 1972. Ruth Nomura Tanbara passed away on January 4, 2008.

Portrait of Ruth Nomura in a kimono, ca. 1928. Physics faculty member John Garman, who taught photography classes, took this portrait of Nomura. (P95:93)

Ruth Nomura (third from right) and classmates at commencement, 1930. (P25:596)

Bob Lundeen studying, 1942. Robert W. Lundeen graduated from OSC in 1942 with a degree in chemical engineering. He was a member of several honorary societies at Oregon State, including Phi Kappa Phi (multi-disciplinary), Tau Beta Pi (engineering), and Pi Mu Epsilon (mathematics). After serving in the US Army Air Corps during World War II, he was hired by Dow Chemical as a research engineer. He served as executive vice president and chairman of the board before retiring in 1986. He later served as CEO and board chairman of Tektronix, Inc. Lundeen has also served on several OSU advisory boards. (1942 *Beaver* Yearbook, p. 91)

Edwin Russell Jackman, ca. 1960. Jackman was both an Oregon State alumnus (class of 1921, BS in agronomy) and a longtime Extension faculty member. He served as Wasco County agent, farm crops specialist (1929 to 1953), and range crops management specialist (1953 to 1959). He helped to organize both the Oregon Wheat League and Oregon Seed Growers' League. It was said that Jackman knew more ranchers by their first names than anyone in Oregon. Jackman authored several books, including *Steens Mountain: Oregon's High Desert Country, The Oregon Desert*, and *Blazing Forest Trails*. Jackman died in 1967; the E. R. Jackman Foundation, an affiliate of the OSU Foundation, was established in his memory. (P89:11)

Dr. Clara Storvick in her lab, 1953. Storvick joined the OSC faculty in 1945 as a professor of nutrition. During her twenty-seven years she became internationally known for her work in vitamin nutrition. At Oregon State she served as head of home economics research and as the first director of the Nutrition Research Institute (1965–1972). She won many awards and was elected a fellow of the American Academy for the Advancement of Science. Storvick received her PhD from Cornell. Prior to coming to OSC, she taught at Iowa State, Oklahoma State, and the University of Washington. (P82:70 #1464)

Loren L. "Stub" Stewart, 1976. Stewart (left) was a 1932 Oregon State graduate in forestry. He and his brother, Faye (class of 1938), acquired the Bohemia Lumber Company in 1946 and turned it into one of Oregon's most successful and diversified lumber companies. Stub served as its president and CEO from 1946 to 1976. Shortly after his death, the *Oregon Stater* characterized Stub as an "'Oregon Titan'—pioneer in the forest industry who was a tireless public servant, philanthropist and advocate." The Stewart family provided funding for OSU's conference center in the early 1980s. It was named the LaSells Stewart Center in honor of Stub and Faye's father. L. L. Stub Stewart State Park west of Portland was established in 2007 and named for him in recognition of his many years on the Oregon Parks and Recreation Commission. (P57:5135)

Douglas Engelbart at OSU, recipient of the E. B. Lemon Distinguished Alumni Award, 1987. Engelbart, a native of Portland, graduated from OSC in 1948 with a bachelor's degree in electrical engineering. He worked for the Stanford Research Institute and the SRI's Augmentation Research Center, where he and his research team made significant contributions to computer technology, including the computer mouse, hypertext, bitmapped screens, and what would become graphical user interfaces. He died in July 2013. (P195)

Mercedes Bates receiving OSU's Distinguished Service Award from President Robert MacVicar, 1973. Bates graduated from OSC in 1936 with a degree in food and nutrition. She was appointed vice president of General Mills' Betty Crocker Division in 1967, becoming the first female corporate officer of the company. Her work helped make Betty Crocker a household name. In addition to the Distinguished Service Award, she also received OSU's Distinguished Alumni Award in 1969. In 1989 Bates made a large contribution to the university, which helped to fund the Mercedes A. Bates Family Study Center. (P92:1179)

BERNARD MALAMUD

Award-winning novelist Bernard Malamud (1914–1986) began his collegiate teaching career at Oregon State College in 1949. He grew up in Brooklyn, New York, attended the City College of New York (BA 1936), and received an MA from Columbia University in 1942. Malamud taught evening classes in English at Erasmus Hall High School, his alma mater, from 1940 to 1949.

While at OSC, Malamud mostly taught freshman composition and grammar classes, though he was able to teach other classes toward the end of his time at Oregon State. He maintained a rigid schedule, teaching on Mondays, Wednesdays, and Fridays, and writing on Tuesdays, Thursdays, Saturdays, and Sunday mornings. Out of his time in Corvallis came some of his most famous works, including *The Natural* (1952), *The Assistant* (1957), *The Magic Barrel* (1958; National Book Award winner), and *A New Life* (1961). The latter is a thinly veiled novel based upon his experiences at Oregon State.

Malamud left OSU in 1961 to take a position at Bennington College in Vermont; he remained affiliated with that institution until his death in 1986. He also was a visiting lecturer at Harvard from 1966 to 1968. Malamud returned to Corvallis on several occasions to lecture and visit old friends. He won the Pulitzer Prize and a second National Book Award for his 1966 novel, *The Fixer*, and was awarded the American Academy and Institute of Arts and Letters' Gold Medal for fiction in 1983.

OSC English faculty members Bernard Malamud and Faith Norris, 1955. Malamud and Norris were good friends. Both had attended graduate school at Columbia University in the 1940s. Norris taught at Oregon State from 1947 to 1979. (P35:35 #1902c)

Portrait of Bernard Malamud, 1949. This portrait was likely appended to Malamud's application to Oregon State. (P92:393)

Bernard Malamud during a visit to OSU, 1972. (P195, Acc. 88:02)

Wayne Burt conducting oceanography field research in Yaquina Bay from a small motorboat, 1957. Burt came to OSU in 1954 with a grant from the Office of Naval Research (ONR) to establish oceanographic studies. With additional funding from the ONR, he established OSU's Department of Oceanography in 1959. In 1966 he was appointed the first director of OSU's Marine Science Center, established in Newport to create additional research opportunities for the new department, and served in that capacity until 1972. Burt Hall, which houses many of the programs of the College of Earth, Ocean, and Atmospheric Sciences on the Corvallis campus, is named for him. (HC 1830)

J. Kenneth Munford with OSU Press books, 1962. Munford, a 1934 Oregon State graduate, was the first director of the OSU Press, 1961 to 1977. From 1939 to 1941 he was an English instructor at OSC, and in 1948 he began working as an editor for the college's Office of Publications. He was appointed director of that office in 1956 and helped with the establishment of the press. After retiring from the press, Munford volunteered at the Horner Museum, organizing historical tours around the state. He received the Oregon Historical Society's Henry Clinton Collins Award in 1978. Munford also authored a popular local history column in the *Corvallis Gazette-Times* in the 1980s and 1990s. (P17:3808)

Coed Cottage graduates, 1961. Darlene Olson, who later became Darlene Hooley, is in the front row, right. Hooley graduated from Oregon State in 1962, earning a degree in education. While at OSU, she participated in a variety of sports. Hooley served as US Representative from Oregon's Fifth Congressional District from 1997 to 2009. Prior to her congressional career, Hooley represented Clackamas County in the state legislature and served on the Clackamas County Board of Commissioners. (MSS–Coed Cottage)

Dr. C. Warren Hovland and students, winter 1963. Hovland taught religious studies at Oregon State from 1948 until his retirement in 1987. In this photo he is talking to students during the filming of the television show *Meet the Professor*, which aired on KOAC-TV. Hovland won many awards during his career at OSU, including the Alumni Association Distinguished Professor Award (1971) and the D. Curtis Mumford Faculty Service Award (1986). Hovland created a bioethics course that was the foundation for subsequent interdisciplinary courses at OSU, and he was known as "OSU's Conscience" because of his concerns during the Vietnam era. Hovland Hall is named in his honor. (P82:35 #2811)

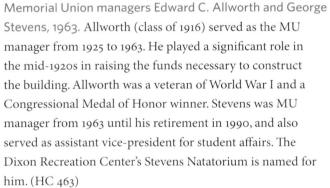

Memorial Union managers Edward C. Allworth and George Stevens, 1963. Allworth (class of 1916) served as the MU manager from 1925 to 1963. He played a significant role in the mid-1920s in raising the funds necessary to construct the building. Allworth was a veteran of World War I and a Congressional Medal of Honor winner. Stevens was MU manager from 1963 until his retirement in 1990, and also served as assistant vice-president for student affairs. The Dixon Recreation Center's Stevens Natatorium is named for him. (HC 463)

Radiation Center Director Chih H. Wang, 1970. Wang, who received his PhD from OSC in 1950, was a founding member of OSU's Nuclear Engineering Department and the Radiation Center. He became the center's director in 1964. In 1998 Wang was inducted into OSU's Engineering Hall of Fame. (P151:1017)

Plant physiologist Harold J. Evans injecting bacterial extract into a test tube, ca. 1972. Evans held professorships in plant physiology and biochemistry during his career at OSU (1961 to 1988) and studied processes related to nitrogen fixation. In 1972 Evans became the first OSU faculty member elected to the National Academy of Sciences, one of the highest honors bestowed on US scientists. (P120:5166)

Chris Johns, OSU freshman class president, 1970–71. Johns attended OSU from 1970 to 1974. Though he came to OSU to study agriculture, he discovered a passion for photography. After graduating from Oregon State and earning a master's degree at the University of Minnesota, Johns embarked on a successful career as a photojournalist. He was named the National Newspaper Photographer of the Year in 1979. After a number of years as a freelance photographer, he joined National Geographic's staff in 1995. In 2003 he became editor-in-chief of *National Geographic* magazine. That same year he was also named as one of the twenty-five most important photographers in the world. Johns was OSU's 2005 commencement speaker. (P3:3731)

Founders of the CH2M engineering firm, ca. 1970. In January 1946, three OSC engineering alumni from the class of 1938 and one of their major professors established the CH2M engineering consulting firm. The founders were (from left) James C. Howland, Professor Fred Merryfield, Holly Cornell, and Burke Hayes. In 1971 the firm merged with another engineering firm, Clair A. Hill and Associates, to become CH2M HILL. Hill also attended Oregon State in the early 1930s. (MSS–Howland)

OSU historian William Appleman Williams near his home at Waldport, ca. 1978. Williams was a prominent historian who focused on United States diplomacy. He came to OSU in 1968 after having taught the previous eleven years at the University of Wisconsin-Madison, where he published his most famous and popular work, *The Tragedy of American Diplomacy* (1959). As an historian, Williams was known for his "intellectual independence and moral seriousness." Williams retired in 1986 and died in 1990. (MSS—Williams, 5.004.25)

Harley Jessup, ca. 1985. Jessup earned a BFA in graphic design at OSU in 1976. After receiving an MFA from Stanford in 1978, he worked for Korty Films, Lucasfilm, and Industrial Light and Magic. While at ILM, he received an Academy Award for special effects work on the film *Innerspace* and a nomination for *Hook*. In 1996 he joined Pixar, where he worked on many of its successful films, including *Toy Story 2, Monsters, Inc.*, and *Ratatouille*. For the latter he received an ANNIE award for Production Design in an Animated Feature. (P195, Accession 2009:034)

Astronaut Don Pettit during a visit to OSU, 2010. Pettit (class of 1978) was interviewed by a news crew in Kearney Hall. Pettit joined NASA as an astronaut in 1996 and has completed two space missions, including a six-month tour of duty aboard the International Space Station. He was the 2010 OSU commencement speaker and received an honorary doctorate during the ceremony. (Photo by Theresa Hogue, courtesy of OSU News and Research Communications)

Willi Unsoeld demonstrating a rappelling position, ca. 1950. Unsoeld came to OSC in 1944 and earned a BS in physics in 1951. During his time at Oregon State, he helped to establish the OSC Mountain Club. After receiving a PhD from the University of Washington in 1958, Unsoeld returned to OSC to teach religious studies. Unsoeld was a world-class mountain climber best known for his participation in a 1963 climb of Mount Everest, the first by a group from the United States. He was one of the first two climbers to scale Everest's west ridge. Unsoeld died in an avalanche on Mount Rainier in March 1979. Unsoeld's wife, Jolene (class of 1953) served as a US Representative from Washington from 1989 to 1995. This photograph was taken by Jim Hosmer, who attended Oregon State and later worked as a professional photographer. Like Unsoeld, he was an avid mountain climber. (P17:4200)

Warren Kronstad receiving the Alexander von Humboldt Foundation Award, 1981. This $10,000 award is given every five years to the person who has made the most significant contribution to US agriculture. Kronstad (1932–2000) came to Oregon State in 1959 as a doctoral student and remained as an instructor after completing his PhD in 1963. He ultimately led the wheat breeding project, which developed many new varieties of wheat. Among Kronstad's many distinctions were OSU's Distinguished Professor Award and the Alumni Association's Distinguished Professor Award. He was the first to hold the Wheat Research Endowed Chair, established by Oregon wheat producers in his honor. During his career, Kronstad advised more than a hundred graduate students from around the world. He retired in 1998. (P57:7153)

Portrait of Katharine Jefferts Schori, 1990. Jefferts Schori is the Episcopal Church of the United States' twenty-sixth Presiding Bishop. She received MS and PhD degrees in oceanography from Oregon State in 1977 and 1983. After receiving a master of divinity degree in 1994, she became assistant rector of Corvallis's Church of the Good Samaritan. Jefferts Schori later served as the Episcopal Church's Bishop of Nevada before being elected as Presiding Bishop in 2006. (P119, Accession 96:054)

Warren Washington, 1993. Washington, who is from Portland, received a BS in physics (1958) and an MS degree in meteorology (1960) from Oregon State. He joined the staff of the National Center for Atmospheric Research (NCAR) in 1963 and earned his PhD from Penn State University in 1964. He has spent his entire career at NCAR; through his work there, Washington has become an internationally renowned climate scientist focusing on climate modeling. He was awarded the National Medal of Science in 2010, has served as chair of the National Science Board, and received an honorary doctorate from OSU in 2006. He was also that year's commencement speaker. (P195, Accession 2009:034)

Ken and Joan Austin celebrating the dedication of the Austin Family Business Program, 1995. Joining the Austins were OSU president John V. Byrne (left) and program director Pat Frishkoff (cutting the ribbon). The program was established in 1985, just the second of its type in the nation. The Austins founded A-dec, a dental equipment company, in 1964. In addition to the family business program, they were strong supporters of various OSU programs and projects, including the LaSells Stewart Center; the Valley Library; the Austin Entrepreneurship Program; and the new home of the College of Business, Austin Hall. (P194:8)

Roosevelt Credit performing at the Valley Library dedication, May 1999. Credit was a 1990 OSU graduate in music education. In 1996, he performed at the library's groundbreaking ceremony. Credit has performed professionally in many musicals, most notably in Broadway productions of *Porgy and Bess* and *Showboat*. He also performed at President Obama's inauguration and was the featured guest artist during the Jazz at Lincoln Center's Centennial Celebration of Duke Ellington. (P83, Accession 2007:089)

Al and Pat Reser, June 2009. Al and Pat Reser were 1960 graduates of Oregon State. As a teenager, Al worked in his family's prepared foods business, delivering his mother's potato salads to grocery stores. Shortly after graduating from OSC, Al became CEO of the family business, Reser's Fine Foods, and turned it into a nearly billion-dollar business selling salads, salsa, and dips. With that success, the Resers turned to philanthropy, supporting Special Olympics, the Portland Rose Festival Grand Floral Parade, and OSU. Most notably, the Resers' contributions to OSU athletics were acknowledged with the renaming of the football stadium as Reser Stadium in 1999. The Resers also provided significant support for the construction of the Linus Pauling Science Center. Al Reser died in April 2010. (Photo courtesy of OSU News and Research Communications)

DISTINGUISHED PROFESSORS

OSU created the Distinguished Professor designation in order to recognize "individuals who have achieved national/international status as a result of their contributions to scholarship/creative activity, research, education and service, and whose work has been notably influential in their fields of specialization." Since the designation was established, more than forty-five faculty have been honored as Distinguished Professors. See the appendix for a complete list of Distinguished Professors.

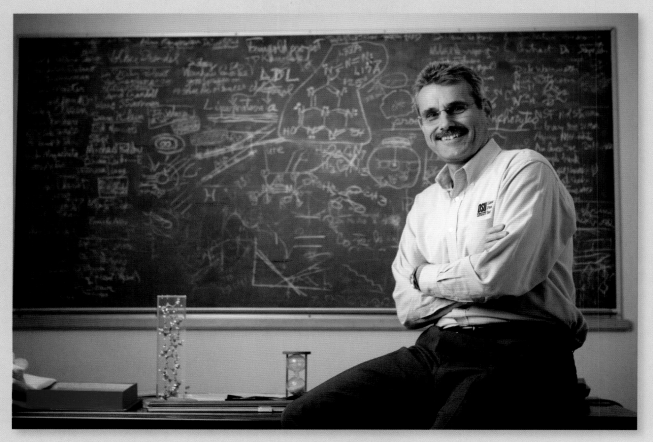

Balz Frei, director of the Linus Pauling Institute, November 2007. Frei was appointed director of the Linus Pauling Institute in 1997, after its move to OSU in 1996. Prior to OSU, he held faculty positions at the Harvard School of Public Health and the Boston University School of Medicine. Frei earned MS and PhD degrees from the Swiss Institute of Federal Technology in Zürich. Frei's research has focused on the role of free radicals and inflammation in human chronic diseases, especially atherosclerosis and cardiovascular disease. He was named an OSU Distinguished Scholar in 2010. (Photo courtesy of OSU News and Research Communications)

Kathleen Dean Moore, 1998. Moore, an Emeritus Distinguished Professor of Philosophy, came to OSU in 1975. An environmental philosopher, she taught many classes about humans' place in the natural world. She co-founded and served as a senior fellow with the Spring Creek Project for Ideas, Nature, and the Written Word. She has won many awards for her writing, including an Oregon Book Award for her 2005 work, *The Pine Island Paradox: Making Connections in a Disconnected World.* (P57, Accession 2006:046)

K. Norman Johnson, August 2010. Johnson, Distinguished Professor of Forest Ecosystems and Society, was one of the architects of the 1993 Northwest Forest Plan, which created policies and guidelines for the use of forest lands in northern California, Oregon, and Washington. Fellow OSU faculty member Jerry Franklin (now affiliated with the University of Washington) was also one of the plan's authors. Johnson received his PhD in forestry from OSU in 1973 and joined the faculty in 1985. (Photo by Danielle White, courtesy of OSU News and Research Communications)

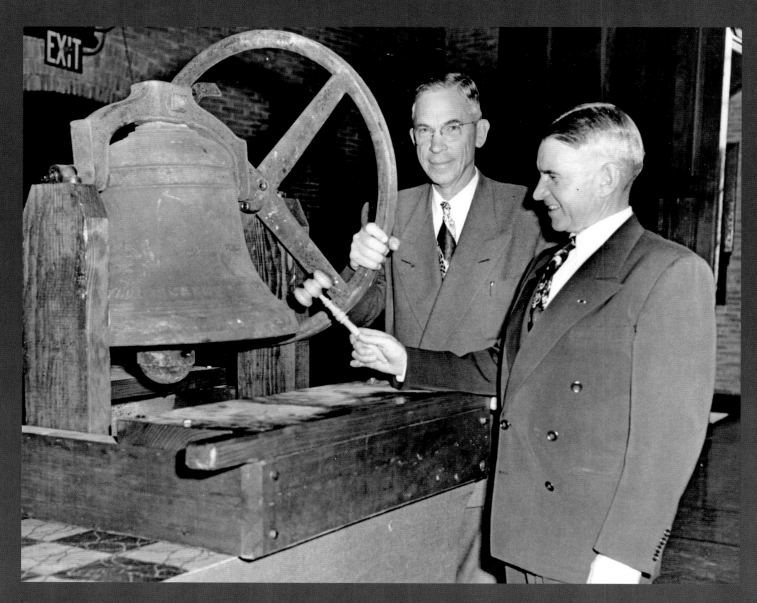

Oregon State College president A. L. Strand and Oregon governor Douglas McKay with the original Corvallis College bell, which was presented to the Horner Museum by the Methodist Church on October 19, 1949, at OSC's first convocation of the 1949–50 academic year. (HC 339)

Afterword

We owe Larry Landis an enormous debt of gratitude for pulling together this monumental work. In what he assures us could have been a book three times the size, he has selected some five hundred photographs documenting the astonishing array of persons, places, and activities that define OSU's nearly 150 years of existence. Open the book at any point and you will be greeted by snapshots of a world in motion that convey the mixture of imagination and execution at the heart of our land-grant university.

The photographs reflect OSU's geographic reach well beyond the campus proper. We see picnic excursions into the countryside, tug-of-war games in local streams, forestry camps, and ROTC military exercises, all taking undergraduates off campus. For faculty, too, the centrifugal force is strong, from Extension faculty in counties throughout Oregon to those whose research takes them much farther afield—oceanographers exploring the seas off the South America aboard submarines; scientists investigating climate change from atop distant mountain ranges. *A School for the People* reminds us just how much of OSU's life has taken place beyond the central campus, just how wide-ranging OSU's presence has been.

As one might expect, many photos document the steady development of the Corvallis campus, the conversion of farmland and dirt roads to groomed landscape. Changes in the institution's built environment, rituals, and academic culture are chronicled in a remarkable array of images, ranging from the familiar to the strange. Next to the ubiquitous beakers and microscopes, greenhouses and dairy farms, and barrels of beer, we encounter a mid-century computer that consumes the better part of a room, a microphone shaped like a teakettle, a fifty-ton magnet being lowered into the

earth. What are we to make of unself-conscious, half-naked cadets engaging in arms exercises on the quad during World War II? Or of contests highlighting swimsuit-clad "wrestling court" beauties, a crowned Forestry Fräulein, a Little Colonel, and a Miss Engineering? Fussing manuals and rook beanies remind us of a world long gone, a world whose wild enthusiasm for rituals has become more muted today (who sanctioned the burning of a two-story, hastily constructed edifice for the homecoming bonfire, one wonders). Those iconic buildings that remain with us—present-day Benton Hall, Kearney Hall, and Furman Hall—acquire new associations when viewed through the years, mounted by eager climbers and surrounded with faculty and students whose fashions signify the passage of time.

One of the key themes that informs this pictorial history is that OSU, however remote geographically, has been caught up in the larger currents of historical change. The Great Depression brought college life to a near standstill; the postwar period saw an enormous surge; and political and cultural ferment of the 1960s and 1970s found its way to campus, too, in sit-ins and walk-outs. Decisions made in Washington, DC, and Salem left their impressions throughout the institution's history: in land-grant acts of the late nineteenth century, in the GI Bill, and in local tax-cutting measures, to name a few. Whatever the local particularities that have shaped this university—the distinctiveness of its physical environment, the demographic profile of the region, the political culture of the state—the changes wrought over the last 150 years are usefully viewed within a larger national and international context.

A second theme concerns the relationship between the individual and the group. OSU has had its share of luminaries—university presidents, distinguished faculty, outstanding students, prominent alumni, and generous supporters. One of this book's great virtues is that it reveals just how much can be accomplished by dedicated individuals. But equally striking is just how much has been done collectively. Teams, clubs, associations, collaborations, and friendships are pervasive in *A School for the People*. The book reveals a world inhabited by people working together earnestly and with good humor and goodwill to get things done.

And it is that collective spirit that may mark the OSU experience most distinctively, underscoring its central mission to create an educated citizenry that will go into the world and change it for the better. The photographs collected in *A School for the People* detail rich and diverse explorations into progressive change—through creative expression, critical imagination, debate and deliberation, and innovation and enterprise. The long history of Oregon State University begins with a land-grant commitment to educating citizens of the state, and, indeed, of the world. If the past is predictor, whatever the next 150 years hold, the university will shine most brightly in holding fast to that original commitment as it negotiates the challenges and opportunities of an uncertain future.

Ben Mutschler
Director, School of History, Philosophy, and Religion
Oregon State University

APPENDIX OSU Quick Facts

PRESIDENTS OF OREGON STATE, 1865–2014

William Asa Finley (1865–1872)

Joseph Emery (1872, acting)

Benjamin Lee Arnold (1872–1892)

John Davidson Letcher (1892, acting)

John McKnight Bloss (1892–1896)

Henry B. Miller (1896–1897)

Thomas Milton Gatch (1897–1907)

William Jasper Kerr (1907–1932)

George Wilcox Peavy (1932–1934, acting; 1934–1940)

Frank Llewellyn Ballard (1940–1941)

Francois Archibald Gilfillan (1941–1942, acting)

August LeRoy Strand (1942–1961)

James Herbert Jensen (1961–1969)

Roy Alton Young (1969–1970, acting)

Robert William MacVicar (1970–1984)

John Vincent Byrne (1984–1995)

Paul G. Risser (1996–2002)

Timothy P. White (2002–2003, acting)

Edward John Ray (2003–present)

MEMBERS OF THE CORVALLIS COLLEGE
BOARD OF TRUSTEES

*The members of this board had varying lengths of service
between 1866 and 1886. The college president served in an
ex-officio capacity.*

Dr. J. M. Applewhite	Corvallis
Benjamin L. Arnold (ex-officio)	Corvallis
Hon. Joseph C. Avery	
Dr. J. R. Bayley	Corvallis
Rev. B. R. Baxter	Dixie
Rev. John R. N. Bell	Corvallis
Benjamin R. Biddle	Corvallis
Judge R. P. Boise	Salem
R. W. Brock	Brownsville
S. T. Brown	Corvallis
William B. Bryan	Corvallis
R. L. Buchanan	Corvallis
Rev. B. F. Burch	Independence
Judge John Burnett	Corvallis
M. Canterbury, MD	Corvallis
J. R. Cardwell, MD	Portland
James A. Cauthorn	Corvallis
A. Cauthorn	Corvallis
Judge F. A. Chenoweth	Corvallis
Rev. J. W. Compton	Eugene
B.F. Crabtree	Scio
Rev. J. W. Compton	——
Rev. E. J. Dawne	Salem
Silas Day	Jacksonville
Rev. Joseph Emery	Corvallis
J. L. Ferguson	Lafayette
Rev. William A. Finley (ex-officio)	Corvallis
J. P. Friedley	Corvallis
Charles Gaylord	Corvallis
W. B. Hamilton	Corvallis
A. Holder	Corvallis
M. Jacobs	Corvallis
Pres. J. W. Johnson	Eugene
Rev. James Kelsay	Corvallis
Robert C. Kinney	Lafayette
Dr. J. B. Lee	Corvallis
Joseph Liggett	Corvallis
A. N. Locke	Corvallis
Hon. E. B. McElroy	Salem

Rev. D. C. McFarland	Tangent	J. M. Church	La Grande, Oregon
R. A. McFarland	Albany	J. A. Churchill (2)	Salem, Oregon
Rev. R. C. Martin	Junction City	Rev. J. W. Compton	Eugene, Oregon
Rev. E. G. Michaels	——	William W. Cotton	Portland, Oregon
Rev. C. H. E. Newton	Umatilla	John D. Daly	Corvallis, Oregon
Rev. R. C. Oglesby	Dallas	T. W. Davenport	Silverton, Oregon
J. M. Osburn	Corvallis	P. I. Dunbar (2)	Salem, Oregon
J. S. Palmer	Corvallis	H. J. Elliott	Perrydale, Oregon
E. T. Perkins	Corvallis	Rev. Joseph Emery	Klamath, Oregon
Harry Pineston	Roseburg	John Emmett	Umpqua Ferry, Oregon
Jackson Rader	Jacksonville	T. T. Geer (1)	Salem, Oregon
A. Roberts	Portland	J. W. Grimm	Aurora, Oregon
Rev. A. E. Sears	Dixie	C. L. Hawley	McCoy, Oregon
G. B. Smith	Corvallis	H. E. Hayes (4)	Oswego, Oregon
Rev. J. W. Stahl	Harrisburg	William H. Hilleary (4)	Turner, Oregon
Hon. R. S. Strahan	Corvallis	Hal E. Hoss (2)	Salem, Oregon
Hon. A. J. Thayer	Corvallis	Charles A. Howard (3)	Salem, Oregon
Rev. T. B. White	Corvallis	M. Jacobs	Corvallis, Oregon
W. A. Willis	Roseburg	B. F. Irvine	Corvallis, Oregon
A. M. Witham	Corvallis	G. M. Irwin (3)	Salem, Oregon

MEMBERS OF THE OREGON AGRICULTURAL COLLEGE BOARD OF REGENTS

The members of the board of regents served terms of various lengths between the board's creation in 1886 and its dissolution in 1929. Ex-officio members are indicated by a number following their names: Governor (1), Secretary of State (2), Superintendent of Public Instruction (3), and State Grange Master (4).

J. H. Ackerman (3)	Salem
E. B. Aldrich	Pendleton
John T. Apperson, President 1896–1901	Oregon City
F. A. Bailey, MD	Hillsboro
Harry Bailey	Lakeview
Dr. J. R. Bayley	Corvallis
Rev. J. R. N. Bell	Corvallis
F. W. Benson (1) (2)	Salem
Judge R. F. Boise (4)	Salem, Oregon
R. W. Brock	Corvallis, Oregon
Sam H. Brown	Gervais, Oregon
R. L. Buchanan	Corvallis, Oregon
B. F. Burch	Independence, Oregon
Austin Buxton (4)	Forest Grove, Oregon
Thomas E. Cauthorn	Corvallis, Oregon
George E. Chamberlain (1)	Salem, Oregon

W. P. Keady	Portland, Oregon
Benton Killin	Portland, Oregon
H. R. Kincaid (2)	Salem, Oregon
Mrs. W. S. Kinney	Astoria, Oregon
Sam A. Kozer (2)	Salem, Oregon
Wm. S. Ladd, President 1888–1896	Portland, Oregon
Dr. J. B. Lee	Corvallis, Oregon
B. G. Leedy (4)	Tigardville, Oregon
William P. Lord (1)	Salem, Oregon

Regent Mary Edna Strong Kinney, ca. 1925. Kinney was the second woman named to the OAC board of regents and served from 1925 to 1929. She had been involved in Oregon's suffrage movement in the 1900s and 1910s and later served in the Oregon House of Representatives and Senate in the late 1910s through the mid-1920s. She was the first woman elected to the Oregon Senate. Kinney was also active in business and civic affairs in Astoria. A World War II Liberty ship built in Portland was named in her honor. (HC 1956)

George W. McBride (2)	Salem, Oregon	1910–1911	R. L. Davidson
E. B. McElroy (3)	Salem, Oregon	1911–1912	L. C. Keene
Rev. D. C. McFarland	Tangent, Oregon	1912–1913	E. G. Rice
Rev. E. G. Michaels	Eugene, Oregon	1913–1914	Ralph A. Blanchard
H. B. Miller	Grants Pass, Oregon	1914–1915	Chester Allen Dickey
N. R. Moore	Corvallis, Oregon	1915–1916	Roy E. Miller
Jefferson Myers	Portland, Oregon	1916–1917	Godfrey R. Hoerner
Wallis Nash	Corvallis, Oregon	1917–1918	J. Douglas McKay
R. G. Oglesby	Eugene, Oregon	1918–1919	Theodore P. Cramer
Ben W. Olcott (1) (2)	Salem, Oregon	1919–1920	George M. Schwarz
John D. Olwell	Central Point, Oregon	1920–1921	William Teutsch
J. M. Osburn	Corvallis, Oregon	1921–1922	Roy S. Keene
B. S. Pague	Portland, Oregon	1922–1923	Harold H. Readen
George A. Palmiter (4)	Hood River, Oregon	1923–1924	John B. Alexander
Isaac L. Patterson (1)	Salem, Oregon	1924–1925	Percy P. Locey
Sylvester Pennoyer (1)	Salem, Oregon	1925–1926	Waldo Stoddard
Walter M. Pierce (1)[1]	La Grande, Oregon	1926–1927	Vernon Jenkins
A. R. Shipley	Oswego, Oregon	1927–1928	Ursel C. Narver
Charles E. Spence (4)	Oregon City	1928–1929	Grant McMillan
Judge R. S. Strahan	Albany, Oregon	1929–1930	Ranson Meinke
H. Von Der Hellen	Wellen, Oregon	1930–1931	George Knutson
Jacob Voorehees (4)	Woodburn, Oregon	1931–1932	Milton Leishman
Clara H. Waldo	Corvallis, Oregon	1932–1933	Elmer Buckhorn
James K. Weatherford, President 1901–1929	Corvallis, Oregon	1933–1934	Fred Saling
		1934–1935	Willard S. White
Oswald West (1)	Salem, Oregon	1935–1936	Jack Graham
E. E. Wilson, Esq.	Corvallis, Oregon	1936–1937	John Gallagher
A. M. Witham	Corvallis, Oregon	1937–1938	Robert Henderson
James Withycombe (1)	Salem, Oregon	1938–1939	Robert Walker
M. S. Woodcock	Corvallis, Oregon	1939–1940	Ralph D. Floberg
William E. Yates	Corvallis, Oregon	1940–1941	Douglas Chambers
		1941–1942	Andy Landforce
		1942–1943	Dave Baum

PRESIDENTS OF THE OAC STUDENT ASSEMBLY/ ASSOCIATED STUDENTS OF OREGON STATE UNIVERSITY

1900–1901	Charles Horner	1943–1944	Donald G. Hall
1901–1902	Edgar Tulley	1944–1945	George Dewey
1902–1903	W. T. Dickey	1945–1946	Robert F. Stevens
1903–1904	Bert Pilkington	1946–1947	Don Moyer
1904–1905	Fred C. Stimpson	1947–1948	Bill Proppe
1905–1906	A. L. Bradley	1948–1949	Tom House
1906–1907	M. E. Forsythe	1949–1950	James W. Hanker
1907–1908	E. P. W. Harding	1950–1951	Donald Hays
1908–1909	T. J. Autzen	1951–1952	Donn Black
1909–1910	T. J. Autzen	1952–1953	D. E. Van Allsburg
		1953–1954	Donald Foss
		1954–1955	Stanley Blinkhorn
		1955–1956	Johnnie Rice

Dean Francois Gilfillan administers a loyalty pledge to the officers of Oregon State's student government, May 10, 1941. Andy Landforce, front row left, was the president of the Associated Students of Oregon State College for 1941–42. He later served as a longtime Extension wildlife specialist. (HC 1535)

1956–1957	Lt. Col. Charles Atticott	1985–1986	David Crowell
1957–1958	Charlie Dunn	1986–1987	Nicholas Van Vleet
1958–1959	Larry McKennon	1987–1988	Bob Mumford
1959–1960	Wilmer H. Post	1988–1989	Christopher H. Voigt
1960–1961	Richard Seideman	1989–1990	Shahid Yusaf
1961–1962	George Abed	1990–1991	Shahid Yusaf
1962–1963	Mike Burton	1991–1992	Todd Mickey
1963–1964	Grant Watkinson	1992–1993	Brad Fields
1964–1965	Jud Blakely	1993–1994	Brian Clem
1965–1966	Roy Ventura	1994–1995	April Diane Waddy
1966–1967	Husnu Ozyegin	1995–1996	Jon Isaacs
1967–1968	Paul Schaber	1996–1997	Libby Mitchell
1968–1969	John Fraser	1997–1998	Matt DeVore
1969–1970	Harold Britton	1998–1999	Mike Caudle
1970–1971	David Hall	1999–2000	Melanie Spraggins
1971–1972	Ronald Wilkinson	2000–2001	Justin Roach
1972–1973	David Dietz	2001–2002	Justin Geddes
1973–1974	John Gartland	2002–2003	Bridget Burns
1974–1975	Robert Kingzett	2003–2004	Andy Saultz
1975–1976	William P. Mumford	2004–2005	Kristen Downey
1976–1977	David Gomberg	2005–2006	Dan McCarthy
1977–1978	Stan McGehee	2006–2007	Mike Olson
1978–1979	Melvin Ferguson	2007–2008	Greg Purdy
1979–1980	Cynthia J. Whilhite	2008–2009	Ryan Mann
1980–1981	Jeffrey Mengis	2009–2010	Chris Van Drimmelen
1981–1982	Jeffrey P. Strickler	2010–2011	Andrew Struthers
1982–1983	Shawn Dooley	2011–2012	Tonga Hopoi
1983–1984	Sharon Wolford	2012–2013	Amelia Harris
1984–1985	Michael Witteman	2013–2014	Brett Deedon

Knute Buhler, 1988

Wesley Sand, 1991

Debra Walt, 1995

PULITZER PRIZE WINNERS

This is an incomplete list.

Chris Anderson	1985, News Photography; 1989, Specialized Reporting
George Oppen	1969, Poetry
Roger Werth	1981, Local General Reporting[2]
Jon D. Franklin	1979, Feature Writing; 1985, Explanatory Journalism

ACADEMY/EMMY/TONY/GRAMMY AWARD WINNERS

This is an incomplete list.

Harley Jessup	1987, Oscar, Best Visual Effects (*Innerspace*)
Scott Baker	2010, Oscar, Best Documentary (*The Cove*)
Roosevelt Credit	2012, Revival (Musical— The Gershwin's *Porgy and Bess*)[3]

AMERICAN ASSOCIATION FOR THE ADVANCEMENT OF SCIENCE FELLOWS

Each fellow's primary section affiliation and year of designation follow his or her name.

Andrew Blaustein, Biological Sciences, 1998

Larry Boersma, Agriculture, Food, and Renewable Resources, 1987

Edward Brook, Geology and Geography, 2011

Stella Melugin Coakley, Agriculture, Food, and Renewable Resources, 1999

Anita Guerrini, History and Philosophy of Science, 2009

John B. Hays, Biological Sciences, 2001

Kenneth Hedberg, Chemistry, 1985

Christopher Mathews, Biological Sciences, 1965

Bruce Menge, Biological Sciences, 1991

Mary Jo Nye, History and Philosophy of Science, 1998

Sastry Pantula, Statistics, 2011

Minocher Reporter, Biological Sciences, 1965

Courtland Smith, Social, Economics and Political Sciences, 1971

Robert Lloyd Smith, Atmospheric and Hydrospheric Sciences, 1990

Steven Strauss, Biological Sciences, 2008

Conrad Weiser, Agriculture, Food, and Renewable Resources, 1988

DISTINGUISHED FACULTY

Alan Acock, Human Development & Family Science

Dan Arp, University Honors College

James Ayres, Pharmacy

George Bailey, Environmental & Molecular Toxicology

Joseph Beckman, Environmental Health Sciences

Luiz Bermudez, Veterinary Medicine

Andrew Blaustein, Environmental Sciences

Larry Boersma, Crop and Soil Science

Marcus Borg, Religious Studies

Arthur Boucot, Zoology

James Carrington, Ag Botany & Plant Pathology

Dudley Chelton, College of Oceanic and Atmospheric Sciences

Tracy Daugherty, English

Thomas Dietterich, Electrical Engineering and Computer Science

Stephen Giovanni, Microbiology

Paul Farber, History

Balz Frei, Linus Pauling Institute

John Fryer, Microbiology

Marie Harvey, Public Health

K. Norman Johnson, Forest Resources

Douglas Keszler, Chemistry

Jo-Ann Leong, Microbiology

Jane Lubchenco, Zoology

Christopher Mathews, Biochemistry/Biophysics

Jeffrey A. McCubbin, Nutrition and Exercise Science

Jeffrey J. McDonnell, Forest Engineering Resources & Management

Bruce Menge, Zoology

Kathleen Dean Moore, Philosophy

Frank Moore, Zoology

Jeffrey J. Morrell, Wood Science and Technology

Michael Oriard, English

Donald Reed, Biochemistry & Biophysics

William Ripple, Forest Ecosystems & Society

William Robbins, History

David Robinson, English Department

William Sandine, Microbiology

Henry Sayre, Art

Lewis Semprini, Civil, Construction and Environmental
Engineering

John Sessions, Forest Engineering Resources & Management

Arthur Sleight, Chemistry

Fred Stormshak, Animal Sciences

Steven Strauss, Forest Ecosystems & Society

Robert Tanguay, Environmental and Molecular Toxicology

T. Darrah Thomas, Chemistry

Kensal Edward Van Holde, Biochemistry/Biophysics

Richard Waring, Forest Science

Patricia Wheeler, College of Oceanic and Atmospheric Sciences

James White, Chemistry

Ronald Wrolstad, Food Science and Technology

HONORARY DEGREE RECIPIENTS

All were presented at the spring commencement exercises unless indicated otherwise.

1923	James Knox Weatherford	LL.D.
1923	Clara Humason Waldo	LL.D.
1927	B.F. Irvine	LL.D.
1929	Hopkin Jenkins	LL.D.
1929	Edward Christopher Allworth	LL.D.
1930	Ben Selling	LL.D.
1930	Edward Charles Elliott	LL.D.
1930	Eva Emery Dye	Litt.D.
1930	Oakes Mortimer Plummer	M. Agriculture
1931	William Lovell Finley	D. Sc.
1931	George B. Herington	D. Eng.
1931	Adolphe Wolfe	LL.D.
1931	William Oxley Thompson	LL.D.
1932	Arthur Burton Cordley	LL.D.
1932	Andrew John Bexell	LL.D.
1932	Henry Joseph Berkowitz	LL.D.
1932	William Arthur Jensen	M.S.
1933	Linus C. Pauling	D.Sc.
1933	D.C. Henny	D. Eng.
1934	Frederick Berchtold	Litt.D.
1934	Louis Gaylord Clarke	LL.D.
1934	Uberto Merson Dickey	LL.D.
1936	Ira N. Gabrielson	D.Sc.
1936	R. K. Brodie	D.Sc.
1936	J. A. Hanson	D.Sc.
1937	Gov. Charles H. Martin	LL.D.

William L. Finley with birds, ca. 1905. Finley was a renowned naturalist photographer, filmmaker and author, and received an honorary degree by Oregon State in 1931. He lived most of his life in the Portland area, was the author of *American Birds* in 1908, and helped to found Oregon's Fish and Game Commission in 1911. He had a close working relationship with the OSC Department of Fish, Game and Fur Animal Management after its founding in 1934. He was a nephew of OSU's first president, William A. Finley. This photo appeared on page 105 of *American Birds*. (MSS—Finley)

1937	Warren Ellsworth Forsythe	D.Sc.
1938	Dr. E. J. Kraus	D.Sc.
1938	Thornton T. Munger	D.Sc.
1938	J. C. Stevens	D.Eng.
1939	Dr. Paul H. Emmett	D.Sc.
1939	Dr. John C. Merriam	D.Sc.
1939	Glen Lukens	Doctor of Ceramics
1939	A. D. Molohon	M.Agr.
1939	J. A. Churchill	LL.D.
1940	John Harrison Belknap	D.Eng.
1940	A. D. Taylor	D.Sc.
1940	Elmer Ivan Applegate	D.Sc.

1940	Brig. Gen. Thomas M. Robins	D.Eng.	
1943	Wm. H. Galvani	D.Eng.	
1943	Wm. Jasper Kerr	LL.D.	
1943	Edwin T. Reed	Litt.D.	
1943	Zed J. Atlee	D.Eng.	
1945	Lucy M. Lewis	D. Library Science	
1945	Melville Eastham	D.Eng.	
1946	Edward Curf Sammons	LL.D.	
1953	Stanley Gordon Jewett	D.Sc.	
Oct. 27 1955	Luang Suwan	D.Sc.	
Oct. 27 1955	Douglas McKay	D.Sc.	
1956	Dr. William Justin Kroll	D.Sc.	
1956	Dr. Roger John Williams	D.Sc.	
1958	Norris Edward Dodd	D.Sc.	
1958	Herman Oliver	D.Sc.	
1959	Yasuo Baron Goto	D.Sc.	
1959	Wilfrid E. Johnson	D.Sc.	
1960	Frank H. Bartholomew	Doctor of Laws	
1960	Harry Richard Wellman	Doctor of Laws	
1961	Stephen Oswald Rice	D.Sc.	
1961	Ralph Alexander Chapman	Mechanical Engineer	
1990	James DePriest	Doctor of Fine Arts	
1990	Jan Karski	Doctor of Humane Letters	
1991	John Hope Franklin	Doctor of Letters	
1991	Betty Friedan	Doctor of Humane Letters	
1991	Gurij Ivanovich Marchuk	Doctor of Science	
1992	Philip C. Habib	Doctor of Humane Letters	
1993	Rajammal P. Devadas	Doctor of Humane Letters	
1994	Douglas E. Engelbart	Doctor of Engineering	
1995	Philip H. Abelson	Doctor of Science	
1995	Sanga Sabhasri	Doctor of Science	
1996	Senator Mark O. Hatfield	Doctor of Laws	
1997	Paul Crutzen	Doctor of Science	
1997	Barrie Gilbert	Doctor of Engineering	
1997	Daniel Callahan	Doctor of Humane Letters	
1999	Paul G. Hawken	Doctor of Letters	
1999	Admiral James D. Watkins	Doctor of Science	
1999	Anne H. and Paul R. Ehrlich	Doctor of Science	
2000	Gordon W. Gilkey	Doctor of Arts & Humanities	
2002	John S. Niederhauser	Doctor of Science	
2003	James W. Poirot	Doctor of Engineering	
2004	Senator John H. Glenn	Doctor of Science	
2004	Sanjaya Rajaram	Doctor of Science	
2005	Ann Roth Streissguth	Doctor of Humanities	
2006	Emery Castle	Doctor of Humane Letters	
2006	Warren Washington	Doctor of Science	
2007	Michael A. Rich	Doctor of Fine Arts	
2007	Mary Carlin Yates	Doctor of English	
2008	Helen E. Diggs	Doctor of Science	
2009	Jen–Hsun Huang	Doctor of Engineering	
2010	Dr. Donald Pettit	Doctor of Science	
2010	Frits Bolkestein	Doctor of Letters	
2011	Jon DeVaan	Doctor of Engineering	
2012	First Lady Michelle Obama	Doctor of Humane Letters	
2013	Brig. Gen. Julie A. Bentz	Doctor of Science	
2014	Ann A. Kiessling	Doctor of Science	

1908	Forrest Smithson	USA	Track: 110 M HH (15.0)	Gold
1920	Louis "Hap" Kuehn	USA	Diving: Springboard (675.4)	Gold
	Clarence Pinkston	USA	Diving: Platform (503.3)	Gold
			Diving: Springboard (655.3)	Silver
1924	Robin Reed	USA	Wrestling: 134.5 Free	Gold
	Chet Newton	USA	Wrestling: 134.5 Free	Silver
	David Fall	USA	Diving: Platform (97.3)	Silver
	Ray Dodge	USA	Track: 800 M	6th
	Clarence Pinkston	USA	Diving: Springboard (653 pts)	Bronze
		USA	Diving: Platform (94.6 pts)	Bronze
1948	Lew Beck	USA	Basketball (8 wins, 0 losses)	Gold
1960	Lynn Eves	Canada	Track: 100 M (10.8)/200 M (21.9)/4x100 (41.1)	
	Fritz Fivian	USA	Wrestling: Greco (160.75/73 kg)	20th
1964	Mel Counts	USA	Basketball (9 wins, 0 losses)	Gold
	Ron Finley	USA	Wrestling: Greco (138.75/63 kg)	4th
	Morgan Groth	USA	Track: 800 M (1:51.4)	
	Jean Saubert	USA	Skiing (Giant Slalom): 1:53.11	Silver
			Skiing (Slalom): 1:31.36	Bronze
1968	Dick Fosbury	USA	High Jump (7-4 1/2)	Gold
	Jess Lewis	USA	Wrestling: Freestyle (213.5/97 kg)	6th
	Bob McLaren	Canada	Track: 400 M Hurdles (51.8)	
	Hank Schenk	USA	Wrestling: Greco (213.5/97 kg)	
	Tracy Smith	USA	Track: 10,000 M (30:14.6)	11th
	Gary Stenlund	USA	Track: Javelin (241-2.5)	
1972	Hailu Ebba	Ethiopia	Track: 1,500 M (3:43.7)	Semis
	Ed Bennett	Yachting		
	Lahcen Samsame	Morocco	Track: Shot Put (63-6 1/4)	15th
	Hank Schenk	USA	Wrestling: Free (220/100 kg)	
	Tim Vollmer	USA	Discus (197-7 1/2/60.24 m)	8th

Olympic skier Jean Saubert, 1964.
Saubert (class of 1966) won silver and
bronze medals in women's slalom
skiing at the 1964 Winter Olympics in
Innsbruck, Austria. (HC 2299)

1976	Hailu Ebba	Ethiopia	Track: 1,500 M	Boycotted
	Kasheef Hassan	Sudan	Track: 400 M	Boycotted
	Joni Huntley	USA	High Jump (6-2 1/2/1.89 m)	5th
	Kathy Weston	USA	Track: 800 M (2:03.31)	
	Lynne Winbigler	USA	Discus (158 2 1/2/48.22 m)	14th
	Robert Zagunis	USA	Rowing (men's 4/6:54.92)	11th
1980	Kasheef Hassan	Sudan	Track: 400 M	Boycotted
	Thomas Woodman	USA	Rowing (men's 8)	Boycotted
	Patti Jo Knorr	Canada	Gymnastics	Boycotted
1984	Cynthia Greiner	USA	Heptathlon (6281 pts)	4th
	Carol Menken-Schaudt	USA	Basketball	Gold
	Joni Huntley	USA	High Jump (6-5 1/1.97 m)	Bronze
	Kasheef Hassan	Sudan	Track: 400 M	Boycotted
	Ron Finley	USA	Wrestling - Greco Coach	
1988	Cynthia Greiner	USA	Heptathlon (6297 pts)	8th
	Horst Niehaus	Costa Rica	Swimming: Back (100 M/1:01.91)	
			Swimming: Back (200 M/2:12.83)	
			Swimming: Ind. Medley (2:16.16)	
	Jose Ortiz	Puerto Rico	Basketball (4 wins, 4 losses)	7th
1992	Cynthia Greiner	USA	Heptathlon (6300 pts)	9th
	Jose Ortiz	Puerto Rico	Basketball (3 wins, 5 losses)	8th
1996	Les Gutches	USA	Wrestling - 180.5 Free	7th
	Gary Payton	USA	Basketball	Gold
	Jose Ortiz	Puerto Rico	Basketball (2 wins, 5 losses)	10th
	Greg Strobel	USA	Wrestling: Freestyle Co-Coach	
	Mike R. Jones	USA	Wrestling: Freestyle Asst. Coach	
2000	Amy Martin	USA	Rowing (women's 8)	6th
	Gary Payton	USA	Basketball (7 wins, 0 losses)	Gold
	Greg Strobel	USA	Wrestling: Freestyle Co-Coach)	
	Selina Scoble	Australia	Volleyball	
2002	Jill Bakken	USA	Bobsled (2-women)	Gold
2004	Oscar Wood	USA	Wrestling: 145.5 Greco	
	Birte Steven	Germany	Swimming: 200 M Breast (2:29.22)	
	Joey Hansen	USA	Rowing+8 (5:42.48)	Gold
	Crystal Draper	Greece	Softball	
	Jose Ortiz	Puerto Rico	Basketball (3 wins, 4 losses)	6th
2008	Saori Haruguchi	Japan	Swimming: 200 IM (4:45.22)	
	Heinrich Barnes	South Africa	Wrestling (141.5/66 kg)	
	Robbie Findley #	USA	Soccer	
	Josh Inman	USA	Rowing (men's 8/5:23.34)	Bronze
	Olivia Vivian*	Australia	Gymnastics: Artistic/uneven, 14.92	
	Brian Barden	USA	Baseball (6 wins, 3 losses)	Bronze
2012	Kim Butler	England	Basketball	
	Patricia Obee	Canada	Rowing	
	Olivia Vivian #	Australia	Gymnastics	

* Before her freshman year at OSU
# Alternate

Notes

FOREWORD

1   Earle D. Ross, *The Land Grant Idea and Iowa State College* (Ames: Iowa State College Press, 1958), 5.

2   *Biennial Report of Oregon State College, 1951–1952*, 79, box 10, subgroup 12, RG 013.

3   For an article on Art Shay, see Dean Reynolds, *CBS News,* February 13, 2014, http://www.cbsnews.com/news /photographs-tell-story-of-decades-long-romance/, accessed Oct. 3, 2014.

CHAPTER 1

1   Morrill first proposed legislation of this type in 1857. It passed in Congress, but President James Buchanan vetoed it.

2   Corvallis College was in competition with Willamette University for the land-grant designation. See chapter 2 for more detail on the designation of the state's land-grant institution.

3   Although created in 1885, the board of regents first met on February 10, 1886, and began governance of the college in June 1887.

4   The Hatch Act of 1887 provided federal funding ($15,000 initially) to land-grant colleges for creation of agricultural experiment stations at each institution. Although the primary impetus of the Second Morrill Act of 1890 was to allow for the creation of separate land-grant institutions for people of color, it also provided the original land-grant colleges with $15,000 per year in 1890, increased yearly by $1,000, reaching $25,000 annually in 1900.

5   A student from Japan had enrolled as early as 1902, but did not graduate.

6   John Olmsted of the Olmsted Brothers firm, founded by the brothers' father, Frederic Law Olmsted, created the first campus plan in 1909. Noted landscape architect Albert D. Taylor of Cleveland, Ohio, expanded and revised the Olmsted plan in 1926. See chapter 3 for information on both plans.

7   This excludes barns, athletic fields, greenhouses, and buildings at the branch experiment stations.

8   KFDJ became KOAC in 1925.

9   Even though the official name of the institution had been changed to Oregon State Agricultural College in 1927, by 1932 the common name used for the institution was Oregon State College. This name was formally adopted in 1937.

10 OSU's tuition rose by more than 50 percent between 1980 and 1985, and its student enrollment fell from a high of 17,689 in 1980–81 to 15,220 in 1986–87.

11 Title IX of the Education Amendments of 1972, also known as the Patsy Mink Equal Opportunity in Education Act, states that "no person in the United States shall, on the basis of sex, be excluded from participation in, be denied the benefits of, or be subjected to discrimination under any education program or activity receiving federal financial assistance."

12 The review was completed by the KPMG Peat Marwick professional services company.

13 The foundation was established by alumni Wayne and Gladys Valley, who attended Oregon State in the 1930s. See chapter 11 for more information on the Valleys.

14 OSU Cascades Campus enrollment of 487 in 2001 included 414 students who enrolled from OSU partner institutions and non-OSU institutions, and COCC students admitted as OSU students.

15 The enrollment number for 2013 includes all sources—the Corvallis campus, Ecampus, and Cascades Campus.

CHAPTER 2

Parts of this chapter were excerpted from "The Early Years" by Rebecca L. Landis, written for the *Oregon Stater.*

1   The territorial legislature "located and established" the territorial university at Marysville (Corvallis) in 1851. A site was selected in 1853, near where Ballard Extension Hall is located today. Materials for constructing a building were assembled at the site, but the structure was never built.

2   The original trustees of the college included Corvallis founders Joseph C. Avery and William F. Dixon, as well as other prominent local citizens such as Bushrod W. Wilson, J. A. Hanna, and W. L. Cardwell.

3   Willamette University, founded in 1842, was one of a very few institutions that offered collegiate-level courses in the late 1850s. Willamette bestowed its first collegiate degree in 1859.

4   The college's second catalog, issued in 1867, listed 167 students, although only eight were enrolled in the Collegiate Department. The other 159 students were enrolled in either the Primary or Preparatory departments.

5   Bellinger had been elected earlier in 1868 to the Legislative Assembly in a hotly disputed election, adding more intrigue to the circumstances surrounding Corvallis College's designation as the state's land-grant institution.

6   Oregon's Democratic Party in the late 1860s was generally sympathetic to pro-Southern issues, and therefore would have been supportive of an institution affiliated with the Methodist Episcopal Church, South. Willamette University was affiliated with the Methodist Episcopal Church, North.

7   It is not known why the lands were located in a remote part of Oregon that was not particularly desirable in the 1870s. It is possible that the railroads viewed this land grant as a potential impediment to their own land grants and pressured the commission to seek lands other than the high-value timber and agricultural areas in western and southern Oregon. Ten thousand acres subsequently proved to be within the boundaries of the Klamath Reservation. On June 30, 1915, 920 acres still remained unsold. The capital of the endowment was a little over $202,000, yielding a very modest $11,600 in income annually.

8   Finley publicly stated his reason for resigning as the poor condition of Mrs. Finley's health, necessitating their return to California.

9   In early 1873, $1,500 was still due on the purchase price, and on March 1 the college undertook another campaign to solicit subscriptions to underwrite the amount.

10   In 1876 two acres were reserved for agricultural experimentation; the remainder was leased out. Wallis Nash, who was named secretary of the board of regents in 1886 and assisted with the effort to place the college under full state control, leased the farm beginning in 1879.

11   The Methodist Episcopal Church, South's local conference was the Columbia Conference, established at Corvallis in 1866.

12   The new board of regents held its first meeting on February 10, 1886, approximately one year after the passage of Cauthorn's legislation. Cauthorn was one of the first regents.

13   One of the leaders of the State Agricultural College Association was M. M. Jacobs of Corvallis, who was also a member of the board of trustees.

14   William S. Ladd of Portland was the president of the board of regents.

15   The annual appropriation from the Second Morrill Act increased yearly until it reached $25,000.

CHAPTER 3

1   The minutes of the board of regents indicate that a Mr. Pugh and Mr. Boothby were to be solicited for designs for the buildings. These references are probably to Salem architects Walter D. Pugh and Wilbur F. Boothby. Pugh designed OAC's Cauthorn (Fairbanks) Hall.

2   These included Cauthorn (Fairbanks) Hall, 1892; the Horticulture Building, 1894; Gymnasium and Armory (Valley Gymnastics Center), 1898; a new Mechanical Hall (Kearney Hall), 1899; Agriculture (Furman) Hall, 1902; and Waldo Hall, 1907.

3   Olmsted's report was narrative only. Kerr opted not to pay for a visual plan, but instead had landscape architecture faculty member Arthur L. Peck design a campus-planning map based on Olmsted's recommendations. That map was completed in 1910. John Olmsted was a stepson and nephew of Frederick Law Olmsted Sr. and half brother of Frederick Law Olmsted Jr.

4   Olmsted also recommended removing the trees planted along the central pathway through Lower Campus. Fortunately they remained and are still enjoyed by the OSU community.

5   These included branch stations at Hermiston (1909), Moro (1909), Harney (1911), Talent (1911), Hood River (1913), Astoria (1913), Pendleton (1927), Medford (1931, relocation

of the Talent station), Squaw Butte (1935), Klamath Falls (1937), and Oregon City (1939).

6   John Olmsted died in 1920.

7   Taylor called for Administration and Academic quads—the East and West quads in the Olmsted plan. Today those are the Library and Memorial Union quads.

8   LEED is the Leadership in Energy and Environmental Design certification of the US Green Building Council. When it opened, the Kelley Engineering Center was the greenest academic engineering building in the United States.

9   Restore Oregon, formerly known as the Historic Preservation League of Oregon, established the DeMuro Awards to honor extraordinary historic rehabilitation projects and compatible infill development in Oregon. It is named in honor of the late Art DeMuro, whose historic redevelopment projects "set the standard for quality, creativity, persistence and business acumen."

CHAPTER 4

1   Frank Ballard (1940–41) and Francois Gilfillan (acting, 1941–42) were the two presidents who held OSU degrees.

2   This position, first held by William A. Jensen, was initially called the "Recorder of the Faculties."

CHAPTER 5

1   The first master of arts degree was awarded to Franklin Cauthorn in 1876. The first doctoral degrees conferred by the college would not occur for nearly sixty more years.

2   The remaining acreage was leased out to raise funds for the college.

3   Edgar Grimm, in his section of the 1882–84 biennial report, had suggested that farmers' institutes should be implemented as one means for the college to have an agriculture school that was as successful as others in the United States; that success was "due to their cooperation with the farmers, through farmers institutes, societies and co-operative field experiments."

4   The Salem farmers' institute was held in the senate chamber of the state capitol.

5   Literary commerce referred to early business-related classes such as bookkeeping, stenography, and typewriting, and included an emphasis on English classes every term during a student's course of study.

6   This funding was for oceanographic research, which laid the foundation for subsequent funding and the establishment of graduate-level instruction.

7   As rated by *US News & World Report*.

8   Text by Kip Carlson, reproduced courtesy of OSU Athletic Communications.

CHAPTER 6

1   White soil is poorly drained soil that tends to build up soluble salts. Marl is a soil type that contains lime-rich clays and silt.

2   Although Oregon governor Sylvester Pennoyer signed legislation formally creating OAC's Agricultural Experiment Station on February 25, 1889, the work of the station had begun in 1888.

3   Hops were first planted on the college farm in the early 1890s.

4   The National Science Foundation was established in 1950.

5   The *Acona* was purchased with an ONR grant of $250,000. It was the first of several OSU research vessels. Others have been the 180-foot *Yaquina* (1964), the 80-foot *Cayuse* (1968), the 180-foot *Wecoma* (1976), and the 54-foot *Elakha* (2000). The 177-foot *Oceanus* is also part of OSU's current fleet; it is owned by the NSF and was transferred from Woods Hole Oceanographic Institute to OSU in 2012.

6   This program evolved into today's food science and technology department.

CHAPTER 7

1   This feature is a condensed version of a paper written by Backen for her fall 2013 History 407 seminar class, Untold History of OSU. The paper, titled "Coed Cheesecake: The 1959 Wrestling Court and the Politics of the Marriage Market at Oregon State College," was a winner of the OSU Libraries and Press's 2013 Library Undergraduate Research Award. It is available online at http://ir.library.oregonstate.edu/xmlui/handle/1957/46927.

CHAPTER 8

1   An earlier version of the Adelphian Literary Society was listed in college catalogs from 1868 to about 1877. A second literary society, Gamma Chi, was first listed in the 1871–72 catalog. Both societies may have disbanded in the late 1870s due to the college's financial difficulties.

2   Two short-lived publications preceded the 1890s. A handwritten publication, the *Student Offering*, first

appeared in 1868 and was offered occasionally over the next two years. It was created by the earlier version of the Adelphian Literary Society. In February 1883, *The Gem,* a monthly journal, was first published.

3   OSU paid $1,000 in settlement fees and $100,000 in legal fees in 2013 to end the lawsuit. The university did not admit to any wrongdoing.

4   Four of the fraternities in 1920 were local organizations, unaffiliated with a national fraternity.

5   During the 1940s and 1950s, cooperative houses such as the Campus Club were among the few living alternatives for students of color. OSU's first African American male graduate, Bill Tebeau, was strongly discouraged from living in OSU housing; he ultimately lived in the Hamer House cooperative, which included many international students.

6   This feature is a condensed version of a paper written by Moore for his fall 2013 History 407 seminar class, Untold History of OSU. The full paper was titled "Eugene Okino and Sigma Chi: The Fraternity Antidiscrimination Debate and Oregon State University."

CHAPTER 9

1   Bloss was the son of OAC's president, John Bloss.

2   Two of the bowl games, in 1940 and 1949, were the Pineapple Bowl, where the University of Hawaii invited a team from the mainland to play against it on New Year's Day.

3   Because of World War II, Oregon State did not play football in 1943 and 1944.

4   Robinson is President Barack Obama's brother-in-law.

5   This refers to being named to any type of All-American team.

6   No relation to football coach Mike Riley.

7   OSU did not participate in intercollegiate wrestling from 1927 to 1933 and from 1943 to 1947.

8   As of Spring 2014.

CHAPTER 10

1   "State" students were those appointed from each county to attend the college and study agriculture and mechanic arts—those subjects mandated by the Morrill Act.

2   College catalogs in the 1880s stated that "state" students were required to furnish their own uniforms, but did not indicate what they were to look like. Not until 1888 would the board of regents prescribe a specific uniform—one that was gray in color.

3   The 1918–1920 biennial report lists 2,067 men as having been part of the SATC, but this figure included 502 men who participated in "war emergency courses" at OAC during the summer of 1918 prior to the establishment of the SATC unit.

4   Marion Carl died in June 1998 during a robbery at his home in Roseburg, Oregon. He was inducted posthumously into OSU's Engineering Hall of Fame in 1998 and received the E. B. Lemon Distinguished Alumnus Award in 1990.

CHAPTER 11

1   Gatch earned two doctorates: a doctor of divinity from Lane Theological Seminary in Cincinnati, Ohio, and a doctor of philosophy from Indiana Asbury University (now Depauw University).

2   Their son, Bill, became the iconic track and field coach at the University of Oregon and was a cofounder of Nike.

APPENDIX

1   Walter Pierce also served on the board of regents in a non-ex-officio capacity prior to being elected governor in 1922 This is an incomplete list.

2   Werth won the award along with other staff of the Longview (WA) Daily News for their coverage of the eruption of Mount St. Helens, including his photographs.

3   The award went to the production; Credit was part of the cast.

Sources

The following list includes the major sources used to compile the chapter narratives and the captions.

Baker, John H. *Camp Adair: The Story of a World War II Cantonment: Today, Oregon's Largest Ghost Town.* Newport, OR: John H. Baker, 2003.

Board of Regents Records (RG 8). Special Collections & Archives Research Center. Oregon State University Libraries and Press. Minutes. Boxes 5 and 6.

Board of Trustees Records (RG 33). Special Collections & Archives Research Center. Oregon State University Libraries and Press. Minutes. Box 1.

Forgard, Benjamin. "The Evolution of School Spirit and Tradition at Oregon State University." Corvallis, OR, 2012. http://hdl.handle.net/1957/29283.

Gearhart, Richard C., ed. *The Orange and Black.* Corvallis, OR: Oregon State College Alumni Association, 1938. http://hdl.handle.net/1957/9287.

Groshong, James W. *The Making of A University, 1868-1968.* Corvallis, OR: Oregon State University, 1968. http://hdl.handle.net/1957/11270.

Keyser, Helen. "The History of Oregon's Land Grant College: 1850-1892." Corvallis, OR. 1958. http://hdl.handle.net/1957/13398.

Landis, Lawrence A. "John Bennes and OSU's Architectural Legacy." 2007. http://hdl. handle.net/1957/7760.

Memorabilia Collection. Special Collections & Archives Research Center. Oregon State University Libraries and Press.

McIlvenna, Don E., and Darold Wax. "W. J. Kerr, Land-Grant President in Utah and Oregon, 1900–1908." Part II. *Oregon Historical Quarterly*, 86 (Spring 1985): 4–22.

Morris, James Madison. *The Remembered Years.* Corvallis, OR: Continuing Education Publications, 1972. http://hdl.handle.net/1957/6780.

Oregon Agricultural College. *Alumni Directory.* Corvallis, OR.: Oregon Agricultural College, 1910. http://hdl.handle.net/1957/35058.

Oregon Agricultural College. *Annual Report of the Oregon Agricultural College and Experiment Station.* Corvallis, OR: Oregon Agricultural College. 1893–1910.

Oregon Agricultural College. *Biennial Report of the Oregon Agricultural College.* Corvallis, OR: Oregon Agricultural College. 1872–1912.

Oregon Agricultural College. *Orange* Yearbook. Corvallis, OR: Oregon Agricultural College. 1907–1915.

Oregon State College. *Sixty Years of Growth in Home Economics.* Corvallis, OR: Oregon State College, 1950.

Oregon State College. *Golden Jubilee of Basketball at Oregon State, 1901-1951: Washington vs. Oregon State, January 12–13, 1951, Souvenir Program.* Corvallis, OR.: Oregon State College, 1951. http://hdl.handle.net/1957/14472.

Oregon State University. Agricultural Experiment Station. *100 Years of Progress: The Oregon Agricultural Experiment Station, Oregon State University, 1888–1988.* Corvallis, OR: Agricultural Experiment Station, Oregon State University, 1990. http://hdl.handle.net/1957/31252.

Oregon State University. Alumni Association. *Oregon Stater.* Corvallis, OR: Alumni Association, Oregon State University. 1915–2013.

Oregon State University. *Beaver* Yearbook. Corvallis, OR: Oregon State University. 1916–2012

Oregon State University. *Daily Barometer.* Corvallis, OR: Oregon State University. 1896–2014.

Oregon State University. *General Catalog.* Corvallis, OR: Oregon State University. 1866–2013.

Oregon State University. Institutional Research and Planning. *2001 Fact Book.* Corvallis, OR: Institutional Research and

Planning, Office of Budgets and Planning, Oregon State University, 2001.

Oregon State University. Intercollegiate Athletics. *Media Guides.* Corvallis, OR: Intercollegiate Athletics, Oregon State University. 1960–2014.

Oregon State University. School of Forestry. *75 Years of Continuing Progress in Forestry Education.* Corvallis, OR: The School, 1981. http://hdl.handle.net/1957/11322.

Oregon State University. Libraries and Press. Special Collections & Archives Research Center. "Chronological History of Oregon State University." http://scarc.library.oregonstate.edu/chronology/chron_head.html.

Oregonian (Portland, OR). 1858–2000.

President's Office Records (RG13). Special Collections & Archives Research Center. Oregon State University Libraries and Press.

Salem (OR) Willamette Farmer. Salem, OR. 1869–1887. http://oregonnews.uoregon.edu/lccn/sn85042522/

Smith, John E. *Corvallis College.* Corvallis, OR. 1953.

Van Loan, Lillian. "Historical Perspective of Oregon State College." Corvallis, OR. 1959. http://hdl.handle.net/1957/11629.

Photos used in this book were drawn from several collections that are a part of the holdings of the Special Collections & Archives Research Center at OSU Libraries and Press and from outside sources.

SCARC COLLECTIONS

Beaver and *Orange* Yearbooks

HC	Harriet's Photograph Collection

A History of Benton County, Oregon, Including its Geology, Topography, Soil and Productions

MAPS	Oregon State University Campus Maps
MC	Oregon State University Memorabilia Collection
MSS	Ava Milam Clark Papers
MSS	Coed Cottage Records
MSS	Co-Signers Engineering Students Wives Club Collection
MSS	Iona Irving Ferguson Collection
MSS	James C. Howland Papers
MSS	Lora Lemon Scrapbook
MSS	Harvey L. McAlister Collection
MSS	Maple Manor Cooperative House Collection

MSS	Ava Helen and Linus Pauling Papers
MSS	Talons Records
MSS	William Appleman Williams Papers
MSS	Withycombe Family Collection
MSS	World War I Poster Collection

Photographic Business and Professional Directory

Portrait and Biographical Record of the Willamette Valley, Oregon

P1	Presidents of OSU Photographic Collection
P2	Oregon State University Military Photographs Collection
P3	*Beaver* Yearbook Photographs
P4	Football Photograph Collection
P7	Baseball Photographs
P15	Rowing (Crew) Photograph Collection
P16	Buildings Photographs
P17	Alumni Relations Photographs
P25	Oregon State University Historical Photographs
P35	*Barometer* Photographs
P36	College of Agricultural Sciences Photographs
P42	Ruby Breithaupt Photograph Collection
P44	College of Home Economics Photograph Collection
P46	Faculty and Staff Photograph Collection
P47	Class Sessions Photograph Collection
P55	Entomology Department Photograph Collection
P57	News and Communication Services Photograph Collection
P61	College of Forestry Photograph Collection
P82	Gwil Evans Photographic Collection
P83	Library Photograph Collection
P84	College of Science Photograph Collection
P89	Edwin Russell Jackman Photographic Collection
P92	President's Office Photographs
P94	University Publications Photographs
P95	John Garman Photographic Collection
P96	Sydney Trask Photograph Collection
P98	Robert W. Henderson Photograph Collection
P101	E.E. Wilson Photographic Collection
P103	Ray Stout Photographic Collection
P104	OSU Bands Photographs
P109	C.A. Vincent Photographs
P111	Poultry Science Department Photograph Collection
P114	Business Affairs Photographic Collection

P116   Alva Aitken Photograph Collection

P119   Media Services Photographs Collection

P120   Extension and Experiment Station Communications Photograph Collection

P125   Larry Kirkland Photographs

P126   David Little Photographs

P128   Jerry D. Belcher Collection of Oregon Agricultural College Track Photographs

P135   William F. Groves Photographs

P146   4-H Photograph Collection

P151   Bill Reasons Photograph Collection

P158   Henry C. Gilbert Photograph Collection

P161   Robert "Wally" Reed Photographs

P170   KBVR Photographs

P176   Oversized Photographic Collection

P182   Student Affairs Photographic Collection

P187   LaSells Stewart Center Photographs

P190   Harold Troxel Vedder Photograph Collection

P191   James G. Arbuthnot Photograph Collection

P194   College of Business Photographs

P195   *Oregon Stater* Photograph Collection

P220   Pernot Family Photographic Collection

P222   English Department Photographs

P224   Ellis Samuel Dement Photograph Collection

P252   Richard W. Gilkey Photographs

P247   Finance and Administration Photographs

P257   Army ROTC Photographs

P281   Air Force ROTC Photographs

P295   John L. Robbins Photographs

PUB10-13c   *Orange Owl*

RG7   Intercollegiate Athletics Records

RG25   Agricultural Experiment Station Records

RG32   Administrative Council Records

RG48   Adelphian Literary Society Records

RG244   Lonnie B. Harris Black Cultural Center Records *Willamette Farmer*

OTHER SOURCES

Benton County Historical Society and Museum

Jane Aune Essig

National Archives, Record Group 11, General Records of the United States Government

OSU Alumni Association

OSU Army ROTC

OSU Athletic Communications

OSU Extension and Experiment Station Communications

OSU Foundation

OSU IMC Network

OSU News and Research Communications

OSU Press

OSU Pride Center

Index